Computer Fundamentals:
English for Computer Engineering

COMPUTER FUNDAMENTALS: ENGLISH FOR COMPUTER ENGINEERING

Mohammad Mehdi Hassani, Hamed Barjesteh and Mehdi Manoochehrzadeh

ARCLER PRESS

www.arclerpress.com

Computer Fundamentals: English for Computer Engineering

Mohammad Mehdi Hassani, Hamed Barjesteh and Mehdi Manoochehrzadeh

Arcler Press
224 Shoreacres Road
Burlington, ON L7L 2H2
Canada
www.arclerpress.com
Email: orders@arclereducation.com

ISBN: 978-1-77469-923-2 (Hardcover)

ABOUT THE AUTHORS

Mohammad Mehdi Hassani received his M.Sc. degree in computer engineering from Iran University of Science and Technology, Tehran, Iran, and the Ph.D. degree in computer engineering from Iran University of Science and Technology, Tehran, Iran. He is an assistant professor and a faculty member of Islamic Azad University, Ayatollah Amoli branch. Mohammad Mehdi Hassani has published several books and articles in computer engineering and presented at conferences at various national and international levels. His research interests are Cognitive Radio Network, Network on Chip and Mobile communications including adaptive algorithms, smart antenna, and cognitive radio networks.

Hamed Barjesteh is an associate professor of Education, Professor of applied linguistics, and a faculty member of Islamic Azad University, Ayatollah Amoli branch, Amol, Iran. A teacher educator for 20 years, Hamed Barjesteh has published several books and articles on teaching English to young and adult language learners and presented at conferences at various national and international levels. He has trained teachers and supervised many MA theses and Ph.D. dissertations. He serves as the head of English Language department, an editor and a reviewer for various journals and conferences. His research interests lie in the field of critical language pedagogy, thinking skills in language learning, Critical Language testing, dynamic assessment, and corrective feedback.

Mehdi Manoochehrzadeh is a Ph.D. candidate in Teaching English as a foreign language. He is the head of English language institute in Tehran. He trained many students and worked as a TTC teacher at different English language institutes. He presented different papers at national and international conferences. He is interested in language learning strategy, teacher education, and Willingness to communicate

TABLE OF CONTENTS

LIST OF FIGURES

LIST OF TABLES

LIST OF ABBREVIATIONS

ADALINE	Adaptive Linear Element
ALU	Arithmetic/Logic Unit
AMD	American Micro Devices
ANN	Artificial Neural Network
ANSI	American National Standards Institute
ARPANET	Advanced Research Projects Agency Network
ART	Adaptive Resonance Theory
ASICs	Application-Specific Integrated Circuits
BNC	Bayone-Neill-Concelman
CAN	Campus Area Network
CDMA	Code Division Multiple Access
CD-R	CD-Recordable
CD-R/W	CD-Read/Write
CMOS	Complementary Metal Oxide Silicon
COTS	Commercial Off-the-Shelf
CPU	Central Processing Unit
CRC	Cyclic Redundancy Check
CRT	Cathode Ray Tube
CSD	Circuit Switched Data
CSMA/CD	Carrier Sense Multiple Access Collision Detect
DD	Double-Density
DRAM	Dynamic Random Access Memory

DS	Differentiated Services
DSL	Digital Subscriber Line
DSPs	Digital Signal Processors
DTEs	Data Terminal Equipment
EEPROM	Electrically Erasable Programmable Read Only Memory
EIA	Electronic Industries Alliance
EIA	Electronic Industry Association
EPROM	Electrically Programmable Read Only Memory
FET	Field-Effect Transistor
FPGA	Field-Programmable Gate Array
FSMs	Finite State Machines
GAN	Global Area Networks
GHZ	Gigahertz
GPRS	General Packet Radio Service
GSM	Global System for Mobiles
HD	High-Density
HDML	Handheld Device Markup Language
HDTP	Handheld Device Transport Protocol
HLR	Home Location Register
HTML	Hypertext Markup Language
HTTP	Hypertext Transfer Protocol
I/O	Inputs and Outputs
IC	Integrated Circuit
IEEE	Institute of Electrical and Electronics Engineers
IP	Internet Protocol
IPSec	Internet Protocol Security
IPX	Internetwork Packet Exchange
ISA	Instruction Set Architecture

ISO	International Organization for Standardization
LAN	Local Area Network
LCD	Liquid Crystal Display
LLC	Logical Link Control
LMS	Least Mean Square
MAC	Media Access Control
MAN	Metropolitan Area Network
MCP	McCulloch and Pitts
MexE	Mobile Station Application Execution Environment
MFD	Multifunction Device
MFP	Multifunction Printer
MOS	Metal-Oxide-Silicon
MRAM	Magneto Resistive Random Access Memory
NRE	Nonrecurring Engineering
NSF	National Science Foundation
NTQ	Near-Typeset Quality
OLPC	One Laptop per Child
OSI	Open Systems Interconnection
PAN	Personal Area Network
PC	Program Counter
PDAs	Personal Digital Assistants
PDL	Page Description Language
PROM	Programmable Read Only Memory
QoS	Quality of Service
RAM	Random Access Memory
ROM	Read Only Memory
RTP	Real-Time Protocol
RWM	Read Write Memory

SAPs	Service Access Points
SDRAM	Synchronous DRAM
SiO_2	Silicon Dioxide
SLA	Service Level Agreement
SMS	Short Message Service
SPX	Sequenced Packet Exchange
SRAM	Static Random Access Memory
SSG	Service Selection Gateway
STP	Shielded Twisted Pair
TCP	Transmission Control Protocol
TIA	Telecommunication Industry Association
TIA	Telecommunications Industries Alliance
TLS	Transport Layer Security
TVs	Televisions
UDP	User Datagram Protocol
UMTS	Universal Mobile Telephone System
URL	Uniform Resource Locator
USSD	Unstructured Supplementary Services Data
UTP	Unshielded Twisted Pair
VPN	Virtual Private Networking
WANs	Wide Area Networks
WAP	Wireless Application Protocol
WEP	Wired Equivalent Privacy
Wi-Fi	Wireless Fidelity
WML	Wireless Markup Language
WPA	Wi-Fi Protected Access
WTA	Wireless Telephony Application
WWW	World Wide Web

PREFACE

Through years of teaching at different educational levels, we found some basic concepts in computers being repeatedly asked by the students. Some fundamental concepts were still vague for higher education. To ensure the consistency of the points posed by the learners, we found similar problems in different interview sessions. We found that the interviewees were confused in distinguishing some basic issues in computer science. Accordingly, we started to collect different key concepts and asked about the fundamentals of computer knowledge in different classrooms with the objective of uncovering the main concerns of the computing students. We asked our colleagues to help and share their knowledge and experience in the key terms which may help computer students to cope with computer fundamentals. The computer fundamentals aim to clarify some basic functions of computers, starting from computer hardware components to neural networks. Notably, this book is outlined into three chapters dealing with hardware, memory, and networks. Study of basic concepts in hardware such as computer components, central processing unit (CPU), CMO CIRCUITS, and FPGA are included in the hardware section. Besides, some fundamentals in system memory, Random access memory (RAM), and types of ROM are included in the memory section. Finally, the last part deals with the network. It begins with the history of networks, common types of computer networks, different types, layers, and the basic internet concept. This book ends with an introduction to neural networks. There is no special prerequisite to learning computer fundamentals. This book was designed for computer students and those who are interested to learn the fundamental concepts of computing engineering. This book can be used as a special English course for students of computers. The contents can help beginner and professional learners to master their computer knowledge or brush up on their information in the basic concept of computer knowledge. School students, those who plan to learn English for a specific purpose, and to have practical knowledge of computer science, can take advantage of this book.

We hope the computer fundamentals help the intended readers consolidate the problematic concepts in computer science. We cordially expect to receive critical comments from the esteemed readers, which will help us to promote the quality of the book for the further edition.

—Mohammad Mehdi Hassani, PhD

Hamed Barjesteh, PhD

Mehdi Manoochehrzadeh, PhD

CHAPTER

1 Hardware

Contents

1.1. COMPUTER COMPONENTS

1.1.1. Hardware

A computer system has two basic parts: hardware and software. The equipment associated with a computer system is the hardware. Computer hardware is responsible for performing four basic functions: input, processing, output, and storage. Let's go back to the basic definition of a computer. A computer is an electronic device that is programmed to accept data (input), process it into useful information (output), and store it for future use (storage). The processing function is under the control of a set of instructions (software); we will explore this later.

The four primary components of a computer system are:

1. **Input:** These devices send data and instructions to the central processing unit (CPU).
2. **Processing:** CPU executes computer instructions. Memory holds data and programs temporarily.
3. **Output:** These devices make processed data available to the user.
4. **Secondary Storage:** These devices store data and programs permanently.

In order to function properly, a computer system must have all four types of hardware: input, processing, output, and storage. In this example, the mouse and keyboard are the input devices, and the monitor and speakers are output devices. The processor is contained inside the tower unit and the storage devices are the hard drive, CD-ROM drive and the diskette drive. Let's explore each of the devices in detail.

1.1.2. Input Devices

An input device consists of external devices – that is, devices outside of the computer's CPU – that provide information and instructions to the computer. Input devices accept data in a form that the computer can utilize. Also, the input devices send the data or instructions to the processing unit to be processed into useful information. There are many examples of input devices, but the most commonly used input devices are shown below:

1. **Light Pen:** It is a stylus with a light sensitive tip that is used to draw directly on a computer's video screen or to select information on the screen by pressing a clip in the light pen or by pressing the

light pen against the surface of the screen. The pen contains light sensors that identify which portion of the screen it is passed over.

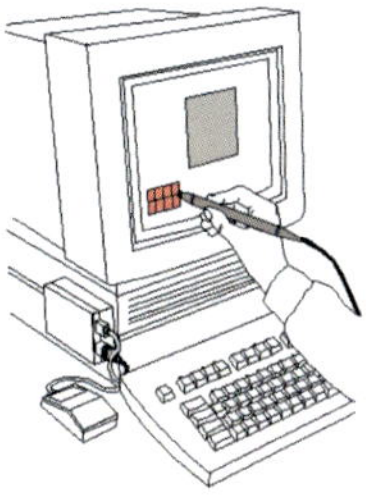

2. **Mouse:** A mouse is a pointing device designed to be gripped by one hand. It has a detection device (usually a ball) on the bottom that enables the user to control the motion of an on-screen pointer, or cursor, by moving the mouse on a flat surface. As the device moves across the surface, the cursor moves across the screen. To select items or choose commands on the screen, the user presses a button on the mouse.

3. **Joystick:** It is a pointing device composed of a lever that moves in multiple directions to navigate a cursor or other graphical object on a computer screen.

4. **Keyboard:** It is a typewriter-like device that allows the user to type in text and commands to the computer. Some keyboards have special function keys or integrated pointing devices, such

as a trackball or touch-sensitive regions that let the user's finger motions move an on-screen cursor.

5. **Optical Scanner:** It uses light-sensing equipment to convert images such as a picture or text into electronic signals that can be manipulated by a computer. For example, a photograph can be scanned into a computer and then included in a text document created on that computer.

The two most common scanner types are the flatbed scanner, which is similar to an office photocopier, and the handheld scanner, which is passed manually across the image to be processed.

6. **Microphone:** It is a device for converting sound into signals that can then be stored, manipulated, and played back by the computer.

7. **Voice Recognition:** This module is a device that converts spoken words into information that the computer can recognize and process.

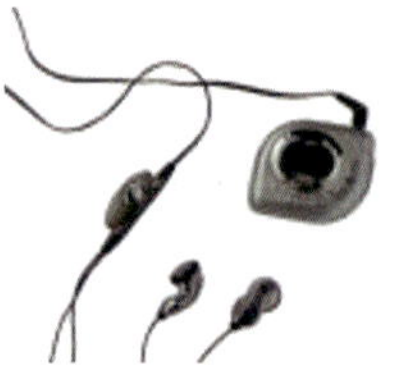

8. **Modem:** A modem, which stands for modulator-demodulator, is a device that connects a computer to a telephone line or cable

television network and allows information to be transmitted to or received from another computer. Each computer that sends or receives information must be connected to a modem. The digital signal sent from one computer is converted by the modem into an analog signal, which is then transmitted by telephone lines or television cables to the receiving modem, which converts the signal back into a digital signal that the receiving computer can understand.

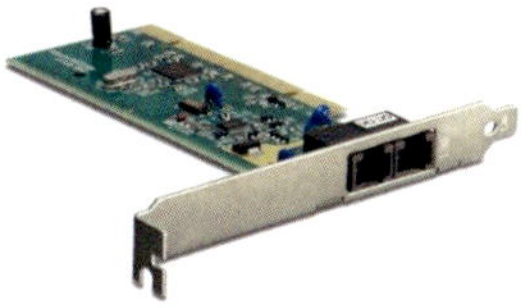

There are few different types of modems including:

i. **Analog:** 56 K (52 K top speed) using telephone line.

ii. **DSL/ADSL:** Top speed can reach as high as 5 Mb in residential using telephone line.

iii. **Cable:** Top speed about 8 Mb using Cable.

iv. **Fiber Optic:** Can reach 30 Mbps depend on your available provider.

Modem is input device as well as output device. So, we will place detailed articles about modems under "Networking" category.

The input device feeds data, raw unprocessed facts, to the processing unit. The role of the processing unit or CPU is to use a stored program to manipulate the input data into the information required. In looking at the computer system below, the CPU, is not exactly visible. The CPU is found inside the tall, vertical unit, called a tower, located just to the right of the monitor.

9. **CPU:** It is the brain of the computer. The CPU consists of electronic circuits that interpret and execute instructions; it communicates with the input, output, and storage devices. The CPU, with the help of memory, executes instructions in the repetition of machine cycles. A machine cycle consists of four steps:

- The control unit fetches an instruction and data associated with it from memory;
- The control unit decodes the instruction;

- The arithmetic/logic unit (ALU) executes the instruction; and
- The ALU stores the result in memory.

The first two instructions are called instruction time, I-time. Steps 3 and 4 are called execution time, E-time. The speed of computer is measured in megahertz, MHz.

A MHz is a million machine cycles per second. A personal computer listed at 500 MHz has a processor capable of handling 500 million machine cycles per second. Another measure of speed is gigahertz (GHZ), a billion machine cycles per second. A third measure of speed is a megaflop, which stands for 1 million floating-point operations per second. It measures the ability of the computer to perform complex mathematical operations.

1.1.3. Output Devices

Output hardware consists of external devices that transfer information from the computer's CPU to the computer user. A video display, or screen, converts information generated by the computer into visual information.

1. **Display:** This commonly take one of two forms: a video screen with a cathode ray tube (CRT) or a video screen with a liquid crystal display (LCD).
2. **CRT:** A CRT-based screen, or monitor, looks similar to a television set. Information from the CPU is displayed using a beam of electrons that scans a phosphorescent surface that emits light and creates images.

3. **Flat Panel or LCD:** An LCD-based screen displays visual information on a flatter and smaller screen than a CRT-based video monitor. LCDs are frequently used in laptop computers.

4. **Printers:** It take text and image from a computer and print them on paper. Dot-matrix printers use tiny wires to impact upon an inked ribbon to form characters. Laser printers employ beams of light to draw images on a drum that then picks up fine black particles called toner. The toner is fused to a page to produce an image. Inkjet printers fire droplets of ink onto a page to form characters and pictures.

Memory, or primary storage, works with the CPU to hold instructions and data in order to be processed. Memory keeps the instructions and data for whatever programs you happen to be using at the moment. Memory is the first-place data and instructions are placed after being input; processed information is placed in memory to be returned to an output device. It is very important to know that memory can hold data only temporarily because it requires a continuous flow of electrical current. If current is interrupted, data is lost. Memory is in the form of a semiconductor or silicon chip and is contained inside the computer.

There are two types of memory: ROM and RAM. ROM is read only memory. It contains programs and data that are permanently recorded when the computer is manufactured. It is read and used by the processor but cannot be altered by the user. RAM is random access memory. The user can access data in RAM memory randomly. RAM can be erased or written over at will by the computer program or the computer user. The amount of RAM has increased dramatically in recent years.

Memory is measured in bytes. A byte is usually made up of 8 bits and represents one character—a letter, digit, or symbol. The number of bytes that can be held is a measure of the memory and storage capacity. Bytes are usually measured in groups of kilobytes, megabytes, gigabytes, and terabytes. The following chart defines each term.

Kilobyte	KB	Roughly 1,000 bytes
Megabyte	MB	Roughly 1,000,000 bytes
Gigabyte	GB	Roughly 1,000,000,000 bytes
Terabyte	TB	Roughly 1,000,000,000 bytes

Memory is usually measured in Megabytes; a typical personal computer will have 64 MB or more. Storage is usually measured in Gigabytes.

Since we have said that memory is in the form of chips and must maintain a constant flow of electricity, there must be a more permanent form of storage that does not depend on a constant flow of electricity. That form of storage is called secondary or auxiliary storage. The benefits of secondary storage are large space capacity, reliability, convenience, and economy.

Magnetic disk storage is a very popular type of secondary storage—the floppy disk drive is an external disk drive, while a hard disk drive is an internal disk drive. The floppy disk drive is usually a 3½" drive and uses a diskette made of flexible Mylar and coated with iron oxide, a substance that can be magnetized. A diskette records data as magnetized spots on the tracks of its surface. A floppy disk can hold 1.44 MBs, or a 'Zip' drive can hold 100 MBs.

A hard disk, an internal disk, is a metal platter coated with magnetic oxide that can be magnetized to represent data. Hard disks come in a variety of sizes and can be assembled into a disk pack. Hard disks for personal computers are 3 ½" disks in sealed modules. A hard disk is capable of holding a great deal more than floppy disks. Hard disks for personal computers are measured in gigabytes. (Remember, a gigabyte is roughly a 1,000 megabytes or a 1,000 floppy disks.)

While the size or data capacity of a hard drive is very important, the speed of accessing that data is equally as important. Files on hard drives can be accessed significantly faster and more conveniently than floppy drives.

5. **Hard Drive:** The ever-demanding need for storage has required even better storage capacity than that of magnetic disks. Optical disk technology meets that need. Included in the list of this type of technology is the optical disk, the CD-ROM or DVD-ROM. The CD-ROM, compact disk read-only memory can hold up to 660 MBs per disk or the equivalent of more than 400 standard 3 ½" diskettes. The new storage technology that outpaces all others is called DVD-ROM, digital versatile disk. The DVD has a 4.7 GB capacity, which is about seven times that of the CD-ROM.

In order to protect the data on your hard drive, you should have a backup system. A backup system is way of storing data in more than one location. Magnetic tape is usually used for this purpose. Magnetic tape is an inexpensive type of storage; it looks like the tape used in audiocassettes.

- Find the *synonyms* for the underlined words.

1. The equipment associated with a computer system is the hardware.
2. A light pen is a stylus with a light sensitive tip that is used to draw directly on a computer's video screen.
3. The pen contains light sensors that identify which portion of the screen it is passed over.

4. A mouse is a pointing device designed to be gripped by one hand. It has a detection device on the bottom that enables the user to control the motion of an on-screen pointer, or cursor, by moving the mouse on a flat surface.
5. A joystick is a pointing device composed of a lever that moves in multiple directions to navigate a cursor or other graphical object on a computer screen.
6. The two most common scanner types are the flatbed scanner, which is similar to an office photocopier, and the handheld scanner, which is passed manually across the image to be processed.
7. Modem is input device as well as output device. So, we will place detailed articles about modems under "Networking" category.
8. The CPU is found inside the tall, vertical unit, called a tower, located just to the right of the monitor.
9. Memory keeps the instructions and data for whatever programs you happen to be using at the moment.
10. If current is interrupted, data is lost. Memory is in the form of a semiconductor or silicon chip and is contained inside the computer.

➢ Fill in the blank with the following words.

Keyboard, Covered, Carrying-out, External devices, Electrical, Save, Programs, Identification.

1. Computer hardware is responsible for ………… four basic functions: input, processing, output, and storage.
2. Secondary storage devices ………. data and programs permanently.
3. Input devices consists of ………. – that is, devices outside of the computer's CPU – that provide information and instructions to the computer.
4. A ………. is a typewriter-like device that allows the user to type in text and commands to the computer.
5. A voice ………. module is a device that converts spoken words into information that the computer can recognize and process.
6. It is very important to know that memory can hold data only temporarily because it requires a continuous flow of ………. current.
7. It contains ………. and data that are permanently recorded when the computer is manufactured.
8. Floppy disk drive is usually a 3 ½" drive and uses a diskette made of flexible Mylar and ………. with iron oxide.

➢ Write *antonyms* of following words.

1. Future ....
2. Continuous ....
3. Properly ....
4. Light ....
5. Flat........................
6. Manually ....
7. Exactly ....

1.1.4. Additional Information about Keyboards

Keyboard is the main input device of a computer. Without a keyboard it is impossible to imagine working on a computer. Keyboard is a lot similar to a typewriter but has added keys that enhance the features and capabilities of a user working on a computer.

The today's keyboards consist of about 101 to 106 keys. The layouts are basically the same with the odd key situated differently. It is generally connected to the PS2 or the USB ports of the motherboard. There are many types of keyboards available these days, but one should always buy that is suitable and comfortable. Some are springy others have mushy feeling.

Yes, you get a keyboard when you buy a computer, but it is not necessary that you have to use it. Keyboards are an inexpensive item that can be replaced easily. But it doesn't mean that all keyboards are inexpensive as today's markets have very hi-tech keyboards.

Once you've found a keyboard that you find it comfortable, one of your main concerns should be proper typing form. Repetitive stress injuries are a concern and poor posture can also result in back and neck pain. Sit up straight and find yourself a chair that supports the natural curve in your back. It should be adjusted to your keyboard so that you don't have to lean forward or hunch to type. Your shoulders should be relaxed with your forearms and wrists fairly level, fingers slightly curved. Wrist pads are made for you to rest your wrists on while taking short breaks, your wrists shouldn't be on them while you type. Don't sit and type constantly, try to take a few breaks every now and then and have a stretch.

1.2. CENTRAL PROCESSING UNIT (CPU)

CPU is an acronym that stands for central processing unit. The CPU is responsible for performing all of the mathematical calculations that are required for a computer to function properly. Because a computer cannot function without the CPU (which may also be referred to as the central processor or just the processor), it is not uncommon to hear people refer to the CPU as the "brains" of a computer.

The CPU is the brain of the computer – it is the 'compute' in computer. Modern CPUs are what are called 'integrated chips.' The idea of an integrated chip is that several processing components are integrated into a single piece of silicon. Without the CPU, you have no computer. The CPU is composed of thousands (and soon billions) of transistors.

Each transistor is a set of inputs and outputs (I/O). When the inputs receive electricity, the combined charge changes the state of the transistor internally and you get a result out the other side. This simple effect of the transistor is what makes it possible for the computer to count and perform logical operations, all of which we call processing.

The first CPUs were used in the early 1960s. They were custom designed as part of a larger computer, making them prohibitively expensive. Once engineers figured out how to mass produce the CPU, personal computers became more affordable for the average American. With the introduction of the integrated circuit (IC) in the late 1970s, it became possible for smaller CPUs to be manufactured as well. This helped transform computers from large, bulky devices that took up entire rooms to more manageable desktop and laptop models.

Early CPUs were custom designed as a part of a larger, usually one-of-a-kind, computer. However, this costly methodology of designing custom CPUs for a particular application has largely given way to the development of inexpensive and standardized classes of processors that are suited for one or many purposes. This standardization trend generally began in the era of discrete transistor mainframes and minicomputers and has rapidly accelerated with the popularization of the IC. The IC has allowed increasingly complex CPUs to be designed and manufactured in very small spaces (in the order of millimeters). Both the miniaturization and standardization of CPUs have increased the presence of these digital devices in modern life far beyond the limited application of dedicated computing machines. Modern microprocessors appear in everything from automobiles to cell phones to children's toys.

It is composed of three units:

1. **The Control Unit:** This maintains order and controls activity in the CPU. It does not process or store data. Rather, it directs the

sequence of operations. The control unit interprets the instruction of a program in storage and produces signal that act as command circuits to execute the instructions. Other function of the control unit includes communicating with an input device in order to begin the transfer of instruction and data into storage ad, similarly, communicating with an output device to initiate the transfer of results from storage.

2. **The Arithmetic/Logic Unit (ALU)**: It performs arithmetic computations and logical operations. For example, the computer can be instructed to branch to one of three operations, depending on whether a value being tested is greater than, equal to, or less than another value.
3. **The Primary Storage Unit:** It holds instructions, data, and intermediate and final results. It is a reusable, fast storage medium, directly accessible by the control unit. Each storage cell is capable of storing one bit of data. A bit is the smallest unit of information that ca be held in memory. Bit of data are generally stored in groups, called bytes.

The CPUs in most PC's and servers are general purpose integrated chips composed of several smaller dedicated-purpose components which together create the processing capabilities of the modern computer. For example, Intel makes a Pentium, while AMD makes the Athlon, and Duron (no memory cache).

1.2.1. CPU Components

A lot of components go into building a modern processor and just what goes in changes with every generation as engineers and scientists find new, more efficient ways to do old tasks:

- Execution core(s);
- Data bus;
- Address bus;
- Math co-processor;
- Instruction sets / microcode;
- Multimedia extensions;
- Registers;
- Flags;

- Pipelining;
- Memory controller;
- High-speed cache memory;
- Measuring speed: Bits, cycles, and execution cores;
- Bit width.

The first way of describing a processor is to say how many bits it processes in a single instruction or transports across the processor's internal bus in a single cycle (not exactly correct, but close enough). The number of bits used in the CPU's instructions and registers and how many bits the buses can transfer simultaneously is usually expressed in multiples of 8 bits. It is possible for the registers and the bus to have different sizes. Current chip designs are 64-bit chips (as of 2008).

1.2.2. Clock Cycles

The second way of describing a processor is to say how many cycles per second the chip operates at. This is how many times per second a charge of electricity passes through the chip. The more cycles, the faster the processor. Currently, chips operate in the billions of cycles per second range. When you're talking about billions of anything in computer terms, you're talking about 'GIGA' something. When you're talking about how many cycles per second, you're talking about 'hertz.' Putting the two together, you get GHZ.

1.2.3. Execution Cores

The third way of describing a processor is to say how many execution cores are in the chip. The most advanced chips today have eight execution cores. More execution cores mean you can get more work done at the same time, but it doesn't necessarily mean a single program will run faster. To put it another way, a processor with one execution core might be able to run your MP3 music, your web browser, a graphics program, and that's about where it starts to slow down enough, it's not worth it running more programs. A system with a processor with 8 cores could run all that plus 10 more applications without even seeming to slow down (of course, this assumes you have enough RAM to load all of this software at the same time).

As of 2008, the most advanced processors available are 64-bit processors with 8 cores, running as fast as 3–4 gigahertz. Intel has released quad-core 64-bit chips as has AMD. Multi-Processor Computers And if you're still needing more processing power, some computers are designed to run more than one processor chip at the same time. Many companies that manufacture servers make models that accept 2, 4, 8, 16 even 32 processors in a single chassis. The biggest supercomputers are running hundreds of thousands of quad-core processors in parallel to do major calculations for such applications as thermonuclear weapons simulations, radioactive decay simulations, weather simulations, high energy physics calculations and more.

1.2.4. CPU Speed Measurements

The main measurement quoted by manufacturers as a supposed indication of processing speed, is the clock speed of the chip measured in hertz. The theory goes that the higher the number of mega or GHZ, the faster the processor.

However, comparing raw speeds is not always a good comparison between chips. Counting how many instructions are processed per second (MIPS, BIPS, TIPS for millions, billions, and trillions of instructions per second) is a better measurement. Still others use the number of mathematical calculations per second to rate the speed of a processor.

Of course, what measurement is most important and most helpful to you depends on what you use a computer for. If you primarily do intensive math calculations, measuring the number of calculations per second is most important. If you are measuring how fast the computer runs an application, then instructions per second are most important.

1.2.5. Processor Manufacturers

- American micro devices (AMD);
- Intel;
- IBM;
- Motorola;
- Cyrix;
- Texas instruments.

AMD and Intel have pretty much dominated the market. AMD and Intel are for IBM compatible machines. Motorola chips are made for Macintoshes. Cyrix (another IBM compatible chip maker) runs a distant fourth place in terms of number of chips sold.

Today all chip manufacturers produce chips whose input and output are identical, though the internal architecture may be different. This means that though they may not be built the same way, they DO all run the same software. The CPU is built using logic gates and contains a small number of programs called 'microcode' built into the chip to perform certain basic processes (like reading data from the bus and writing to a device). Current chips use a 'reduced instruction set' or RISC architectures. Chips can also be measured in terms of instructions processed per second (MIPS).

1.2.6. CPU Operation

The fundamental operation of most CPUs, regardless of the physical form they take, is to execute a sequence of stored instructions called a program. Discussed here are devices that conform to the common Von Neumann architecture. The program is represented by a series of instructions (represented by a number or sequence of numbers) that are kept in some kind of computer memory. There are four steps that nearly all von Neumann CPUs use in their operation: fetch, decode, execute, and write back.

The first step, fetch, involves retrieving an instruction from program memory. The location in program memory is determined by a program counter (PC), which stores a number that identifies the current position in the program. In other words, the program counter keeps track of the CPU's place in the current program. After an instruction is fetched, the PC is incremented by the length of the instruction word in terms of memory units. Often the instruction to be fetched must be retrieved from relatively slow memory, causing the CPU to stall while waiting for the instruction to be returned. This issue is largely addressed in modern processors by cache and superscalar architecture.

In the decode step, the instruction is broken up into parts that have significance to other portions of the CPU. The way in which the numerical instruction value is interpreted is defined by the CPU's instruction set architecture (ISA). Often, one group of numbers in the instruction, called the opcode, indicates which operation to perform. The remaining parts of the number usually provide information required for that instruction, such as operands for an addition operation. Such operands may be given as a constant value, or as a place to locate a value: a register or a memory address. In older designs the portions of the CPU responsible for instruction decoding were unchangeable hardware devices. However, in more abstract and complicated CPUs and ISAs, a micro program is often used to assist in translating instructions into various configuration signals for the CPU. This micro program is often rewritable and can be modified to change the way the CPU decodes instructions even after it has been manufactured.

After the fetch and decode steps, the execute step is performed. During this step, various portions of the CPU are connected, so they can perform the desired operation. If, for instance, an addition operation was requested, an ALU (Arithmetic Logic Unit) will be connected to a set of inputs and a set of outputs. The inputs provide the numbers to be added, and the outputs will contain the final sum.

The final step, write back, simply "writes back" the results of the execute step to some form of memory. Very often the results are written to some internal CPU register for quick access. In other cases they may be written to slower, but cheaper and larger, main memory. Some types of instructions manipulate the PC rather than directly produce result data. These are generally called "jumps" and facilitate behavior like loops, conditional program execution, and functions in programs.

After the execution of the instruction and write back the resulting data, the entire process repeats, with the next instruction cycle normally fetching the next-in-sequence instruction. In more complex CPUs than the one described here, multiple instructions can be fetched, decoded, and executed simultaneously. Many instructions will also change the state of digits in a "flags" register. These flags can be used to influence how a program behaves, since they often indicate the outcome of various operations. For example, one type of "compare" instruction considers two values and sets a number in the flags register according to which one is greater. This flag could then be used by a later jump instruction to determine program flow.

➢ Find the *synonyms* for the underlined words.

1. CPU is an acronym that stands for central processing unit.
2. This simple effect of the transistor is what makes it possible for the computer to count and perform logical operations, all of which we call processing.
3. They were custom designed as part of a larger computer, making them prohibitively expensive.
4. This helped transform computers from large, bulky devices that took up entire rooms to more manageable desktop and laptop models.
5. This standardization trend generally began in the era of discrete transistor mainframes and minicomputers and has rapidly accelerated with the popularization of the integrated circuit (IC).

6. A system with a processor with 8 cores could run all that plus ten more applications without even seeming to slow down (of course, this assumes you have enough RAM to load all of this software at the same time).
7. The most advanced processors available are 64-bit processors with 8 cores, running as fast as 3–4 gigahertz. Intel has released quad-core 64-bit chips as has AMD.
8. The biggest supercomputers are running hundreds of thousands of quad-core processors in parallel to do major calculations for such applications as thermonuclear weapons simulations, radioactive decay simulations, weather simulations.
9. If you primarily do intensive math calculations, measuring the number of calculations per second is most important.
10. The first step, fetch, involves retrieving an instruction from program memory.

➢ Fill in the blank with the following words.

Brains, RISC, Control unit, Hertz, Transistors, Flags, Superscalar, Cell

1. It is not uncommon to hear people refer to the CPU as the .... of a computer.
2. The CPU is composed of thousands (and soon billions) of ....
3. .... directs the sequence of operations and maintains order and controls activity in the CPU.
4. Each storage .... is capable of storing one bit of data.
5. When you're talking about how many cycles per second, your talking about ....
6. Current chips use a 'reduced instruction set' or .... architectures.
7. This issue is largely addressed in modern processors by cache_and .... architecture.
8. Many instructions will also change the state of digits in a .... register.

- Write *antonyms* of following words.

1. Properly ....
2. Uncommon ....
3. Internally ....
4. Early ....
5. Discrete ....
6. Intensive ....
7. Unchangeable ....

1.2.7. Additional Information about Processors

The processor (really a short form for microprocessor and also often called the CPU) is the central component of the PC. It is the brain that runs the show inside the PC. All work that you do on your computer is performed directly or indirectly by the processor. Obviously, it is one of the most important components of the PC, if not the most important. It is also, scientifically, not only one of the most amazing parts of the PC, but one of the most amazing devices in the world of technology.

The processor plays a significant role in the following important aspects of your computer system:

1. **Performance:** The processor is probably the most important single determinant of system performance in the PC. While other components also play a key role in determining performance, the processor's capabilities dictate the maximum performance of a system. The other devices only allow the processor to reach its full potential.
2. **Software Support:** Newer, faster processors enable the use of the latest software. In addition, new processors such as the Pentium with MMX Technology, enable the use of specialized software not usable on earlier machines.
3. **Reliability and Stability:** The quality of the processor is one factor that determines how reliably your system will run. While most processors are very dependable, some are not. This also depends to some extent on the age of the processor and how much energy it consumes.
4. **Energy Consumption and Cooling:** Originally processors consumed relatively little power compared to other system devices. Newer processors can consume a great deal of power.

Power consumption has an impact on everything from cooling method selection to overall system reliability.

5. **Motherboard Support:** The processor you decide to use in your system will be a major determining factor in what sort of chipset you must use, and hence what motherboard you buy. The motherboard in turn dictates many facets of your system's capabilities and performance.

1.3. WHAT IS A PRINTER?

A printer is an output device that produces text and graphics on paper. In computers, a printer is a device that accepts text and graphic output from a computer and transfers the information to paper, usually to standard size sheets of paper. Printers are sometimes sold with computers, but more frequently are purchased separately. Printers vary in size, speed, sophistication, and cost. In general, more expensive printers are used for higher-resolution color printing.

1.3.1. Printer Qualities

The four printer qualities of most interest to most users are:

1. **Color:** It is important for users who need to print pages for presentations or maps and other pages where color is part of the information. Color printers can also be set to print only in black-and-white. Color printers are more expensive to operate since they use two ink cartridges (one color and one black ink) that need to be replaced after a certain number of pages. Users who don't have a specific need for color and who print a lot of pages will find a black-and-white printer cheaper to operate.
2. **Resolution:** Printer resolution (the sharpness of text and images on paper) is usually measured in dots per inch (dpi). Most inexpensive printers provide sufficient resolution for most purposes at 600 dpi.
3. **Speed:** If you do much printing, the speed of the printer becomes important. Inexpensive printers print only about 3 to 6 sheets per minute. Color printing is slower. More expensive printers are much faster.
4. **Memory:** Most printers come with a small amount of memory (for example, one megabyte) that can be expanded by the user.

Having more than the minimum amount of memory is helpful and faster when printing out pages with large images or tables with lines around them (which the printer treats as a large image).

1.3.2. Printer I/O Interfaces

The most common I/O interface for printers are described below:

1. **Parallel:** In the context of the Internet and computing, parallel means more than one event happening at a time. It is usually contrasted with *serial*, meaning only one event happening at a time. In data transmission, the techniques of time division and space division are used, where time separates the transmission of individual bits of information sent serially and space (in multiple lines or paths) can be used to have multiple bits sent in parallel.

   In the context of computer hardware and data transmission, serial connection, operation, and media usually indicate a simpler, slower operation (think of your serial mouse attachment). Parallel connection and operation (think of multiple characters being sent to your printer) indicates faster operation. This indication doesn't always hold since a serial medium (for example, fiber optic cable) can be much faster than a slower medium that carries multiple signals in parallel.

   A conventional phone connection is generally thought of as a serial line since its usual transmission protocol is serial.

   Conventional computers and their programs operate in a serial manner, with the computer reading a program and performing its instructions one after the other. However, some of today's computers have multiple processors that divide up the instructions and perform them in parallel.

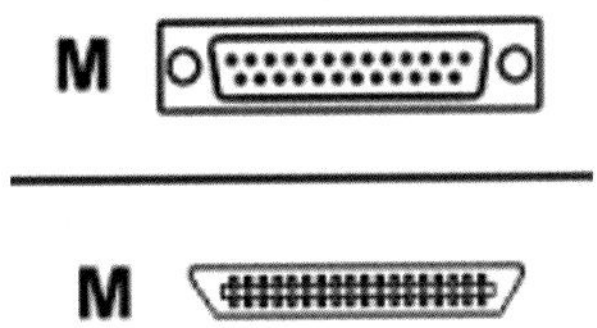

2. **Parallel Interfaces:** USB (universal serial bus) is a plug-and-play interface between a computer and add-on devices (such as audio players, joysticks, keyboards, telephones, scanners, and printers).

With USB, a new device can be added to your computer without having to add an adapter card or even having to turn the computer off. The USB peripheral bus standard was developed by Compaq, IBM, DEC, Intel, Microsoft, NEC, and Northern Telecom and the technology is available without charge for all computer and device vendors.

USB supports a data speed of 12 megabits per second. This speed will accommodate a wide range of devices, including MPEG video devices, data gloves, and digitizers. It is anticipated that USB will easily accommodate plug-in telephones that use ISDN and digital PBX. Since October 1996, the Windows operating systems have been equipped with USB drivers or special software designed to work with specific I/O device types. USB is integrated into Windows 98 and later versions. Today, most new computers and peripheral devices are equipped with USB.

3. **FireWire:** It is Apple Computer's version of a standard, IEEE 1394, High Performance Serial Bus, for connecting devices to your personal computer. FireWire provides a single plug-and-socket connection on which up to 63 devices can be attached with data transfer speeds up to 400 Mbps (megabits per second). The standard describes a serial bus or pathway between one or more peripheral devices and your computer's microprocessor. Many peripheral devices now come equipped to meet IEEE 1394.
4. **Infrared:** Printers can also be attached with the help of infrared adapter. A simple diagram of a printer with an infrared adapter is shown below.

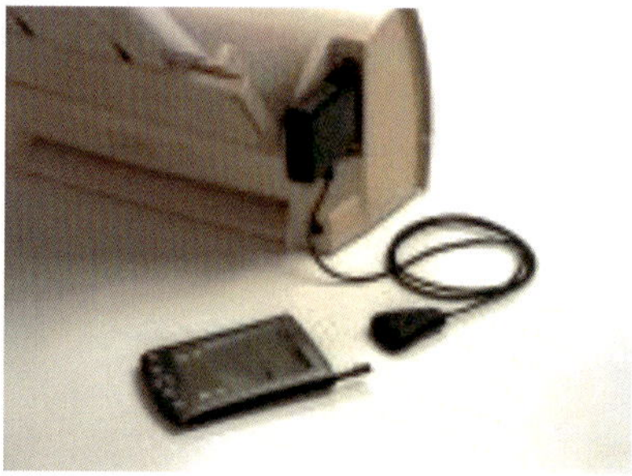

1.3.3. Printer Languages

Printer languages are commands from the computer to the printer to tell the printer how to format the document being printed. These commands manage font size, graphics, compression of data sent to the printer, color, etc. The two most popular printer languages are Postscript and Printer Control Language.

Postscript is a printer language that uses English phrases and programmatic constructions to describe the appearance of a printed page to the printer. This printer language was developed by Adobe in 1985. It introduced new features such as outline fonts and vector graphics. Printers now come from the factory with or can be loaded with Postscript support. Postscript is not restricted to printers. It can be used with any device that creates an image using dots such as screen displays, slide recorders, and image setters.

PCL (Printer Command Language) is an escape code language used to send commands to the printer for printing documents. Escape code language is so-called because the escape key begins the command sequence followed by a series of code numbers. Hewlett Packard originally devised PCL for dot matrix and inkjet printers. Since its introduction, it has become an industry standard. Other manufacturers who sell HP clones have copied it. Some of these clones are very good, but there are small differences in the way they print a page compared to real HP printers. In 1984, the original HP LaserJet printer was introduced using PCL. PCL helped change the appearance of low-cost printer documents from poor to exceptional quality.

1.3.4. Fonts

A font is a set of characters of a specific style and size within an overall typeface design. Printers use resident fonts and soft fonts to print documents. Resident fonts are built into the hardware of a printer. They are also called internal fonts or built-in fonts. All printers come with one or more resident fonts. Additional fonts can be added by inserting a font cartridge into the printer or installing soft fonts to the hard drive. Resident fonts cannot be erased unlike soft fonts. Soft fonts are installed onto the hard drive and then sent to the computer's memory when a document is printed that uses the particular soft font. Soft fonts can be purchased in stores or downloaded from the Internet.

There are two types of fonts used by the printer and screen display, bitmap fonts and outline fonts. Bitmap fonts are digital representations of fonts that are not scalable. This means they have a set size or a limited set of sizes. For example, if a document using a bitmap font sized to 24 point is sent to the printer and there is not a bitmap font of that size, the computer will try to guess the right size. This results in the text looking stretched-out or squashed. Jagged edges are also a problem with bitmap fonts. Outline fonts are mathematical descriptions of the font that are sent to the printer. The printer then rasterizes or converts them to the dots that are printed on the paper. Because they are mathematical, they are scalable. This means the size of the font can be changed without losing the sharpness or resolution of the printed text. TrueType and Type 1 fonts are outline fonts. Outline fonts are used with Postscript and PCL printer languages.

1.3.5. Major Types of Printer

Printers can be divided into two main groups, impact printer and non-impact printer. Impact printer produces text and images when tiny wire pins on print head strike the ink ribbon by physically contacting the paper. Non-impact printer produces text and graphics on paper without actually striking the paper.

1. **Non-Impact Printers:** Non-impact printers are much quieter than impact printers as their printing heads do not strike the paper. Most non-impact printers produce dot-matrix patterns. Several different technologies have been used to provide a variety of printers.

   The main types of non-impact printer are:

   - Thermal printer;
   - Laser printer;
   - Ink jet printer.

2. **Impact Printers:** These use a print head containing a number of metal pins which strike an inked ribbon placed between the print head and the paper. Some print heads have only 9 pins to make the dots to build up a character; some have 24 pins which produce a better resolution. Impact printers are the oldest print technologies still in active production. Some of the largest printer vendors continue to manufacture, market, and support impact printers, parts, and supplies. Impact printers are most functional in specialized environments where low-cost printing is essential. The three most common forms of impact printers are dot-matrix, daisywheel, and line printers.

Printers can also be categorized based on the print method or print technology. The most popular ones are inkjet printer, laser printer, dot-matrix printer, and thermal printer. Among these, only dot-matrix printer is impact printer, and the others are non-impact printers. Some printers are named because they are designed for specific functions, such as photo printers, portable printers, and all-in-one / multifunction printers (MFP). Photo printers and portable printers usually use inkjet print method whereas MFPs may use inkjet or laser print method.

Inkjet printers and laser printers are the most popular printer types for home and business use. Dot matrix printer was popular in 70's and 80's but has been gradually replaced by inkjet printers for home use. However, they are still being used to print multi-part forms and carbon copies for some businesses. The use of thermal printers is limited to ATM, cash registers and point-of-sales terminals. Some label printers and portable printers also use thermal printing.

Due to the popularity of digital camera, laptop, and SoHo office (small office / home office), the demand for photo printers, portable printers and MFPs has also increased substantially in recent years.

- **Popular Printers:**
  - Inkjet printers;
  - Laser printers.
- **Less Popular Printers:**
  - Dot-matrix printers;
  - Thermal printers.
- **Specialty Printers:**
  - Photo printers;
  - Portable printers.

1.3.5.1. Inkjet Printers

Inkjet printers are non-impact printers which print text and images by spraying tiny droplets of liquid ink onto paper. They are the most popular printers for home use.

Currently, most inkjet printers use either thermal inkjet or piezoelectric inkjet technology. Thermal inkjet printer uses heating element to heat liquid ink to form vapor bubble, which forces the ink droplets onto the paper through the nozzle. Most inkjet manufacturers use this technology in consumer inkjet printers.

Piezoelectric inkjet technology is used on all Epson printers and industrial inkjet printers. Instead of using heating element, these printers use a piezoelectric crystal in each nozzle. The piezoelectric crystal changes shape and size based on the electric current received and forces tiny droplets of ink onto the paper from the nozzle.

Thermal inkjet printers use aqueous ink which is a mixture of water, glycol, and dyes. These inks are inexpensive, but they can only be used on paper or specially coated materials. Piezoelectric inkjet printers allow the use of a wider range of inks, such as solvent inks, UV-curable inks, dye sublimation inks, and can print text and graphics on different uncoated materials.

The inkjet head design is also divided into two main groups: fixed-head and disposable head. Fixed head is built into the printer and should last for the whole life of the printer. It produces more accurate output than cheap disposable head. The ink cartridges for fixed head printers are also cheaper as the print head does not need to be replaced. However, if the head is damaged, the entire printer has to be replaced.

Disposable head is included in replacement ink cartridge. It is replaced each time an ink cartridge runs out of ink. This increases the cost of ink cartridges and also limits the use of high-quality print head in these cartridges. However, a damaged print head is not a problem as one can easily replace it with a new ink cartridge.

Some printer manufacturers use disposable ink and disposable print head separately. The print head can last much longer than cheap disposable head and is suitable for high volume printing. However, it can also be replaced easily if the head is clogged or damaged.

Although inkjet printers are generally used in home and small businesses, some manufacturers, such as Hewlett Packard, have produced high end inkjet printers for industrial use. These professional inkjet printers are usually used to print advertising graphics or technical drawings.

Ø **Advantages of Inkjet Printers:**

- Low cost;

- High quality of output, capable of printing fine and smooth details;
- Capable of printing in vivid color, good for printing pictures;
- Easy to use;
- Reasonably fast;
- Quieter than dot matrix printer;
- No warmup time.

Ø **Disadvantages of Inkjet Printers:**

- Print head is less durable, prone to clogging and damage;
- Expensive replacement ink cartridges;
- Not good for high volume printing;
- Printing speed is not as fast as laser printers;
- Ink bleeding, ink carried sideways causing blurred effects on some papers;
- Aqueous ink is sensitive to water, even a small drop of water can cause blurring;
- Cannot use highlighter marker on inkjet printouts.

Many consumer inkjet printers are selling at very low price (under $100) these days. It is the printer manufacturer's marketing strategy to reduce the price of the printers but dramatically mark up the price of replacement cartridges. However, consumers still have the options to buy cheap compatible and remanufactured inkjet cartridges or ink refill kits to cut down printing cost.

1.3.5.2. Laser Printers

Laser printers are non-impact printers which can print text and images in high speed and high-quality resolution, ranging from 600 to 1,200 dpi.

Unlike inkjet printers, laser printer use toner (black or colored powder) instead of liquid inks. A laser printer consists of these major components: drum cartridge, rotating mirror, toner cartridge and roller. The drum cartridge rotates as the paper is fed through. The mirror deflects laser beam across the surface of the drum. Laser beam creates charge that causes the toner to stick to the drum. As the drum rotates and presses on paper, toner is transferred from the drum to paper, creating images. Rollers then use heat and pressure to fuse toner to paper. Colored laser printers add colored toner in three additional passes.

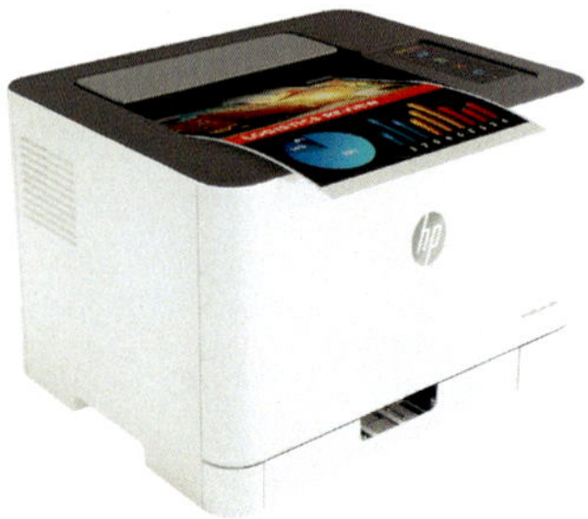

Ø **Advantages of Laser Printers:**
- High resolution;
- High print speed;
- No smearing;
- Low cost per page (compared to inkjet printers);
- Printout is not sensitive to water;
- Good for high volume printing.

Ø **Disadvantages of Laser Printers:**
- More expensive than inkjet printers;
- Except for high end machines, laser printers are less capable of printing vivid colors and high-quality images such as photos;
- The cost of toner replacement and drum replacement is high;
- Bulkier than inkjet printers;
- Warm up time needed.

1.3.5.3. Dot-Matrix Printer

Dot-matrix printer is an impact printer that produces text and graphics when tiny wire pins on the print head strike the ink ribbon. The print head runs back and forth on the paper like a typewriter. When the ink ribbon presses on the paper, it creates dots that form text and images. Higher number of pins means that the printer prints more dots per character, thus resulting in higher print quality.

Dot-matrix printers were very popular and the most common type of printer for personal computer in 70's to 80's. However, their use was gradually replaced by inkjet printers in 90's. As of today, dot matrix printers are only used in some point-of-sales terminals, or businesses where printing of carbon copy multi-part forms or data logging are needed.

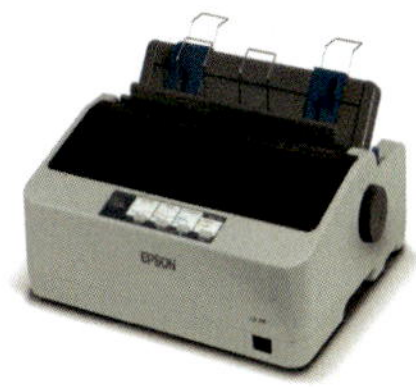

Ø **Advantages of Dot Matrix Printer:**

- Can print on multi-part forms or carbon copies;
- Low printing cost per page;
- Can be used on continuous form paper, useful for data logging;
- Reliable, durable.

Ø **Disadvantages of Dot Matrix Printer:**

- Noisy;
- Limited print quality;
- Low printing speed;
- Limited color printing.

1.3.5.4. Thermal Printers

Thermal printers use two types of printing technologies: direct thermal and thermal transfer printing. Traditional thermal printers use direct thermal method by pushing electrically heated pins against heat-sensitive paper (thermal paper). The coating on the thermal paper turns black in the areas where it is heated, producing characters or images. Direct thermal printers have no ink, toner, or ribbon. These printers are durable, easy to use and cost less to print than other printers. However, the thermal paper is sensitive to heat, light, water, and abrasion and the text and images may fade over time.

In thermal transfer printing, a thermal print head applies heat to a heat-sensitive ribbon, which melts ink onto paper and a wide range of materials to form text and images. The printouts can be extremely durable and can be stored over long period of time.

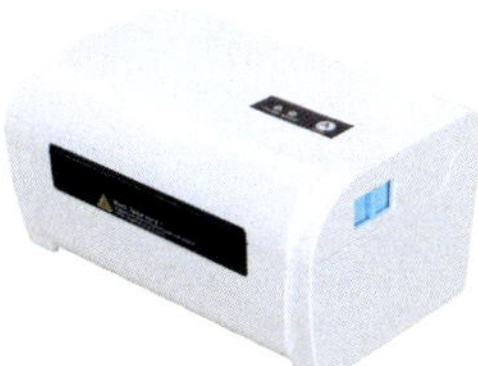

Thermal printers are often used in cash registers, ATM, and point-of-sales terminals. Direct thermal printing was used in some older fax machines before the 21st-century. However, these old models are now replaced by new machines which use laser and inkjet printing. Thermal printing is still considered as the best technology for bar code printing because it produces accurate, high-quality images with exact bar widths. Some portable printers and most label printers still use thermal printing method.

Thermal printer is not the same as thermal inkjet printer. The latter uses inkjet print technology by heating liquid ink to form vapor bubble, which forces the ink droplet onto the paper from the nozzle.

1.3.5.5. Photo Printer

Photo printers are color printers that produce photo lab quality pictures on photo paper. They can also be used to print documents. These printers have a very high number of nozzles and can print very fine droplets for improved image quality. Some photo printers also have media card readers. They can print 4" x 6" photos directly from the media card of digital cameras without a computer in between.

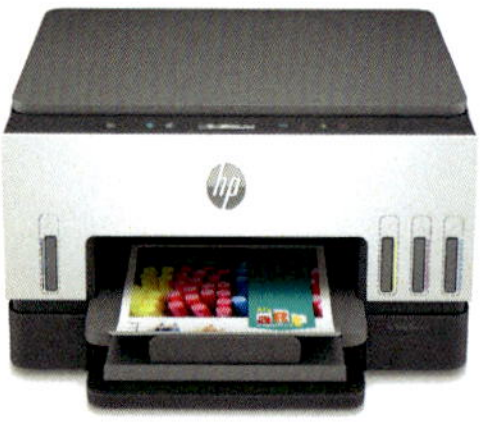

Theoretically, most inkjet printers and high-end laser printers are capable of printing high quality pictures. Sometimes, these printers are marketed as "photo printers." However, a dedicated photo printer is designed to print photos effectively and economically. Apart from a higher number of nozzles and very fine droplets, these printers also use additional cartridges, such as photo cyan, light magenta and light black. These additional color cartridges allow the printing of more vivid and realistic photos, and the result is better than ordinary inkjet and laser printers.

1.3.5.6. Portable Printer

Portable printers are small, lightweight inkjet or thermal printers that allow computer users to print from laptop computers when traveling. They are easy to carry, convenient to use but generally more expensive than normal inkjet printers due to the compact design. Their printing speed is also lower than normal printers. Some portable printers are designed to print photos immediately from digital cameras and are known as portable photo printers.

1.3.5.7. Multifunction Printer (MFP)

Multifunction printer (MFP) is also known as all-in-one printer or multifunction device (MFD). It is a machine that includes several functionalities including printer, scanner, copier, and fax.

MFP is very popular in SoHo (small office / home office) offices. It can use either inkjet or laser print method. Some MFPs also have media card readers, allowing printing of pictures directly from digital cameras without using a computer.

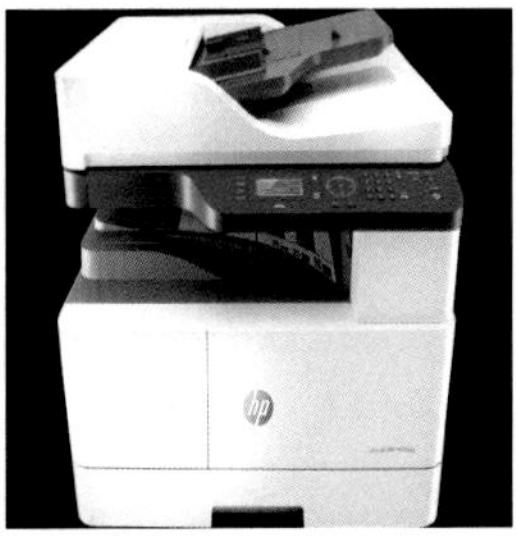

Ø **Advantages of Multifunction Printers (MFPs):**

- Low cost – it is often cheaper to buy an MFP than individual components (fax machine, scanner, printer, copier) separately;
- Take up less room.

Ø **Disadvantages of Multifunction Printers (MFPs):**

- If one component is broken, the entire machine has to be replaced;
- Failure in any component will affect other functions;
- The print quality and speed may be lower than some standalone components.

- Find the *synonyms* for the underlined words.

1. Impact printer produces text and images when tiny wire pins on print head strike the ink ribbon by physically contacting the paper.
2. Non-impact printers are much quieter than impact printers as their printing heads do not strike the paper.
3. Some printers are named because they are designed for specific functions, such as photo printers, portable printers and all-in-one / multifunction printers.
4. The use of thermal printers is limited to ATM, cash registers and point-of-sales terminals.
5. the demand for photo printers, portable printers and multifunction printers has also increased substantially in recent years.
6. Thermal inkjet printer uses heating element to heat liquid ink to form vapor bubble, which forces the ink droplets onto the paper through the nozzle.
7. Thermal inkjet printers use aqueous ink which is a mixture of water, glycol and dyes.
8. Consumers still have the options to buy cheap compatible and remanufactured inkjet cartridges or ink refill kits to cut down printing cost.
9. A laser printer consists of these major components: drum cartridge, rotating mirror, toner cartridge and roller.
10. The drum cartridge rotates as the paper is fed through. The mirror deflects laser beam across the surface of the drum. Laser beam creates charge that causes the toner to stick to the drum. As the drum rotates and presses on paper, toner is transferred from the drum to paper, creating images.
11. Piezoelectric inkjet printers allow the use of a wider range of inks, such as solvent inks, UV-curable inks, dye sublimation inks, and can print text and graphics on different uncoated materials.

> ➢ Fill in the blank with the following words.

Classified, Hit, Substitution, Daisy-wheel, Forward, Regular, Disposable, Sturdy

1. Impact Printers use a print head containing a number of metal pins which ……… an inked ribbon placed between the print head and the paper.
2. The three most common forms of impact printers are dot-matrix, ………, and line printers.
3. Printers can also be ……… based on the print method or print technology.
4. It is the printer manufacturer's marketing strategy to reduce the price of the printers but dramatically mark up the price of ……… cartridges.
5. The print head can last much longer than cheap ………head and is suitable for high volume printing.
6. The print head runs back and ……… on the paper like a typewriter.
7. These printers are ………, easy to use and cost less to print than other printers.
8. These additional color cartridges allow the printing of more vivid and realistic photos and the result is better than ……… inkjet and laser printers.

➢ Write *antonyms* of following words.

1. Actually ………………………
2. Active ………………………
3. Gradually ………………………
4. Durable………………………
5. Aqueous ………………………
6. Curable………………………
7. Exact ………………………

1.3.6. Additional Information about Impact and Non-Impact Printers

What are printers? A printer is an output device that prints characters, symbols, and perhaps graphics on paper. The printed output is generally referred to as hardcopy because it is in relatively permanent form. Softcopy refers to temporary images such as those displayed on a monitor. Printers are categorized according to whether or not the image produced is formed by physical contact of the print mechanism with the paper. Impact printers have contact; nonimpact printers do not.

1.3.6.1. Impact Printers

An impact printer has mechanisms resembling those of a typewriter. It forms characters or images by striking a mechanism such as a print hammer or wheel against an inked ribbon, leaving an image on paper. Impact printers are dying out; however, you may still come in contact with a dot-matrix printer. A dot-matrix printer contains a print head of small pins that strike an inked ribbon, forming characters or images. Print heads are available with 9, 18, or 24 pins; the 24-pin head offers the best print quality. Dot-matrix printers permit a choice between output of draft quality; a coarser-looking 72 dots per inch vertically, which may be acceptable for drafts of papers and reports, and near-letter-quality, a crisper-looking 144 dots per inch vertically, which is more suitable for a finished product to be shown to other people.

Dot-matrix printers print about 40–300 characters per second (cps) and can print some graphics, although the reproduction quality is poor. Color ribbons are available for limited use of color. Dot-matrix printers are noisy, inexpensive, and they can print through multipart forms, creating several copies of a page at the same time, which nonimpact printers cannot do.

Another type of impact printer is not used with microcomputers. Large computer installations use high-speed line printers, which print a whole line of characters at once rather a single character at a time. Some, called chain printers, contain characters on a rotating chain; others, called band printers, contain characters on a rotation band. Speeds of up to 3,000 lines a minute may be possible with these machines.

1.3.6.2. Nonimpact Printers

Nonimpact printers, used almost everywhere now, are faster and quieter than impact printers because they have fewer moving parts. Nonimpact printers form characters and images without direct physical contact between the printing mechanism and the paper.

Two types of nonimpact printers often used with microcomputers are laser printers and ink-jet printers:

1. **Laser Printer:** Like a dot-matrix printer, a laser printer creates images with dots. However, as in a photocopying machine, these

images are created on a drum, treated with a magnetically charged ink-like toner (powder), and then transferred from drum to paper.

There are good reasons why laser printers are so popular. They produce sharp, crisp images of both text and graphics, providing resolutions from 300 dpi up to 1,200 dpi, which is near-typeset quality (NTQ). They are quiet and fast. They can print 4–32 text-only pages per minute for individual microcomputers, and more than 120 pages per minute for mainframes. (Pages with more graphics print more slowly.) They can print in many fonts (type styles and sizes). The more expensive models can print in different colors. Laser printers have built-in RAM chips to store documents output from the computer. If you are working in desktop publishing and printing complicated documents with color and many graphics, you will need a printer with a lot of RAM. Laser printers also have their own ROM chips to store fonts and their own small dedicated processor. To be able to manage graphics and complex page design, a laser printer works with a page description language (PDL), a type of software that has become a standard for printing graphics on laser printers. A PDL is software that describes the shape and position of letters and graphics to the printer. PostScript, from Adobe Systems, is one common type of PDL; HPGL, Hewlett-Packard Graphic Language, is another.

2. **Ink-Jet Printer:** Like laser and dot-matrix printers, ink-jet printers also form images with little dots. Ink-jet printers spray small, electrically droplets of ink from four nozzles through holes in a matrix at high speed onto paper. Ink-jet printers can print in color and are quieter and much less expensive than a color laser printer. However, they are slower and print in a somewhat lower resolution (300-720 dpi) than laser printers. Some new, expensive ink-jet printers print up 1200 or 1400 dpi. High-resolution output requires the use of special coated paper, which costs more paper that is regular. If you are printing color graphics at a high resolution on an ink-jet printer, it may take 10 minutes or more for a single page finish printing.

1.4. CMOS CIRCUITS

Over the past two decades, complementary metal oxide silicon (CMOS) technology has played a very important role in the global IC industry.

Although the basic principle of the MOS field-effect transistor (FET) was explained by J. Lilienfeld in 1925, commercial success of MOS devices could be ensured only during the 1960s with the invention of the silicon planar process. Nevertheless, the nMOS devices, fabricated by the nMOS-silicon-gate technology, came to be used in the early 1970s, prior to which only single-polarity p-type transistors were in use. At the same time, P. K. Weimer & F. Wanlass demonstrated the possibility of using both polarity devices on the same substrate.

With the implementation of the CMOS inverter, NOR gate and NAND gate, initially using discrete transistors however, the CMOS concept took root, demonstrating the low power dissipation characteristics. Initially, requirement of more complex processing technology and larger silicon area compared to the single polarity transistors led to limited application of CMOS transistors to general system designs. However, as CMOS technology rapidly improved to support large chip sizes, and the issue of power consumption became more and more critical, CMOS technology has firmly established itself as the dominant VLSI technology. This first chapter introduces the reader to CMOS logic design and design representations.

1.4.1. MOS Transistors and Switches

Silicon is predominantly used in the fabrication of semiconductor devices and microcircuits. A MOS (metal-oxide-silicon) transistor structure is built by stacking several layers of conducting, insulating, and semiconductor materials. This structure is produced involving a series of chemical processing steps such as oxidation of silicon, diffusion of impurities into silicon following etching of silicon oxide from selected locations, and deposition and etching of aluminum on silicon to provide connections with the external environment of the transistor. The fabrication process is carried out on a single crystal of silicon available as thin circular wafers of diameter about 10 cm. CMOS technology makes way for two kinds of transistors, namely nMOS (n-channel) transistor and pMOS (p-channel) transistor built by using negatively diffused silicon (rich in electrons) and positively doped silicon respectively. Some of the distinct layers resulting after the fabrication of a MOS transistor happen to be diffusion, polysilicon, and metal (aluminum), separated by insulating layers.

Figure 1.1 depicts the physical structures and circuit symbols of an n-channel and a p-channel transistor. The structure of the n-channel transistor is made of a p-type silicon substrate accommodating two diffused islands of n-type silicon. Selected areas of the p-substrate are altered by a chemical process into n-type silicon. On top of the area separating the n-type islands lies a thin insulating layer of silicon dioxide (SiO_2) above which there is a conducting layer (usually made of polycrystalline silicon) called the gate.

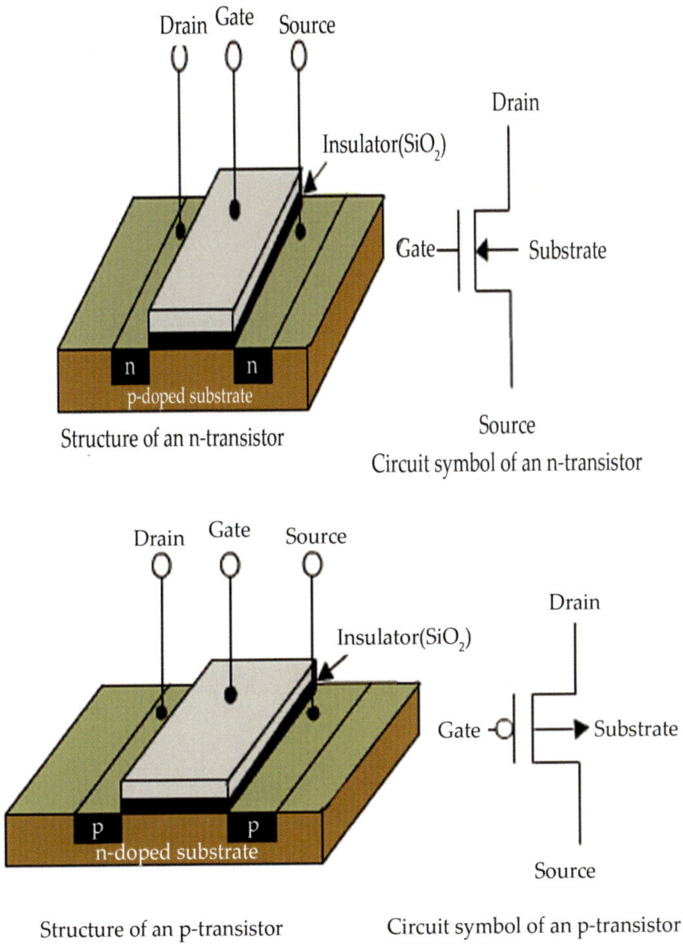

Figure 1.1. Physical structure and schematic representation of MOS transistors.

A p-channel transistor, on the other hand, is made of an n-substrate separating two diffused p-type islands. Like an n-transistor, it too has a gate electrode. Apart from the gate electrode, an nMOS transistor has two more terminals known as the source and the drain which connect the two n-diffused regions (p-diffused regions in a pMOS transistor) with the external environment of the device. The gate acts as a control input, regulating the current flow between the source and the drain. Although the source and the drain are physically equivalent, the name source is reserved for the terminal by which the current carriers enter the device, whereas the drain refers to the terminal by which the carriers leave the device. As shown in Figure 1.1, the substrate (also called the body) happens to be the fourth terminal of a MOS transistor. The voltage applied at the gate terminal regulates the flow of current between the source and the drain. In this way, a MOS transistor may be viewed as a simple on/off switch.

Assume that '1' or POWER (PWR) or VDD denotes a high voltage normally between 1.5 and 15 volts, and '0' or GROUND (GND) or VSS stands for a low voltage normally set to zero volt. The "strength" of a signal denotes its ability to source or sink current. The strength of '1' and '0' signal can vary. One may distinguish between an output and an input in that an output is a source of stronger '1's and '0's than an input.

The switch models of both nMOS and pMOS transistors are depicted in Figure 1.2. As shown in Figure 1.2(a), an nMOS switch is deemed closed or `ON' if the gate voltage is at logic '1' voltage, or more precisely if the potential between the gate and the source terminals, namely VGS happens to be greater than a threshold voltage VT. A closed nMOS switch implies the existence of a continuous channel between the source and the drain terminals. On the other hand, an 'OFF' or open nMOS switch indicates the absence of a connecting channel between the source and the drain. Similarly, a pMOS switch is considered 'ON' or closed if the potential VGS is smaller or more negative than the threshold voltage VT. Threshold voltage and related issues will be dealt with in detail in the next chapter.

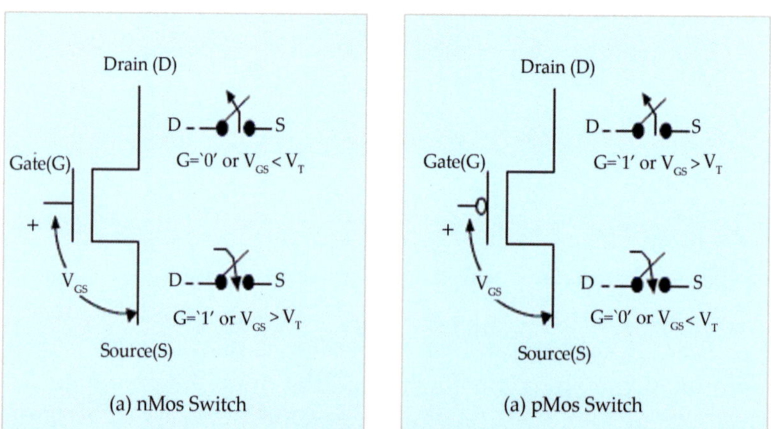

Figure 1.2. Switch models of MOS transistors.

1.4.2. CMOS Logic – Inverters, Combinational Logic, NAND, and NOR Gates, Compound Gates and Multiplexers, Memories

This section gives an overview of CMOS logic elements that find use in different applications.

1.4.2.1. Inverter

The inverter is universally accepted as the most basic logic gate doing a Boolean operation on a single input variable. Figure 1.3 depicts the symbol, truth table and a general structure of a CMOS inverter. As shown, the simple structure consists of a combination of an pMOS transistor at the top and a nMOS transistor at the bottom.

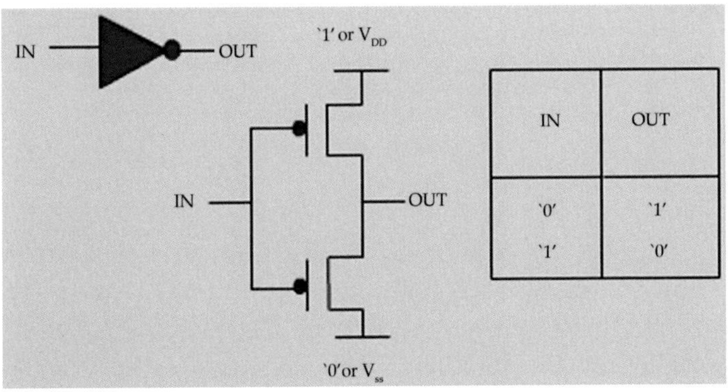

Figure 1.3. Symbol, circuit structure and truth table of a CMOS inverter.

The truth table shows a logic '1' output corresponding to a logic '0' in the input. This can be ensured by the p-transistor whose source is connected to a logic '1' source (VDD) and gate is provided a logic '0' stimulus. Similarly, a logic '0' output will result from a logic '1' input. The nMOS transistor connected in the bottom realizes this when its gate is given a logic '1' input and its source is connected to logic '0' or ground (VSS).

The inverter can best be considered as the central part of digital designs. A thorough understanding of its operation and properties is required to design more complex structures like NAND and NOR gates, adders, and multipliers.

1.4.2.2. Combinational Logic

Combinational logic circuits, rather gates, perform Boolean operations on multiple input variables and determine the outputs as Boolean functions of the inputs. The basic two-input AND- and OR-functions can be realized by series and parallel combinations of nMOS and pMOS transistors as shown in Figure 1.4.

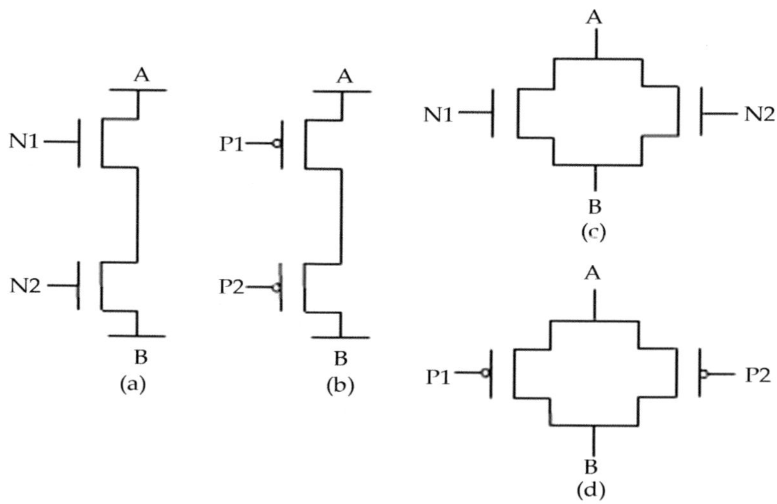

Figure 1.4. Connection of series and parallel n-switches and p-switches.

If two nMOS switches are in series to produce AND function as shown in Figure 1.4(a), both of them should be closed (or ON) by connecting their gates to logic `1.' Similarly, to obtain a two-variable AND function by pMOS switches as shown in Figure 1.4(b), the gates should be fed by logic `0' signals. On the other hand, a two-input OR function is realized by placing two nMOS transistors (Figure 1.4(c)) or two pMOS transistors (Figure 1.4(d)) in parallel. The OR switch by nMOS transistors is closed if any one of the transistors is ON (that is, if any input is at logic `1'). At the same time, the OR function based on pMOS transistors is realized by placing logic `0' at either input.

1.4.2.3. NAND and NOR Gates

Figure 1.5 depicts CMOS implementation of a two-input NAND gate and its typical symbol. The pull-down sub-circuit is made of a series combination of two nMOS transistors. These are responsible for conducting logic '0' to the output node when both of the gates are at logic '1.' The pull-up path on the other hand consists of a parallel combination of two pMOS transistors. If either of the is at logic `0,' the output node assumes the value `1.'

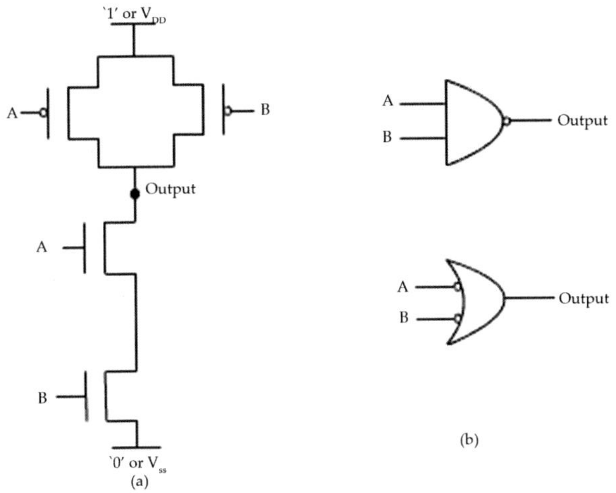

Figure 1.5. A two-input CMOS NAND gate and its symbol.

The two symbols shown in Figure 1.5(b) for a two-input NAND gate is due to the equivalence given by:

$$\overline{AB} \equiv \overline{A} + \overline{B}$$

Figure 1.6 depicts CMOS implementation of a two-input NOR gate and its typical symbol. The pull-up sub-circuit is made of a series combination of two pMOS transistors. These are responsible for conducting logic `1' to the output node when both of the gates are at logic `0.'

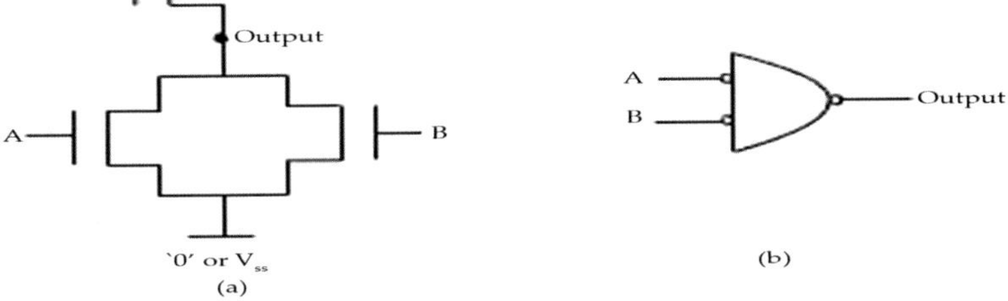

Figure 1.6. CMOS implementation of a two-input NOR gate and its typical symbol.

The pull-down path on the other hand consists of a parallel combination of two nMOS transistors. If either of the is at logic `1,' the output node assumes the value `0.' The two symbols shown in Figure 1.6(b) for a two-input NOR gate is due to the equivalence.

$$\overline{A+B} \equiv \overline{A}\,\overline{B}$$

1.4.2.4. Compound Gate and Multiplexers

Complex Boolean functions of multiple input variables can be realized by simple extension of the circuit structures developed for the basic NAND and NOR gates discussed above.

Consider the Boolean function $z=\overline{(A+B)(C+D)}$ whose CMOS implements is shown in Figure 1.7. The output node attains the logic `1' owing to the pMOS sub-circuit.

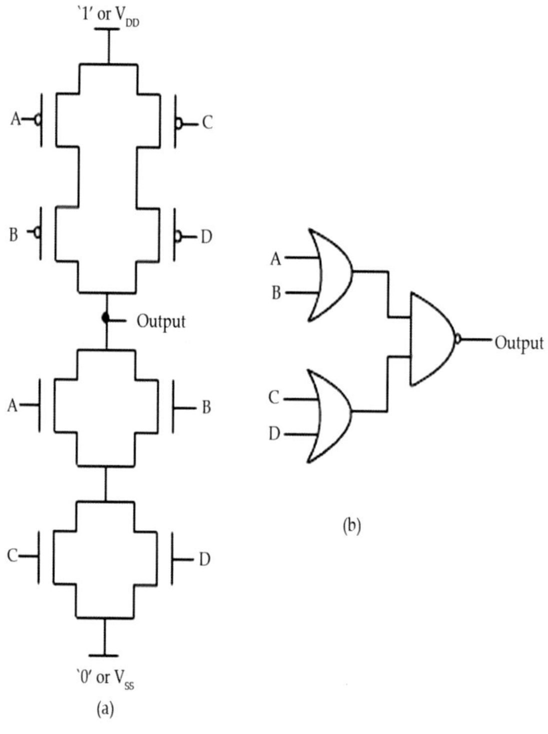

Figure 1.7. CMOS implementation of the function $z=\overline{(A+B)(C+D)}$.

One can easily see that driving both the gate inputs (labeled A and B) of the pMOS transistors or driving the inputs (labeled C and D) of the series pMOS transistors achieves the output `1.' Due to the complementary nature of the pMOS and nMOS transistors, any series combination of transistors in the nMOS tree gets replaced by a parallel connection in the pMOS tree and vice versa. To implement a multiplexer, one can use complementary switches. Figure 1.8 depicts how to realize a 2-input multiplexer in CMOS design style. The circuit shown in Figure 1.8(a) consists of two transmission gates, each consisting of an nMOS and a pMOS transistors. Note that the upper transmission gate allows input A to be passed to the output when the gate control C is at logic '0.' Also, the lower transmission gate transmits the input B to the output when its gate control C is at logic '1.' Thus, both the transmission gates are not simultaneously open for their respective input signals to pass to the common output node. This in essence constitutes a 2-input multiplexer with control input C and two data inputs A and B. Figure 1.8(b) shows the commonly used symbol for a 2-input multiplexer.

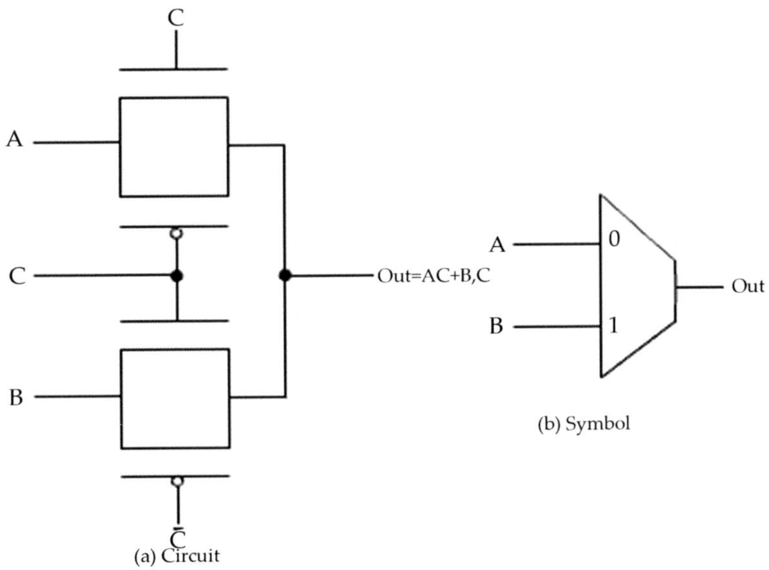

Figure 1.8. CMOS implementation of a 2-input multiplexer.

1.4.2.5. Memory: Latch and Register

Semiconductor memory capable of storing large amount of information are essential to all digital systems. In its simplest form, a single-bit memory element can be realized as a latch or a register. A latch is a level-sensitive circuit for which the state of the output depends on the level of the clock signal. It passes the D input to the Q output when the clock signal is high (for a positive latch) or when the clock is low (in case of a negative latch). This latch is then said to be in transparent mode. During the low state of the clock, for a positive latch, the input data sampled at the falling edge of the clock is held stable at the output; the latch is now said to be in hold mode. The input should be stable for a short period around the falling edge of the clock to meet setup and hold requirements. Figure 1.9 depicts a positive level-sensitive latch implemented using a 2-input multiplexer and two inverters. It has a data input D, a clock input Clk, and two outputs Q and Q. The output Q follows the input D when Clk=`1.' When Clk=`0,' the D input is ignored, and the state of output Q is retained. Similarly, a negative latch passes the D input to the Q output when the clock signal is low.

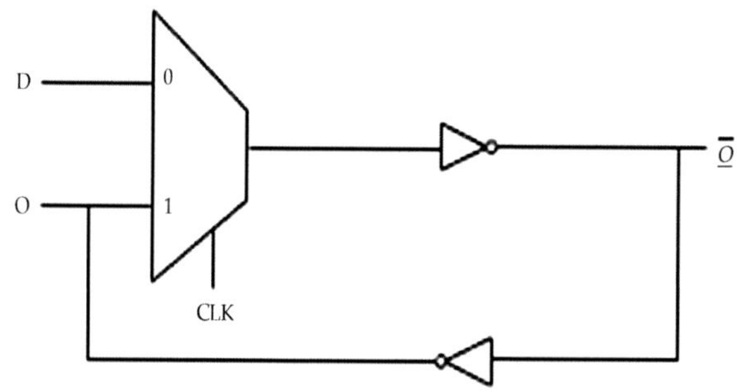

Figure 1.9. A CMOS positive level-sensitive D latch.

One can use a negative latch followed by a positive latch to realize an edge-triggered register, as shown in Figure 1.10. When the clock signal is low, the output of the first stage, normally referred to as the master stage, follows the D input, whereas the output Q of the second stage, commonly known as the slave stage, retains the previous value. When a transition 0 à 1 takes place in the clock input, the value of the slave output Q freezes at the value of D input existing just before the rising edge of the clock. As the sampling of the input takes place on a 0 à 1 clock transition, this register is called a positive edge-triggered register. When the clock remains at logic `1,' the master stops sampling the D input and stores the D value at the time of the clock transition. Now, the slave latch allows the complement of the stored master value to pass to the output Q. The D input cannot affect the output Q as the master stage is disconnected from the D input. When the clock makes a transition from `1' to `0,' the slave stage is disconnected from the master stage and gets locked to its previous value due to the feedback loop. Also, the master stage begins sampling the D input again. A negative edge-triggered register is one in which during a 1 → 0 transition, the value of the output Q freezes at the value of D input existing just before the falling edge of the clock. It is realized by reversing the order of the two latches shown in Figure 1.10.

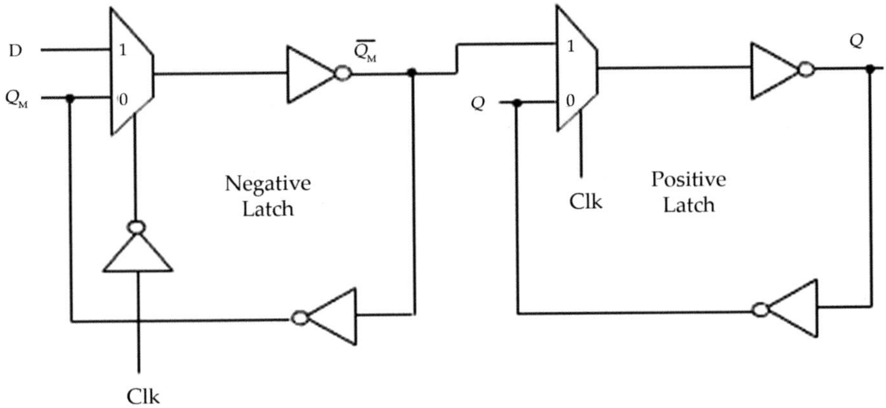

Figure 1.10. A CMOS positive edge-triggered D register.

1.4.3. Circuit and System Representation – Behavioral, Structural, and Physical Representation

A complex digital system is broken down into component gates and memory elements by splitting the system in a hierarchical manner. A set of requirements is envisaged. Guided by these, an initial design is developed and subsequently tested against the requirements. Design is made to improve in case the requirements are not met. The Y-chart (first conceived by D. Gajski) shown in Figure 1.11 demonstrates a simplified design flow that is adopted for the majority of logic chips, using the activities on three different axes (domains) which resemble the letter "Y."

The three domains of representation that make up the Y-chart are the behavioral domain, the structural domain, and the physical layout domain. The behavioral view of a digital system describes its function of the system with no regard to its implementation. The structural view of a system describes a system as an interconnection of components. The physical view of a system is concerned with the physical entities, namely the transistors that constitute the circuit.

➢ Find the *synonyms* for the underlined words:

1. Nevertheless, the nMOS devices, fabricated by the nMOS-silicon-gate technology, came to be used in the early 1970s, prior to which only single-polarity p-type transistors were in use.
2. Wanlass demonstrated the possibility of using both polarity devices on the same substrate.
3. Silicon is predominantly used in the fabrication of semiconductor devices and microcircuits.
4. CMOS technology makes way for two kinds of transistors, namely nMOS (n-channel) transistor and pMOS (p-channel) transistor built by using negatively diffused silicon (rich in electrons) and positively doped silicon respectively. Some of the distinct layers resulting after the fabrication of a MOS transistor happen to be diffusion, polysilicon and metal (aluminum), separated by insulating layers.
5. This can be ensured by the p-transistor whose source is connected to a logic '1' source (VDD) and gate is provided a logic '0' stimulus.
6. Complex Boolean functions of multiple input variables can be realized by simple extension of the circuit structures.
7. The input should be stable for a short period around the falling edge of the clock to meet setup and hold requirements.
8. When a transition 0 à 1 takes place in the clock input, the value of the slave output Q freezes at the value of D input existing just before the rising edge of the clock.
9. A complex digital system is broken down into component gates and memory elements by splitting the system in a hierarchical manner.
10. The last major refinement at the behavioral plane is concerned with the detailed Boolean description of the leaf cells followed by a transistor level realization of the leaf cells and mask generation.

- Fill in the blank with the following words.

Boolean, Y-chart Oxidation, P-type, Structural, Transmission, Structural, Discrete

1. With the implementation of the CMOS inverter, NOR gate and NAND gate, initially using .... transistors.
2. This structure is produced involving a series of chemical processing steps such as .... of silicon.
3. The structure of the n-channel transistor is made of a .... silicon substrate accommodating two diffused islands of n-type silicon.
4. Combinational logic circuits, rather gates, perform Boolean operations on multiple input variables and determine the outputs as .... functions of the inputs.
5. Thus both the .... gates are not simultaneously open for their respective input signals to pass to the common output node.
6. The three domains of representation that make up the .... are the behavioral domain.
7. At the .... level, the target chip is now described in terms of the logic gates.
8. The architecture of the corresponding processor in the .... domain is envisaged.

- Write *antonyms* of following words.

1. Complementary ....
2. Dissipation ....
3. Insulating ....
4. Deposition ....
5. Conducting ....
6. Transparent ....
7. Stable ....

1.4.4. Additional Information about Physical Layout Domain

The design flow at the behavioral domain starts from the algorithm that specifies the operation of the target chip. The architecture of the corresponding processor in the structural domain is envisaged. It is projected onto the chip surface in the physical (geometrical) layout domain by floor-planning.

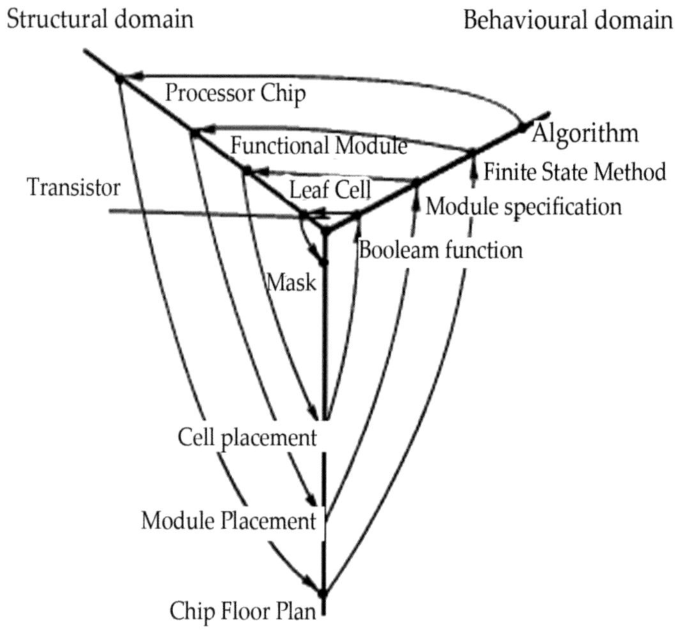

Figure 1.11. Physical layout domain.

The next development along the axis of the behavioral domain happens to be the finite state machines (FSMs) which are realized at the structural plane by functional modules such as registers, adders, multipliers, and arithmetic logic units (ALUs). The automatic placement and routing of these modules are then done on the physical plane with an objective of minimizing the area occupied by the interconnects and signal delay. Next phase of refinement on the behavioral level is the behavioral description of the module. At the structural level, the target chip is now described in terms of the logic gates (or leaf cells) which can be placed and interconnected using a cell placement and routing program. The last major refinement at the behavioral plane is concerned with the detailed Boolean description of the leaf cells followed by a transistor level realization of the leaf cells and mask generation. Actually, the leaf cells are pre-designed at the transistor level in the standard-cell based design style and stored in a library for logic.

1.5. FPGA

Field-programmable gate array (FPGA) technology continues to gain momentum, and the worldwide FPGA market is expected to grow from $1.9 billion in 2005 to $2.75 billion by 2010. Since its invention by Xilinx in 1984,

FPGAs have gone from being simple glue logic chips to actually replacing custom application-specific integrated circuits (ASICs) and processors for signal processing and control applications. Why has this technology been so successful? This article provides an introduction to FPGAs and highlights some of the benefits that make FPGAs unique.

At the highest level, FPGAs are reprogrammable silicon chips. Using prebuilt logic blocks and programmable routing resources, you can configure these chips to implement custom hardware functionality without ever having to pick up a breadboard or soldering iron. You develop digital computing tasks in software and compile them down to a configuration file or bitstream that contains information on how the components should be wired together. In addition, FPGAs are completely reconfigurable and instantly take on a brand new "personality" when you recompile a different configuration of circuitry. In the past, FPGA technology was only available to engineers with a deep understanding of digital hardware design. The rise of high-level design tools, however, is changing the rules of FPGA programming, with new technologies that convert graphical block diagrams or even C code into digital hardware circuitry.

FPGA chip adoption across all industries is driven by the fact that FPGAs combine the best parts of ASICs and processor-based systems. FPGAs provide hardware-timed speed and reliability, but they do not require high volumes to justify the large upfront expense of custom ASIC design. Reprogrammable silicon also has the same flexibility of software running on a processor-based system, but it is not limited by the number of processing cores available. Unlike processors, FPGAs are truly parallel in nature so different processing operations do not have to compete for the same resources. Each independent processing task is assigned to a dedicated section of the chip and can function autonomously without any influence from other logic blocks. As a result, the performance of one part of the application is not affected when additional processing is added.

1.5.1. Top Five Benefits of FPGA Technology

1. **Performance:** Taking advantage of hardware parallelism, FPGAs exceed the computing power of digital signal processors (DSPs) by breaking the paradigm of sequential execution and accomplishing more per clock cycle. BDTI, a noted analyst and benchmarking firm, released benchmarks showing how FPGAs can deliver many times the processing power per dollar

of a DSP solution in some applications. Controlling inputs and outputs (I/O) at the hardware level provides faster response times and specialized functionality to closely match application requirements.

2. **Time to Market:** FPGA technology offers flexibility and rapid prototyping capabilities in the face of increased time-to-market concerns. You can test an idea or concept and verify it in hardware without going through the long fabrication process of custom ASIC design. You can then implement incremental changes and iterate on an FPGA design within hours instead of weeks. Commercial off-the-shelf (COTS) hardware is also available with different types of I/O already connected to a user-programmable FPGA chip. The growing availability of high-level software tools decrease the learning curve with layers of abstraction and often include valuable IP cores (prebuilt functions) for advanced control and signal processing.

3. **Cost:** The nonrecurring engineering (NRE) expense of custom ASIC design far exceeds that of FPGA-based hardware solutions. The large initial investment in ASICs is easy to justify for OEMs shipping thousands of chips per year, but many end users need custom hardware functionality for the tens to hundreds of systems in development. The very nature of programmable silicon means that there is no cost for fabrication or long lead times for assembly. As system requirements often change over time, the cost of making incremental changes to FPGA designs are quite negligible when compared to the large expense of an ASIC.

4. **Reliability:** While software tools provide the programming environment, FPGA circuitry is truly a "hard" implementation of program execution. Processor-based systems often involve several layers of abstraction to help schedule tasks and share resources among multiple processes. The driver layer controls hardware resources, and the operating system manages memory and processor bandwidth. For any given processor core, only one instruction can execute at a time, and processor-based systems are continually at risk of time-critical tasks pre-empting one another. FPGAs, which do not use operating systems, minimize reliability concerns with true parallel execution and deterministic hardware dedicated to every task.

5. **Long-Term Maintenance:** As mentioned earlier, FPGA chips are field-upgradable and do not require the time and expense involved with ASIC redesign. Digital communication protocols, for example, have specifications that can change over time, and ASIC-based interfaces may cause maintenance and forward compatibility challenges. Being reconfigurable, FPGA chips are able to keep up with future modifications that might be necessary. As a product or system matures, you can make functional enhancements without spending time redesigning hardware or modifying the board layout.

1.5.2. FPGA Usage

In the past, FPGAs have been a niche market. Typical applications were prototyping and emulation systems. Complexity was too low to implement real products and pricing was too expensive for moderate volumes. In the past four years, FPGA technology made large success, changing the way FPGAs are used dramatically:

- FPGAs are being used in mainstream products;
- Networking;
- Telecom;
- DSP;
- Consumer electronics.

> Find the *synonyms* for the underlined words.

1. An Artificial Neural Network (ANN) is an information processing paradigm that is inspired by the way biological nervous systems, such as the brain, process information.
2. An ANN is configured for a specific application, such as pattern recognition or data classification, through a learning process.
3. Neural network simulations appear to be a recent development. However, this field was established before the advent of computers, and has survived at least one major setback and several eras.
4. These pioneers were able to develop convincing technology which surpassed the limitations identified by Minsky and Papert. Minsky and Papert, published a book in which they summed up a general feeling of frustration among researchers.

5. Partial destruction of a network leads to the corresponding degradation of performance.
6. When a neuron receives excitatory input that is sufficiently large compared with its inhibitory input, it sends a spike of electrical activity down its axon.
7. Feed-forward ANNs tend to be straight forward networks that associate inputs with outputs.
8. Feedback architectures are also referred to as interactive or recurrent, although the latter term is often used to denote feedback connections in single-layer organizations.
9. The single-layer organization, in which all units are connected to one another, constitutes the most general case and is of more potential computational power than hierarchically structured multi-layer organizations.
10. An important issue concerning supervised learning is the problem of error convergence, ie the minimization of error between the desired and computed unit values.

➢ Fill in the blank with the following words.

Neurons, Synaptic, Mapping, Axon, Odors Weights, Machine code, Hidden

1. Learning in biological systems involves adjustments to the .... connections that exist between the neurons.
2. These instructions are then converted to a high level language program and then into .... that the computer can understand.
3. The neuron sends out spikes of electrical activity through a long, thin stand known as an ...., which splits into thousands of branches.
4. We conduct these neural networks by first trying to deduce the essential features of .... and their interconnections.
5. The MCP neuron has the ability to adapt to a particular situation by changing its .... and/or threshold.
6. The behavior of the output units depends on the activity of the .... units and the weights between the hidden and output units.
7. Associative .... in which the network learns to produce a particular pattern on the set of input units.
8. These identified .... would then be electronically transmitted to another site where a door generation system would recreate them.

> ➢ Write *antonyms* of following words.
> 1. Highly ....
> 2. Boosted ....
> 3. Resurgence ....
> 4. Deduce ....
> 5. Novel ....
> 6. Equilibrium.........................
> 7. Influential ....

1.5.3. Additional Information about FPGA Technology in Detail

FPGAs are chips, which are programmed by the customer to perform the desired functionality. The chips may be programmed either:

- **Once:** Antifuse technology, e.g., devices manufactured by Quicklogic.
- **Several Times:** Flash based, e.g., devices manufacture by Actel.
- **Dynamically:** SRAM based, e.g., devices manufactured by Actel, Altera, Atmel, Cypress, Lucent, Xilinx Each technology has its own advantages, which shall be discussed only very briefly:
- **Antifuse FPGAs:**
  - Devices are configured by burning a set of fuses. Once the chip is configured, it cannot be altered any more.
  - Bug fixes and updates possible for new PCBs, but hardly for already manufactured boards.
  - ASIC replacement for small volumes.
- Flash FPGAs:
  - Devices may be re-programmed several 1,000 times and are non-volatile, i.e., keep their configuration after power-off;
  - With only marginal additional effort, the chips may be updated in the field;
  - Expensive;
  - Re-configuration takes several seconds.
- SRAM FPGAs:
  - Currently the dominating technology;
  - Unlimited re-programming;

- Additional circuitry is required to load the configuration into the FPGA after power on;
- Re-configuration is very fast, some devices allow even partial re-configuration during operation;
- Allows new approaches and applications buzz word "reconfigurable computing," e.g., a circuit, that searches for a specific DNA pattern, or a mobile phone that;
- Downloads the latest protocol update.

CHAPTER

2 Memory

Contents

2.1. SYSTEM MEMORY

The system memory is the place where the computer holds current programs and data that are in use. The term "memory" is somewhat ambiguous; it can refer to many different parts of the PC because there are so many different kinds of memory that a PC uses. However, when used by itself, "memory" usually refers to the main system memory, which holds the instructions that the processor executes and the data that those instructions work with.

Memory plays a significant role in the following important aspects of your computer system: (effect of memory):

1. **Performance:** The amount and type of system memory you have is an important contributing factor to overall performance. In many ways, it is more important than the processor, because insufficient memory can cause a processor to work at 50% or even more below its performance potential. This is an important point that is often overlooked.
2. **Software Support:** Newer programs require more memory than old ones. More memory will give you access to programs that you cannot use with a lesser amount.
3. **Reliability and Stability:** Bad memory is a leading cause of mysterious system problems. Ensuring you have high-quality memory will result in a PC that runs smoothly and exhibits fewer problems. Also, even high-quality memory will not work well if you use the wrong kind.
4. **Upgradeability:** There are many different types of memory available, and some are more universal than others. Making a wise choice can allow you to migrate your memory to a future system or continue to use it after you upgrade your motherboard.

A computer's memory can be viewed as a list of cells into which numbers can be placed or read. Each cell has a numbered "address" and can store a single number. The computer can be instructed to "put the number 123 into the cell numbered 1357" or to "add the number that is in cell 1357 to the number that is in cell 2468 and put the answer into cell 1595." The information stored in memory may represent practically anything. Letters, numbers, even computer instructions can be placed into memory with equal ease. Since the CPU does not differentiate between different types of information, it is up to the software to give significance to what the memory sees as nothing but a series of numbers.

In almost all modern computers, each memory cell is set up to store binary numbers in groups of eight bits (called a byte). Each byte is able to represent 256 different numbers; either from 0 to 255 or –128 to +127. To store larger numbers, several consecutive bytes may be used (typically, two, four or eight). When negative numbers are required, they are usually stored in two's complement notation. Other arrangements are possible but are usually not seen outside of specialized applications or historical contexts. A computer can store any kind of information in memory as long as it can be somehow represented in numerical form. Modern computers have billions or even trillions of bytes of memory.

The CPU contains a special set of memory cells called registers that can be read and written to much more rapidly than the main memory area. There are typically between 2 and 100 registers depending on the type of CPU. Registers are used for the most frequently needed data items to avoid having to access main memory every time data is needed. Since data is constantly being worked on, reducing the need to access main memory (which is often slow compared to the ALU and control units) greatly increases the computer's speed. Your system memory is an important part of the main processing subsystem of the PC, tied in with the processor, cache, motherboard, and chipset.

This section describes various aspects of the system memory, including how the system memory works, the different technologies used, packaging styles and how operating systems and programs organize and use the memory in the PC. Special attention is given to error detection and correction (which is in my opinion a greatly under-emphasized subject today) as well as details on how to know what type of memory works in different kinds of PCs.

2.1.1. Volatile and Nonvolatile Memory

Memory can be split into two main categories: volatile and nonvolatile. Volatile memory loses any data as soon as the system is turned off; it requires constant power to remain viable. Most types of RAM fall into this category. Nonvolatile memory does not lose its data when the system or device is turned off. A number of types of memory fall into this category. The most familiar is ROM.

2.1.2. Primary and Secondary

There are two types of memories: primary and secondary. The primary memory or the main memory is part of the main computer system. The processor or the CPU directly stores and retrieves information from it. This memory is accessed by CPU, in random fashion. That means any location of this memory can be accessed by the CPU to either read information from it, or to store information in it.

The primary memory itself is implemented by two types of memory technologies. The first is called random access memory (RAM) and the other is read only memory (ROM). A more appropriate name for RAM is RWM (read write memory), the CPU can write and read information from any primary memory location implemented using RAM. The other part of primary memory is implemented using ROM which stands for ROM.

The memory subsystem, also known as the secondary storage, allow for extra data, storage exceeding the CPU's primary storage. It I an efficient and compact means of storing large amount of data, ready for retrieval or further processing. It is substantially less expensive than the CPU's primary storage. One limitation, though, of secondary storage, is that its retrieval time is slower than the primary memory.

Primary memory is much faster and also it is more cost effective. But the secondary memory is much slower and also less costly. It stores the data permanently unless it is erased. The secondary memory is usually available in the form of floppy disk storage media, hard disk, CD, DVD, Pen drive (i.e., mass storage devices), memory chips. A 5- and 1/4-inch floppy disk typically stores 1.44 mb of data. The data on the floppy disk is organized in terms of tracks and sectors. Hard disk can have large capacity something like 80–300 GB's or higher. Hard disk itself is made up of, large number of platters. Hard disk is usually much faster compared to floppy disk. CD can store up to 750 mb of data. Information on CD ROM is organized in terms of a spiral track. A DVD is digital Versatile Disk and can store 4.6 Gigabyte of information. All these CD disks are usually writing ones and read many times (if the disk is not multi session and re writable). So are the DVDs.

2.1.3. Primary Memory Types

Most of the system's primary memory is located on the system board. Primary memory typically exists in two or three forms on the system board:

1. **Read-Only Memory (ROM):** It contains the computer's permanent startup programs. ROM devices store information in a permanent fashion and are used to hold programs and data that do not change.
2. **Random Access Memory (RAM):** It is quick enough to operate

directly with the microprocessor and can be read from, and written to, as often as desired. RAM devices retain the information stored in them only as long as electrical power is applied to the IC. Any interruption of power causes the memory contents to vanish.

3. **Cache Memory:** It is a fast RAM system designed to hold data recently accessed from the disk drive that the microprocessor may need again.

2.1.4. Comparing Primary and Secondary Memory

Primary Memory	Secondary Memory
Fast	Slow
Expensive	Cheap
Low capacity	Large capacity
Connects directly to the processor	Not connected directly to the processor

> Find the *synonyms* for the underlined words.

1. The term "memory" is somewhat ambiguous.
2. Memory plays a significant role in the following important aspects of your computer system.
3. Insufficient memory can cause a processor to work at 50% or even more below its performance potential.
4. Making a wise choice can allow you to migrate your memory to a future system.
5. Special attention is given to error detection and correction.
6. Volatile memory loses any data as soon as the system is turned off.
7. The primary memory itself is implemented by two types of memory technologies.
8. It stores the data permanently unless it is erased.
9. Hard disk itself is made up of, large number of platters.
10. RAM devices retain the information stored in them only as long as electrical power is applied to the IC.

➢ Fill in the blank with the following words.

Multi-Purpose, Situated, Form, Suitable, Capability, Nonvolatile, Accidental, Sufficient

1. Random access memory (RAM) is quick .... to operate directly with the microprocessor.
2. Most of the system's primary memory is .... on the system board.
3. Hard disk can have large .... something like 80–300 GB's or higher.
4. ROM devices store information in a permanent .... and are used to hold programs and data.
5. A DVD is digital .... Disk and can store 4.6 Gigabyte of information.
6. More .... name for RAM is RWM.
7. This memory is accessed by CPU, in .... fashion.
8. .... memory does not lose its data when the system or device is turned off.

➢ Write *antonyms* of following words.

1. Primary ....
2. Require ....
3. Effective ....
4. Start up ....
5. Constant ....
6. Familiar ....
7. Permanent ....

2.1.5. Additional Information About Main Memories

A computer system is generally comprised of several component parts including a processor, computer memory, a data bus, and other peripheral devices and components. The processor accesses, modifies, and writes data to RAM. The data contained in computer memory is transferred to the processor through the data bus. Memory is a semiconductor storage device for holding programs or data. There're three basic forms of memories which include dynamic storage in which data must be constantly refreshed and in which data are erased when power is no longer applied to the cell, non-volatile memory in which data remains permanently in the cell even when power is not applied, and static memory which does not need to be refreshed but which loses its data when power is no longer applied to the cell. In a computer system, non-volatile memory is used for long-term storage of programs and data which seldom or never changes, and volatile memory devices are used for the short-term storage of program instructions and data during the execution of a program. According to the application functions, memories can be categorized into ROM and RAM. As the name implies, the ROM is only read accessible. A ROM device cannot be rewritten once it has been programmed.

Embedded software applications use ROM to store embedded code and data records. The processor in an embedded software application retrieves each instruction from ROM and executes it. The RAM can perform both write and read operations. RAM also differs from ROM in that when power is disconnected from RAM, the data stored in RAM is lost whereas when power is disconnected from ROM the data stored in read only memory remains. The ROM is further categorized into a mask read only memory programmable read only memory (PROM), erasable programmable read only memory (EPROM), and electrically erasable programmable read only memory (EEPROM). Whereas the RAM can be further categorized into a static random-access memory (SRAM) and a dynamic random-access memory (DRAM). Static read/write random-access memory (SRAM) is a type of volatile memory in which the data, once it is written to a memory location, remains stored there as long as power is applied to the memory chip. Dynamic random-access memories (DRAMs) are a mainstay in the semiconductor industry. DRAMs are data storage devices that store data as charge on a storage capacitor.

In DRAM, the data stored at each location is periodically refreshed by reading it and then writing it back again to the same location, or else it disappears. One type of DRAM transfers information synchronously with a clock signal. This type of DRAM is referred to as synchronous DRAM (SDRAM). SDRAM transfers information once every clock cycle of the clock signal, such as the rising edge of the clock signal. Nevertheless, DDR DRAM transfers data on each edge of the clock signal, thus doubling the peak throughput of the memory device as compared with SDRAM. The magneto resistive random-access memory (MRAM) is an alternative memory device to DRAM. An MRAM device uses magnetic orientations to retain data in its memory cells. MRAM devices are relatively fast, are nonvolatile, consume relatively little power, and do not suffer from a write cycle limitation. PROM allows the device manufacturer to program the embedded code. This allows for revisions in the code but still does not allow for modification or erasure of the ROM once it has been programmed. Erasable programmable read only memory (EPROM), electronically erasable programmable read only memory (EEPROM) and flash memory are a growing class of non-volatile storage integrated circuits (ICs) based on floating gate transistors. Flash memory devices typically use a one-transistor memory cell that allows for high memory densities, high reliability, and low power consumption. Common uses for flash memory include personal computers, personal digital assistants (PDAs), digital cameras, and cellular phones.

2.2. RANDOM ACCESS MEMORY (RAM)

RAM is an abbreviation for random access memory. It usually refers to "temporary" memory, as when the system is shut down, the memory is lost. This is why the memory is referred to as being "random," as any piece of information can be circulated through the memory regardless of its location and its relation to any other information within the RAM. The first of the many RAMs to come in the future was created in 1951 and was used until the late 1960s and early 1970s.

2.2.1. Types of RAMs

RAM divide into two main categories:

1. **Static RAM (SRAM):** It is a type of RAM that holds its data without external refresh, for as long as power is supplied to the circuit. This is contrasted to dynamic RAM (DRAM), which must be refreshed many times per second in order to hold its data contents. SRAMs are used for specific applications within the PC, where their strengths outweigh their weaknesses compared to DRAM:

i. **Simplicity:** SRAMs don't require external refresh circuitry or other work in order for them to keep their data intact.

ii. **Speed:** SRAM is faster than DRAM.

In contrast, SRAMs have the following weaknesses, compared to DRAMs:

i. **Cost:** SRAM is, byte for byte, several times more expensive than DRAM.

ii. **Size:** SRAMs take up much more space than DRAMs (which is part of why the cost is higher).

These advantages and disadvantages taken together obviously show that performance-wise, SRAM is superior to DRAM, and we would use it exclusively if only we could do so economically. Unfortunately, 32 MB of SRAM would be prohibitively large and costly, which is why DRAM is used for system memory. SRAMs are used instead for level 1 cache and level 2 cache memory, for which it is perfectly suited; cache memory needs to be very fast, and not very large.

SRAM is manufactured in a way rather similar to how processors are: highly integrated transistor patterns photo-etched into silicon. Each SRAM bit is comprised of between four and six transistors, which is why SRAM takes up much more space compared to DRAM, which uses only one (plus a capacitor). Because a SRAM chip is comprised of thousands or millions of identical cells, it is much easier to make than a CPU, which is a large die with a non-repetitive structure. This is one reason why RAM chips cost much less than processors does. See this discussion of how processors are manufactured; this process is similar (but simplified somewhat) for making memory circuits.

2. **DRAM:** Memory devices are used in a wide variety of applications, including computer systems. Computer systems and other electronic devices containing a microprocessor typically include system memory, which is generally implemented using DRAM. A DRAM cell typically includes a memory cell coupled to a storage capacitor. A DRAM includes a large number of memory cells, each of which can store at least one bit of data. The memory cells are arranged in an array having a number of rows and columns. The memory cells of dynamic random-access memories (DRAMs) include two main components, a field-effect transistor (FET) and a capacitor which functions as a storage element. The cells in the array are typically arranged in rows and columns. Each cell is situated at the intersection of a row and a column. Each cell in the DRAM array may be accessed by simultaneously addressing the intersecting row and column. The storage capacitor is accessed using an access transistor which allows charge to be stored in the storage capacitor or retrieves charge from the storage capacitor depending on whether the desired action is a read or write function. Dynamic random-access memories (DRAMs) may have memory pre-charge, activate,

read, and write operations. The primary advantage of DRAM is that it uses relatively few components to store each bit of data and is thus relatively inexpensive to provide relatively high-capacity system memory. A disadvantage of DRAM is that their memory cells must be periodically refreshed.

2.2.2. Security Concerns

SDRAMs are known to not fully shut off when the power is cut. Instead, the stored memory is faded away. While this fading away only takes seconds in a normal room temperature, which is not the case in lower temperatures, which then the fading away can take up to minutes. Therefore, encrypted information could potentially be leaked as it is still stored in the memory.

2.2.3. Recent Developments

Currently non-volatile RAMs are under development, which will mean that memory can still be stored when the power is shut off. The more advanced step yet to have been taken was in 2004 when a fully functioning carbon Nano tube memory type holding 10 GB, have been developed Recently in 2006, "Solid State Drives" with sizes of 150 GB and a faster speed than the normal hard drives have been created.

➢ Find the *synonyms* for the underlined words.

1. It usually refers to "temporary" memory, as when the system is shut down, the memory is lost.
2. Static RAM is a type of RAM that holds its data without external refresh, for as long as power is supplied to the circuit.
3. SRAMs are used for specific applications within the PC.
4. These advantages and disadvantages taken together obviously show that performance-wise, SRAM is superior to DRAM
5. A SRAM chip is comprised of thousands or millions of identical cells.
6. The memory cells are arranged in an array having a number of rows and columns
7. Each cell in the DRAM array may be accessed by simultaneously addressing the intersecting row and column.
8. Dynamic random access memories (DRAMs) may have memory recharge, activate, read, and write operations
9. Currently non-volatile RAMs are under development
10. Unfortunately, 32 MB of SRAM would be prohibitively large and costly.

➢ Fill in the blank with the following words.

Solely, SRAM, Shaped, Renewed, Comparatively, Diversity, Undamaged

1. SRAMs don't require external refresh circuitry or other work in order for them to keep their data.......
2. We would use it .... if only we could do so economically.
3. ....is manufactured in a way rather similar to how processors are: highly-integrated transistor patterns photo-etched into silicon.
4. Memory devices are used in a wide .... of applications, including computer systems.
5. The storage capacitor is .... within a deep trench etched into a semiconductor substrate.
6. The primary advantage of DRAM is that it uses .... few components to store each bit of data
7. A disadvantage of DRAM is that their memory cells must be periodically ....

➢ Write *antonyms* of following words.

1. Disadvantage ....
2. Fade ....
3. Encrypt ....
4. Random ....
5. External ....
6. Strength ....
7. Weaknesses.........................

2.2.4. Additional Information about RAMs

The most widely used RAMs today are SRAMs (static RAMs), which stores data in a state of a flip-flop, or DRAMs (dynamic RAMs), Flash, and EPROM, which stores data as a charge in a capacitor. Another well-known type of RAM, a ROM, is a type of a RAM that has permanently enabled/disabled selected transistors by using a metal mask. ROMs thus cannot store any further charges.

Flash memory is also widely used. Because SRAMs and DRAMs are known to be highly volatile, many new products adopt the flash memory technology. Some examples of devices using flash memory include portable music players, scientific calculators, mobile phones, and even certain types of personal computers such as the one laptop per child (OLPC) devices.

Flash memory is divided into two types: the NOR type and the NAND type. The NOR type is the one able to conduct a random access, therefore being widely used as a ROM in today's market. However, as the NOR is not able to, it is often used in flash USB drives.

In today's computers, RAMs are shipped in a form of module known as DRAM modules or memory modules. It is about the size of a chewing gum and with the Plug n Play technology, these can easily be replaced by taking it out of the port and replacing it with a new one. Not to forget, there is also an extremely small amount of RAM (known as SRAMs) within CPUs, motherboards, hard drives, and other parts of the system.

2.3. TYPES OF ROM

2.3.1. Read-Only Memory

Read-only memory or ROM is an integrated-circuit memory chip that contains configuration data. ROM is commonly called firmware because its programming is fully embedded into the ROM chip. As such, ROM is a hardware and software in one.

Because data is fully incorporated at the ROM chip's manufacture, data stored can neither be erased nor replaced. This means permanent and secure data storage. However, if a mistake is made in manufacture, a ROM chip becomes unusable. The most expensive stage of ROM manufacture, therefore, is creating the template. If a template is readily available, duplicating the ROM chip is very easy and affordable. A ROM chip is also non-volatile, so data stored in it is not lost when power is turned off.

2.3.2. RAM versus ROM

Both RAM and ROM provide the user random access to stored data. However, RAM provides only short-term memory since data stored in RAM is lost when power is turned off. ROM, on the other hand, provides long-term storage since data is permanently etched into the ROM chip. One other difference between the two is that RAM's data can frequently and speedily be altered and changed at will. ROM cannot be reconfigured at all.

2.3.3. ROM Chip Manufacture

The ROM chip has a matrix of columns and rows. The point of intersection between the column and the row is called a cell. Each cell will have a value of either 1 or 0. The manufacturer of the ROM chip has to determine each cell's value before the ROM manufacture ensues.

After the program has been designed, the ROM chip can now be made. At each cell where the value should be 1, a diode is placed to connect column to row. At each cell where the value should be 0, no diode is placed.

2.3.4. The ROM Chip's Diode

The diode is the cell's electronic check valve. Its main function in the ROM chip is to control and direct the flow of electric current in cells. Specifically, it transfers the electric current from column to row.

The diode has a minimum voltage requirement, what is commonly called the forward break over, which needs to be surpassed before the diode will transfer the charge from the column to the row of the cell. The usual ROM diode forward break over voltage is around 0.6 volts.

2.3.5. Programmable Read-Only Memory

PROM stands for Programmable Read-Only Memory. It was invented by Wen Tsing Chow in 1956. Unlike a ROM chip, a PROM chip comes from the manufacturers devoid of any programming. Programming is done by the end user or the makers of electronic devices which require a permanent data storage device. Since it is cheaper than a ROM chip, it is also useful for making experimental programming test runs. Successful programming can later on be applied to a ROM chip at manufacture.

A PROM chip can only be programmed with the desired data once. Data or programming information stored in PROM chips is permanent. A PROM chip is also non-volatile, so data is not lost when power is turned off. The PROM chip is physically similar to a ROM chip as it also has an array of columns and rows. Unlike the ROM chip, however, all columns and rows are connected by a fuse at their points of intersection. Every point of connection determines one cell or one bit. Since connection between the columns and rows is intact and therefore charges can pass unhindered from column to rows, a newly manufactured PROM chip's cells all have a value of 1.

2.3.6. PROM Programmer

A PROM Programmer, also known as a PROM blower, is used in programming a PROM chip. The PROM programmer is a device that can hold and program more than one PROM chip at the same time. Basically, what it does is melt the fuses where the truth table data indicates the value of a cell or bit should be 0.

2.3.7. Programming a PROM

The process of programming a PROM chip is called PROM "burning" or "blowing" because it involves burning or blowing out the fuses of some cells whose value needs to be altered from 1 to 0. Before programming a PROM chip, the PROM programmer is first configured so it contains the desired PROM burning instructions. After this is done, the PROM chip is inserted into one of the PROM programmer slots. The PROM programmer sends a predetermined amount of voltage pulse ranging from 12 to 21 volts. This high voltage is directed only to the fuses belonging to cells whose value has to be changed from 1 to 0.

When the charge reaches the fuse, the high voltage causes this fuse to blow out or burn out. The burned-out fuse no longer connects a column to a row in a cell and the row is rendered incapable of receiving any charge from the column. The cell with a burned-out fuse has a value of 0. PROM programming is irreversible because burning a PROM involves permanent damage to some of the fuses. The cells whose fuses have been burned out will have a permanent value of 0. After PROM programming has been accomplished, there's no returning the altered cells' value back to 1. Thus, the PROM chip's programming cannot be modified, and no new data can be written to an already programmed PROM chip.

2.3.8. Configuring an EPROM

An EPROM is an array of columns and rows. Each intersection is called a cell and each cell has a floating gate transistor and a control gate transistor. These two transistors are separated by a fine oxide layer.

The floating gate is connected to the grid row (wordline) through the control gate. The cell's value is 1 if the floating gate's connection to the wordline through the control gate exists. All cells of a blank EPROM have a value of 1.

To configure an EPROM chip, you need to change certain cells from 1 to 0. The cell value 0 is attained if the connection between the floating gate transistor and the word line is removed. This is done through a process known as Fowler-Nordheim tunneling. To accomplish tunneling, a charge of electricity, typically 10–13 volts, is passed through the column (bit line). This electric charge proceeds to the floating gate. In reaction, the floating gate releases electrons which are in turn trapped on the oxide layer. The electric charge, in effect, rearranges the floating gate's electron configuration. The excited electrons become a barrier between the floating gate and the control gate. The link between the control gate and the word line is subsequently eliminated and the cell's value changes from 1 to 0.

2.3.9. Erasing EPROM Programming

To erase EPROM programming, sufficiently strong energy should be passed through the EPROM to break down the wall of negative electrons blocking the floating gate's link to the word line. Most EPROM chip has a quartz window on top and this is where this energy is directed.

Erasure of EPROM programming is accomplished by using ultraviolet light that belongs to the UVC range and has a frequency of 253.7. Remove the EPROM chip from your computer or electronic device then put it under the EPROM eraser for a number of minutes. The EPROM Eraser will emit UV light which should be directed towards the quartz window from where it proceeds to flow through the cells and unblock the floating gates.

This energy will unblock all cells so that all cell values will return to 1. EPROM programming erasure is non-selective. This means that a specific part of the EPROM chip cannot be selected for reconfiguration. When UV light is directed towards the quartz window of the EPROM, all data will be lost.

It is inadvisable to leave the EPROM chip under the EPROM eraser for too long. This may lead to over erasure. An over-erased EPROM chip can no longer be used for storing data. Due to overcharging of UV light, the EPROM's floating gates become unstable, rendering them incapable of holding any electrons.

2.3.10. Electrically Erasable Programmable Read-Only Memory

EPROM or erasable programmable read only memory was invented by Engr. Dov Frohman. It is a ROM-type chip that can hold data from 10–20 years. It is different from PROM because it can be programmed more than once.

EEPROM stands for Electrically Erasable Programmable Read-Only Memory. An EEPROM is like an EPROM chip since it can be written in or programmed more than once. Unlike the EPROM chip, however, an EEPROM chip need not be taken out of the computer or electronic device of which it is part when a new program or data needs to be written on it. Selective programming can be done to an EEPROM chip. The user can alter the value of certain cells without needing to erase the programming on other cells. Thus, sections of data can be erased and replaced without needing to alter the rest of the chip's programming. Data stored in an EEPROM chip is permanent, at least until the user decides to erase and replace the information it contains. Furthermore, the data stored in an EEPROM chip is not lost even when power is turned off.

2.3.11. History of the EEPROM

The EEPROM is a modification of the EPROM and was designed by George Perlegos. Its development began in 1978 while Perlegos was still employed by Intel. However, the archetypal EEPROM still had to be taken out of the computer or electronic device of which it was part if any reprogramming was necessary.

Perlegos designed the first fully functional EEPROM. To eliminate the necessity of external programming, Perlegos and company made the insulating layer thinner and integrated an oscillator and capacitor circuit into the memory chip itself. This charge pump can produce the necessary programming voltage. Since it is fully integrated in every EEPROM chip, there is no need to take out the EEPROM chip for erasing and programming. To configure an EEPROM chip, an electric field produced by the charge pump is applied locally to cells marked for modification.

2.3.12. EEPROM Structure

The EEPROM chip is physically similar to the EPROM chip. It is also composed of cells with two transistors. The floating gate is separated from the control gate by a thin oxide layer. Unlike the EPROM chip, however, the EEPROM chip's oxide layer is much thinner. In EEPROM chips, the insulating layer is only around 1 nanometer thick whereas in EPROM chips, the oxide layer is around 3 nanometers thick.

The thinner oxide layer means lower voltage requirements for initiating changes in cell value. Tunneling the electrons of the floating gate towards the oxide layer separating the floating gate and the control gate is still the method of changing a bit's value from 1 to 0. To erase EEPROM programming, the electron barrier still has to be overcome by the application of enough programming voltage.

2.3.13. EEPROM Limitations

While the EEPROM can be reprogrammed, the number of times it can be altered is limited. This is the main reason why EEPROM chips are popular for storing only configuration data such as the computer's BIOS code which doesn't require frequent reprogramming. The oxide insulating layer can be damaged by frequent rewrite. Modern-day EEPROMs can be rewritten up to a million times.

> ➢ Find the *synonyms* for the underlined words.
>
> 1. A ROM chip is also nonvolati so data stored in it is not lost when power is turned off.
> 2. The manufacturer of the ROM chip has to determine each cell's value before the ROM manufacture ensues.
> 3. Specifically, it transfers the electric current from column to row.
> 4. APROM chip comes from the manufacturers devoid of any programming.
> 5. It is also useful for making experimental programming test runs. Successful programming can later on be applied to a ROM chip at manufacture.
> 6. All columns and rows are connected by a fuse at their points of intersection.
> 7. Since connection between the columns and rows is intact and therefore charges can pass unhindered from column to rows.
> 8. To configure an EPROM chip, you need to change certain cells from 1 to 0.
> 9. To erase EPROM programming, sufficiently strong energy should be passed through the EPROM to break down the wall
> 10. To eliminate the necessity of external programming, Perlegos and company made the insulating layer thinner and integrated an oscillator and capacitor circuit into the memory chip itself.

➢ Fill in the blank with the following words.

Include, Distinct, EPROM, Dissolve, Unchangeable, Find out, EEPROM, Substitute

1. Thus, sections of data can be erased and .... without needing to alter the rest of the chip's programming.
2. Tunneling the electrons of the floating gate towards the oxide layer .... the floating gate.
3. This is the main reason why .... chips are popular for storing only configuration data.
4. It is inadvisable to leave the EPROM chip under the .... eraser for too long. This may lead to over erasure.
5. PROM programming is .... because burning a PROM involves permanent damage to some of the fuses.
6. . Before programming a PROM chip, the PROM programmer is first configured so it .... the desired PROM burning instructions.
7. Basically, what it does is .... the fuses where the truth table data indicates the value of a cell or bit should be 0.
8. Every point of connection .... one cell or one bit.

➢ Write *antonyms* of following words.

1. Primary ....
2. Require ....
3. Effective ....
4. Start up ....
5. Constant ....
6. Familiar ....
7. Permanent ....

2.3.14. Additional Information about ROMs

One major type of memory that is used in PCs is called read-only memory, or ROM for short. ROM is a type of memory that normally can only be read, as opposed to RAM which can be both read and written. There are two main reasons that read-only memory is used for certain functions within the PC:

1. **Permanence:** The values stored in ROM are always there, whether the power is on or not. A ROM can be removed from the PC, stored for an indefinite period of time, and then replaced, and the data it contains will still be there. For this reason, it is called

non-volatile storage. A hard disk is also non-volatile, for the same reason, but regular RAM is not.

2. **Security:** The fact that ROM cannot easily be modified provides a measure of security against accidental (or malicious) changes to its contents. You are not going to find viruses infecting true ROMs, for example; it's just not possible. (It's technically possible with erasable EPROMs, though in practice never seen.)

Read-only memory is most commonly used to store system-level programs that we want to have available to the PC at all times. The most common example is the system BIOS program, which is stored in a ROM called (amazingly enough) the system BIOS ROM. Having this in a permanent ROM means it is available when the power is turned on so that the PC can use it to boot up the system. Remember that when you first turn on the PC the system memory is empty, so there has to be something for the PC to use when it starts up. See this section for a description of the system BIOS ROM; see here for a description of the system boot sequence.

While the whole point of a ROM is supposed to be that the contents cannot be changed, there are times when being able to change the contents of a ROM can be very useful. There are several ROM variants that can be changed under certain circumstances; these can be thought of as "mostly read-only memory." The following are the different types of ROMs with a description of their relative modifiability.

2.3.15. ROM

A regular ROM is constructed from hard-wired logic, encoded in the silicon itself, much the way that a processor is. It is designed to perform a specific function and cannot be changed. This is inflexible and so regular ROMs are only used generally for programs that are static (not changing often) and mass-produced. This product is analogous to a commercial software CD-ROM that you purchase in a store.

1. **Programmable ROM (PROM):** Semiconductor memory devices can be classified into different types. Among them, there are random access memories (RAMs) and read only memories (ROMs). When the power supply to a memory is interrupted, stored data in the RAM is erased while the ROM maintains stored data. For this reason, memory devices such as read only memories are called "nonvolatile memory devices."

An electrically programmable read only memory (EPROM) device is a non-volatile memory IC which is employed to store a bit of binary data in each cell. An EPROM is widely used in a variety of logic devices because it can electrically store and erase data, and it can retain data when power is turned off. EPROM structures are used to build non-volatile semiconductor memories, especially for ICs (embedded EPROM) and generally in computers or in microprocessor-controlled devices for storing programs and/or data that must be retained without a supply voltage. The EPROM is a core device of a micro controller unit for controlling equipment such as a central processing unit (CPU) and remote controllers for household appliances like televisions (TVs), video, or audio devices. EPROMs are implemented using floating gate field effect transistors in which the binary states of the EPROM cell are represented by the presence or absence of sufficient charge on the floating gate to prevent conduction even when a normal high signal is applied to the gate of the EPROM transistor. Each memory cell of an EPROM structure generally has two transistors, namely a selection or access transistor that selects the memory cell, and a floating gate transistor, whose floating gate represents an erased or programmed state according to its positive or negative charge. The memory cell transistor's state is read by placing an operating voltage across its source and drain and on its control gate, and then detecting the level of current flowing between the source and drain as to whether the device is programmed to be "on" or "off" at the control gate voltage selected.

2. **Electrically Erasable Programmable ROM (EEPROM):** The next level of erasability is Electrical erasable programmable read-only memory (EEPROM) is a type of non-volatile memory with many advantages including a rapid response, a large storage capacity and a small size. Electrically erasable and programmable read only memory (EEPROM) serves for multiple data write/read/rapid erase operations, and the data stored therein stays after supplying power is off. The electrically erasable programmable read-only memory (EEPROM) has proven useful because it combines the convenience of non-volatile data storage with the capability to erase the stored data electrically, then program new data. Electrically erasable and programmable read only

memory (EEPROM) is currently one the most widely used memory devices applied in personal computers and electronic equipment. An EEPROM memory device typically includes EEPROM memory cells arranged in an array and peripheral circuits around the array for accessing the memory cells for program or erase operations. EEPROM cells have floating gates similar to erasable programmable read only memory (EPROM) cells. The basic EEPROM memory cell has a FET with a control gate and a floating gate. The cell is erased and programmed by producing a potential difference between the control gate and the source or drain large enough to cause Fowler-Nordheim tunneling of electrons into or out of the floating gate. EEPROM cells and EPROM cells are programmed or erased by injecting electrons into the floating gates or ejecting the electrons out of the floating gates. A memory cell in an early developed conventional EEPROM comprises a transistor with a floating gate to achieve the operations of writing, erasing, and storing data while electrical shut down. The information is stored in the EEPROM cell as an electrical charge. The electrical charge modifies the electrical characteristics of the EEPROM cell so that the information can be later read back using the modified electrical characteristics. Non-volatile electrically erasable and programmable memory structures, such as a flash memory, utilize a floating gate whose charging is controlled by appropriate biasing of the source, drain, and controlling gate. A flash memory is unique in providing fast compact storage which is both nonvolatile and rewritable. One thing that sometimes confuses people is that since RAM is the "opposite" of ROM (since RAM is read-write and ROM is read-only), and since RAM stands for "random access memory," they think that ROM is not random access. This is not true; any location can be read from ROM in any order, so it is random access as well, just not writeable. RAM gets its name because earlier read-write memories were sequential and did not allow random access.

Finally, one other characteristic of ROM, compared to RAM, is that it is much slower, typically having double the access time of RAM or more. This is one reason why the code in the BIOS ROM is often shadowed to improve performance.

2.4. SECONDARY MEMORY

Secondary memory, in basic terms, is a computer's method of storing data and information on a more long-term basis than primary memory. While primary memory (RAM, for example) is concerned mainly with storing programs currently executing and data currently being accessed, secondary memory is generally intended for storing anything that needs to be kept even if the computer is switched off or no programs are currently executing. Secondary memory (or secondary storage) is the slowest and cheapest form of memory. It cannot be processed directly by the CPU. It must first be copied into primary storage (also known as RAM).

When working on the computer, all work is entered into the computer's memory. In order to store your work for future retrieval, you must "save" your work to a storage device before turning the computer off. When your work is saved it creates a computer "file." The most common storage devices are hard disks and floppy disks. If you only save your work on the hard disk, you run the risk of losing your data, either through viruses, which attack the hard disk, or to hard disk failure or crashes. It's very important to back up your important files onto other media, such as floppy disks.

2.4.1. Floppy Disk

A removable disk that stores information magnetically, also called a diskette. You can use a floppy disk to exchange information between computers, or to make a backup of your files. Floppy disks are 3.5 inches in diameter, and they are enclosed in a rigid plastic shell. A "double density" (DD) diskette has a storage capacity of 740 KB while a "high-density" (HD) diskette has a storage capacity of 1.44 MB. To protect your floppy disks, keep them away from heat, drinks, and magnets. Use a felt tip pen to label a disk and write on the label before you attach it to the disk.

Every disk must be formatted with the operating system used by the computer in order to allow storage of files. The operating system is the "language" of the program—the disk must be in the same language as the computer in order to communicate. Examples of operating systems are DOS, Windows, Macintosh OS, and Windows NT. When you purchase disks, be sure to purchase them for the operating system you are using (IBM/PC Compatible or Apple/Macintosh). Today, most floppy disks come already formatted. However, it is a good idea to run scandisk on a disk before using as a means of checking the disk for bad sectors. See Section M for instructions on how to run scandisk on a floppy. Disks can be reused as long as there are no bad sectors on the disk. Disks are inserted into the disk drive with the metal part first, label up.

Every disk comes with a write-protect tab. The tab provides protection against erasing or replacing information on a floppy disk. You can write-protect a 3.5-inch floppy disk by moving the plastic tab up to the write-protected position (open hole). No information can be altered on the disk when it is write-protected.

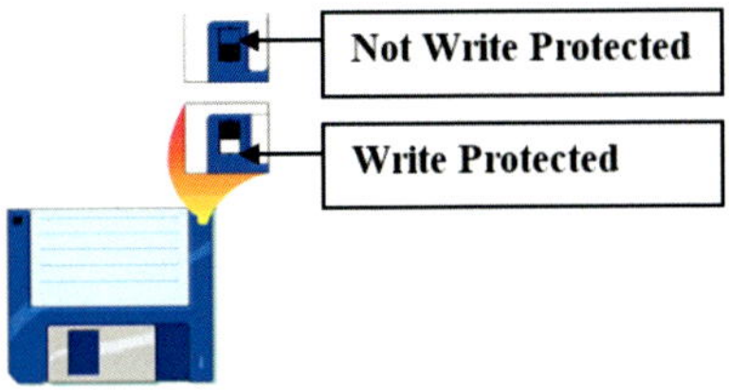

2.4.2. Hard Drive

The primary device that a computer uses to store information. Most computers come with one or two hard drives, called drive C and drive D, located inside the computer case. The terms hard drive and hard disk are used interchangeably. Today's hard disks provide fast retrieval and can hold several gigabytes of information as compared to megabytes on floppy disks.

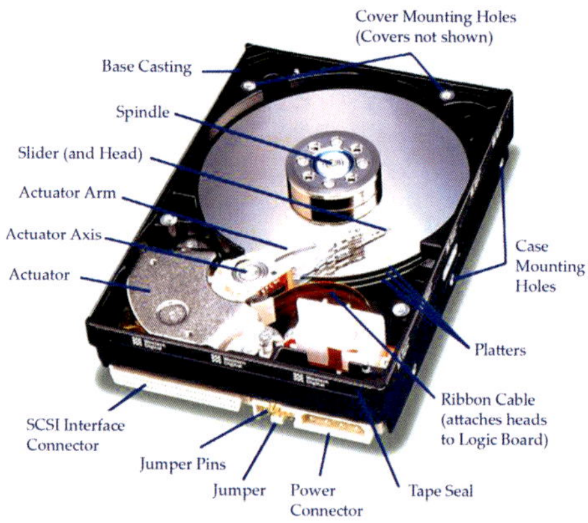

The Read/Write Heads are energy converters: they transform electrical signals to magnetic signals, and magnetic signals back to electrical ones again. They are in essence tiny electromagnets that perform this conversion from electrical information to magnetic and back again. There is normally one head for each surface used on the drive.

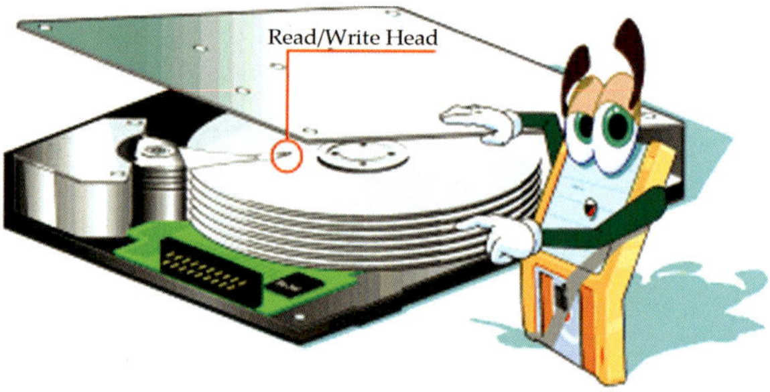

If the heads contact the surface of the disk while it is at operational speed, the result can be loss of data, damage to the heads, damage to the surface of the disk, or all three. This is usually called a head crash, two of the most frightening words to any computer user. :^) The most common causes of head crashes are contamination getting stuck in the thin gap between the head and the disk, and shock applied to the hard disk while it is in operation.

2.4.3. Zip Disks

Zip disks store 100–250 MB of data (depending on the type of drive purchased) and cost about $11 to $19 each. A special 3.5" removable disk drive is needed to retrieve the information from the computer and write to the zip disk. An external zip drive can be moved from one computer to another. Due to the large storage capability of zip disks and mobility of the drives, they are gaining popularity as storage and backup mediums.

2.4.4. CD-ROMS

Compact disks can store approximately 650–800 MB of data or 74–80 minutes of music. Most software programs today are shipped on CD-ROMs instead of floppy disks. All computers today come with CD-ROM drives that are part of the computer's multimedia configuration.

They are connected to a sound card, which provides the computer with stereo speaker capabilities, allowing for musical CD-ROMs to also be played on your computer. These drives are read only and cannot be used for recording data.

- Only retrieve data that's pre-recorded by the manufacturer. Like a musical CD-ROM, the information is pressed on one side (the side opposite the label).
- CD-ROMs are inserted into the CD-ROM drive with the label side up.
- Pressing the button opens and closes the drive.
- Handling and storage of CD-ROM's are the same as musical CD-ROM's and floppy disks.
- Avoid putting fingers on the information side. Hold the CD-ROM by the edges when handling. Protect CD-ROM's by making sure the data side does not get scratched and by providing proper storage (store them in the case they came in).

2.4.5. Read/Write CD-ROMS

CD-ROM drives that write, rewrite, and record data. Two types of CD-ROM disks are used in these drives: CD-recordable (CD-R) and CD-read/write (CD-R/W). CD-R/W's can only be "read" by CD Read/Write drives, while CD-R disks can be read by most CD-ROM drives. You can download CD-RW UDF Reader software from www.zdnet.com (click on the Downloads tab) or http://downloads-zdnet.com.com/2001-20-0.html.

2.4.6. Cartridge Tapes

These are magnetic tapes similar to cassette tapes used as a storage and backup device. Backup and retrieval of stored information is slower with tapes because the information is stored sequentially. The computer must search in sequential order to find the desired information, rather than by sectors. The advantage of tape cassettes is that they can be purchased with large storage capacities (1–4 GB's) allowing the entire contents of the hard drive to easily fit on one tape.

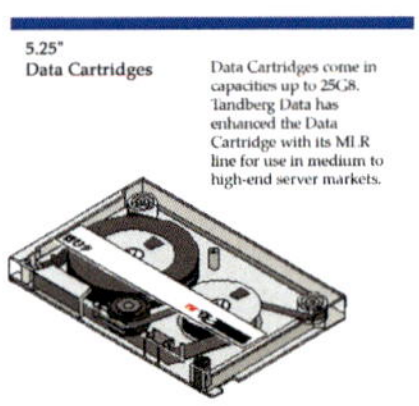

2.4.7. USB/Flash Drive (Jump/Thumb Drive)

It is a plug-and-play portable storage device that uses flash memory and is lightweight enough to attach to a key chain. A keychain drive can be used in place of a floppy disk, Zip drive disk, or CD. When the user plugs the device into their USB port, the computer's operating system recognizes the device as a removable drive. Unlike most removable drives, a keychain drive does not require rebooting after it's attached, does not require batteries or an external power supply, and is not platform dependent. Several keychain drive manufacturers offer additional features such as password protection, and downloadable drivers that allow the key chain drive to be compatible with older systems that do not have USB ports. Keychain drives are available in capacities ranging from 8 MB to 2 gigabytes, depending on manufacturer, in a corresponding range of prices.

> ➢ Find the *synonyms* for the underlined words.
>
> 1. Primary memory (RAM, for example) is concerned mainly with storing programs.
> 2. A removable disk that stores information magnetically, also called a diskette.
> 3. To protect your floppy disks, keep them away from heat, drinks, and magnets.
> 4. When you purchase disks, be sure to purchase them for the operating system you are using.
> 5. Disks are inserted into the disk drive with the metal part first, label up.
> 6. Most computers come with one or two hard drives, called drive C and drive D, located inside the computer case.
> 7. The terms hard drive and hard disk are used interchangeably. Today's hard disks provide fast retrieval and can hold several gigabytes of information as compared to megabytes on floppy disks.
> 8. . They are in essence tiny electromagnets that perform this conversion from electrical information to magnetic and back again.
> 9. All computers today come with CD-ROM drives that are part of the computer's multimedia configuration.
> 10. The computer must search in sequential order to find the desired information.

➢ Fill in the blank with the following words.

Destroy, Analogous, Crashes, reused, Multimedia, Clearly, Zip, Identifies

1. When the user plugs the device into their USB port, the computer's operating system .... the device as a removable drive.
2. Keychain drives are available in capacities ranging from 8 MB to 2 gigabytes, depending on manufacturer, in a .... range of prices.
3. All computers today come with CD-ROM drives that are part of the computer's .... configuration.
4. An external .... drive can be moved from one computer to another.
5. If the heads contact the surface of the disk while it is at operational speed, the result can be loss of data, ... to the heads, damage to the surface of the disk, or all three.
6. Disks can be .... as long as there are no bad sectors on the disk.
7. If you only save your work on the hard disk, you run the risk of losing your data, either through viruses, which attack the hard disk, or to hard disk failure or ....
8. It cannot be processed .... by the CPU. It must first be copied into primary storage.

➢ Write *antonyms* of following words.

1. Important ....
2. Inserted ....
3. Protection ....
4. Interchangeably ....
5. Contamination ....
6. Mobility ....
7. Allowing ....

2.4.8. Additional Information about DRAMs

Flash memories are non-volatile; they do not require power to retain memory content. They can be programmed (erased and written to) and can be accessed (read) at high speed. Longer time periods are required for erasing and writing. Note that erasing is a block-level function for these devices.

By using a single transistor memory cell, the flash memories are currently nearly as dense as DRAMs and potentially denser. The development of flash memories is lagging behind the development of DRAMs because of the need for high internal voltages for writing and erasing, but new approaches (such as multi-level flash memories) are being used which may provide flash memory densities close to those available with DRAMS. Flash memories are beginning to be widely used in the commercial market where they are showing up in applications such as solid-state disks. Flash memories do have a limited life of about 104 to 106 erase and write operations, but this is sufficient for many applications.

Because flash memories are non-volatile, power to the device can be turned off when not in use. This saving in power makes flash memories very attractive to spacecraft designers. As a side benefit, flash memories are immune to single event upset when powered off.

Writing to flash memories is a two-step process. The memory must first be erased as a block, and then written. A write operation only writes a zero into a memory cell. A block erase is required to first put all ones into the cells prior to writing. Flash memories require a long time to erase and write relative to DRAMs. As an example, the Intel 28F016 flash memories require 20 to 30 seconds to erase all 16 Mb (32 blocks), and 5 to 8 μs to write to each cell. However, the time required to read (70 nsec.) is close to DRAMs. For space applications the time to erase/write is probably not the main concern. The main concern would probably be radiation effects: total dose and single event effects sensitivity.

2.5. CACHE

The system cache is responsible for a great deal of the system performance improvement of today's PCs. The cache is a buffer between the very fast processor and the relatively slow memory that serves it.

2.5.1. Layers of Cache

There are in fact many layers of cache in a modern PC. This does not even include looking at caches included on some peripherals, such as hard disks. Each layer is closer to the processor and faster than the layer below it. Each layer also caches the layers below it, due to its increased speed relative to the lower levels:

Level	Devices Cached
Level 1 Cache	Level 2 Cache, System RAM, Hard Disk/CD-ROM
Level 2 Cache	System RAM, Hard Disk/CD-ROM
System RAM	Hard Disk/CD-ROM
Hard Disk/CD-ROM	–

What happens in general terms is this. The processor requests a piece of information. The first place it looks is in the level 1 cache since it is the fastest. If it finds it there (called a hit on the cache), great; it uses it with no performance delay. If not, it's a miss and the level 2 cache is searched. If it finds it there (level 2 "hit"), it is able to carry on with relatively little delay. Otherwise, it must issue a request to read it from the system RAM. The system RAM may in turn either have the information available or have to get it from the still slower hard disk or CD-ROM. The mechanics of how the processor (really the chipset controlling the cache and memory) "look" for the information in these various places is discussed here:

- **Level 1 (Primary) Cache:** Level 1 or primary cache is the fastest memory on the PC. It is in fact, built directly into the processor itself. This cache is very small, generally from 8 KB to 64 KB, but it is extremely fast; it runs at the same speed as the processor. If the processor requests information and can find it in the level 1 cache, that is the external best case, because the information is there immediately, and the system does not have to wait. The level 1 cache is discussed in more detail here, in the section on processors.
- **Level 2 (Secondary) Cache:** The level 2 cache is a secondary cache to the level 1 cache and is larger and slightly slower. It is used to catch recent accesses that are not caught by the level 1 cache and is usually 64 KB to 2 MB in size. Level 2 cache is usually found either on the motherboard or a daughterboard that inserts into the motherboard. Pentium Pro processors actually have the level 2 cache in the same package as the processor itself (though it isn't in the same circuit where the processor and level 1 cache are) which means it runs much faster than level 2 cache that is separate and resides on the motherboard. Pentium II processors are in the middle; their cache runs at half the speed of the CPU.

Ø *Note:* Level 2 cache is also sometimes called "external" cache since it resides outside the processor. (Even on Pentium Pros… it is on a separate chip in the same package as the processor.)

2.5.1.1. Disk Cache

A disk cache is a portion of system memory used to cache reads and writes to the hard disk. In some ways this is the most important type of cache on the PC, because the greatest differential in speed between the layers mentioned here is between the system RAM and the hard disk. While the system RAM is slightly slower than the level 1 or level 2 cache, the hard disk is much slower than the system RAM.

2.5.1.2. Peripheral Cache

Much like the hard disk, other devices can be cached using the system RAM as well. CD-ROMs are the most common device cached other than hard disks, particularly due to their very slow initial access time, measured in the tens to hundreds of milliseconds (which is an eternity to a computer). In fact, in some cases CD-ROM drives are cached to the hard disk, since the hard disk, despite its slow speed, is still much faster than a CD-ROM drive is.

2.5.2. Why Caching Works?

Cache is in some ways a really amazing technology. A 512 KB level 2 cache, caching 64 MB of system memory, can supply the information that the processor requests 90–95% of the time. Think about the ratios here: the level 2 cache is less than 1% of the size of the memory it is caching, but it is able to register a "hit" on over 90% of requests. That's pretty efficient and is the reason why caching is so important.

The reason that this happens is due to a computer science principle called locality of reference. It states basically that even within very large programs with several megabytes of instructions, only small portions of this code generally get used at once. Programs tend to spend large periods of time working in one small area of the code, often performing the same work many times over and over with slightly different data, and then move to another area. This occurs because of "loops," which are what programs use to do work many times in rapid succession.

- Find the *synonyms* for the underlined words.

1. The system cache is responsible for a great deal of the system performance improvement of today's PCs.
2. The processor requests a piece of information.
3. It must issue a request to read it from the system RAM.
4. It is used to catch recent accesses that are not caught by the level 1 cache, and is usually 64 KB to 2 MB in size.
5. It runs much faster than level 2 cache that is separate and resides on the motherboard.
6. While the system RAM is slightly slower than the level 1 or level 2 cache, the hard disk is *much* slower than the system RAM.
7. CD-ROMs are the most common device cached other than hard disks, particularly due to their very slow initial access time, measured in the tens to hundreds of milliseconds
8. Programs tend to spend large periods of time working in one small area of the code.
9. which are what programs use to do work many times in rapid succession.
10. it is able to register a "hit" on over 90% of requests.

- Fill in the blank with the following words:

Basically, Locality, Happens, discussed, Effective, In spite

1. In fact, in some cases CD-ROM drives are cached to the hard disk, since the hard disk, ... its slow speed, is still much faster than a CD-ROM drive is.
2. That's pretty ...., and is the reason why caching is so important.
3. The reason that this happens is due to a computer science principle called .... of reference.
4. It is inadvisable to leave the EPROM chip under the .... eraser for too long. This may lead to over erasure.
5. This .... because of "loops," which are what programs use to do work many times in rapid succession.
6. The mechanics of how the processor "look" for the information in these various places is .... here.

> Write *antonyms* of following words.
>
> 1. Available ....
> 2. Miss ....
> 3. Peripherals ....
> 4. Increased ....
> 5. Fastest ....
> 6. External ....
> 7. Best ....

2.5.3. Additional Information About Main Memories

Computers operate at very high speeds. Current CPUs operate at speeds of 400 million cycles per second or more. What this means is, every 2.5 nanoseconds, the computer can execute a complete processing loop. On modern computers, this means usually executing one or two instructions. This is the speed you will see advertised on a computer – a Pentium III 400. The problem is, while the computer can operate at this speed, it has to get the program and data to execute from somewhere.

What happens is the program and data is loaded from the hard drive into RAM. From RAM it is loaded into cache RAM, and from there it is executed by the CPU.

Hard drives are very slow compared to the CPU. RAM is much faster than a hard drive, but still 4–5 times slower than your CPU. Also, RAM is erased if the power goes off. Cache RAM is extremely fast – it is capable of delivering data at or near the speed of the CPU.

Cache RAM and normal RAM are very similar in the way they work. Cache is just extremely fast, and expensive. That is why there is so very little of cache RAM available – it is expensive. In order to reduce the cost of computers, hard drives are used to store huge amounts of data because they are so cheap – some drives cost less than a penny for a megabyte of storage. RAM is much more expensive – about a dollar for a megabyte of storage. This is over 100 times more expensive than a hard drives. Cache RAM is a lot more expensive than regular RAM – about $15–20 per megabyte of storage.

In order to reduce the cost of computers, engineers have designed controllers that load data and instructions from the hard drive when they may be needed into RAM. When they are not needed in RAM, something else is loaded. Then, as the computer runs, whatever is needed for that time is loaded into cache. When the controller does a pretty good job at predicting what is needed, the computer will operate at close to its full speed. When the controllers don't do a good job, things will slow down while the CPU waits for data to be loaded from the hard drive to RAM, and then into the cache before it can continue.

Cache memory is where the computer gets the program and data it needs to execute. If the cache is slower than your CPU, your computer will be slow. But if it is faster, your computer won't speed up. So, you want to make sure the cache is fast enough for your computer, but getting faster cache memory is a waste of money. The amount of cache memory also affects the speed of your computer. In general, the more cache, the faster your computer will go. Most computers have a fairly small limit on the amount of cache RAM possible. Generally, make sure your computer has as much cache RAM as it can handle.

CHAPTER

3 Network

Contents

3.1. NETWORK HISTORY

The key to the computer revolution of the 1980s was the invention of the microprocessor in the 1970s. This gave rise to the cheap computers which have become ubiquitous in homes, schools, and offices, and to the embedded computers which serve as controllers inside cameras, cars, washing machines and so on. The computer revolution of the late 1990s, now continuing in the 21st-century, involves computer networks, whose existence is enriching our society in countless different ways.

3.1.1. What Is a Network?

In its simplest form, networking may be defined as two computers being linked together, either physically through a cable or through a wireless device. This link allows the computers to share files, printers, and even internet connections. Within small organizations, the two most prevalent types of networks are "peer-to-peer" networks and "client/server" networks. Peer-to-peer networks are the simplest and least expensive type of networks available and are most suitable for organizations with less than 5 computers. A peer-to-peer network will allow an organization to share files, printers, and even modems and Internet connections. In general, a peer-to-peer network does not have a central server and consists of 2 or more computers connecting through a device called a "Hub." The hub allows multiple computers and devices to connect via network cable. While simpler and less expensive, peer-to-peer networks do not offer many of the benefits of client/server networks. And as an organization and network grows, the administration of these peer-to-peer networks becomes more difficult and expensive. Client/server networks are networks that connect individual computers, known as "clients," and one or more central computers, called "servers." There are many types of servers, the most common being a file server. In a client/server network, the file server acts as a shared resource – a repository for files, such as documents, spreadsheets, databases, etc. Instead of storing these files on each individual machine, the file server permits storage on one central computer.

3.1.2. What Are the Benefits of a Network?

Centralized storage of files is often the initial and primary justification for a network. Instead of having multiple iterations of documents and spreadsheets on disparate computers, files can be stored in a centralized location. This then allows another benefit of networking, centralized backup. With a centralized backup system, an organization's files can be backed up daily onto high-capacity tapes. This helps ensure the long-term integrity of the data. The use of dial-up services and the Internet has grown tremendously. This growth has often necessitated the installation of a modem on each computer. Using a network, an organization can share a modem or dial-up connection to access the Internet or other dial up services. An inexpensive device called a router facilitates the sharing of your network's dedicated Internet connection, be it via dialup using a modem, ISDN, DSL, Cable Modem or T-1 line. In addition, networks can help to reduce other capital investment costs as well. For example, modems, printers, scanners, and CD-ROMs are just a few of the devices that can be shared over a network. A more recently developed benefit of networks with the advent of the Internet is the remote access of email and files. Using technology known as virtual private networking (VPN), an organization can access its network remotely via a secure, encrypted channel by means of either a dialup or Internet connection.

3.1.3. What Are Networks Used For?

A simplified but worthwhile description of the uses of computer networks might be as follows:

1. **Sharing of Hardware:** For example, several PCs might be networked together in a wired or wireless local area network (LAN) to share a printer.
2. **Sharing of Information:** Distributed databases, e-mail, the world wide web (WWW) and so on are examples of this. Here the sharing involves both LANs and wide area networks (WANs), especially the latter.

3.1.4. Uses for Networks

Networks are essential for moving data between computers. Without a network, the only way to move data from two computers is through the use of moving physical storage. The prospect of moving information between computers probably doesn't sound very exciting at first, but when you remember what data means – movies, books, and music are all forms of data – then the usage of a network becomes more exciting.

At the home, a network allows the media of one member of a family to become the media for all members of a family. Using a wireless router, everyone in a home can share their movies and music with everyone else.

This makes enjoying media much easier, because it is possible to store a movie in one physical location but enjoy that movie on any computer connected to the network.

For businesses, networks allow the secure and quick transfer of vital information. Accounting documents, new orders for products and inventory reports can instantly be transferred from the employee in a warehouse to an executive in the main office. This drastically increases efficiency and makes work easier for everyone involved.

3.1.5. Future of Networks

Computer networks are a relatively new technology, and they will likely change drastically as technology moves forward. Wireless networks, which have risen to popularity since the turn of the century, have broadened the range of networks substantially. It is now possible for users to take a computer to numerous places and connect to numerous networks without a physical connection. The same goes for other devices that use wireless networking, such as smart phones.

That said, the basics of networks are likely to remain the same, even as the scale of their implementation increases. Networks are a fundamentally scalable concept, and so while computer networks will become larger and more flexible, the basic types of hardware and types of networks will likely persist.

3.1.6. Which Aspects of Networks Are Important to Know?

Networks touch upon virtually every aspect of computing today. A good working knowledge (i.e., not of the "partial credit on an extra problem" type) is of enormous value. It should be noted carefully that it is important to know both the software and non-software aspects of networks the latter meaning the hardware, the protocols, 1 the quantitative performance issues and so on.

If you interview for a job involving networks, you can expect that at least half of the questions will be on the non-software aspects, even if the job itself deals mainly with software. Moreover, many jobs you might interview for might be as system administrators; in such positions, knowing the physical structure of networks is just as important as knowing how the network software works.

3.1.7. Internet Working

The art and science of connecting individual local-area networks (LANs) to create wide-area networks (WANs) and connecting WANs to form even larger WANs. Internetworking can be extremely complex because it generally involves connecting networks that use different protocols. Internetworking is accomplished with routers, bridges, and gateways.

3.1.8. Internet Network

Two or more networks or network segments connected using devices that operate at layer 3 (the 'network' layer) of the OSI Basic Reference Model, such as a router. Any interconnection among or between public, private, commercial, industrial, or governmental networks may also be defined as an internet work. Modern practice, the interconnected networks use the internet protocol (IP). There are at least three variants of internet work, depending on who administers and who participates in them:

- Intranet;
- Extranet; and
- Internet.

Intranets and extranets may or may not have connections to the Internet. If connected to the Internet, the intranet or extranet is normally protected from being accessed from the Internet without proper authorization. The Internet itself is not considered to be a part of the intranet or extranet, although the Internet may serve as a portal for access to portions of an extranet.

3.1.8.1. Intranet

An intranet is a set of interconnected networks, using the IP and uses IP-based tools such as web browsers, which is under the control of a single administrative entity. That administrative entity closes the intranet to the rest of the world and allows only specific users. Most commonly, an intranet is the internal network of a company or other enterprise.

3.1.8.2. Extranet

An extranet is a network or internet work that is limited in scope to a single organization or entity but which also has limited connections to the networks of one or more other usually, but not necessarily, trusted organizations or entities (e.g., a company's customers may be given access to some part of its intranet creating in this way an extranet, while at the same time the customers may not be considered 'trusted' from a security standpoint). Technically, an extranet may also be categorized as a CAN, MAN, WAN, or other type of network, although, by definition, an extranet cannot consist of a single LAN; it must have at least one connection with an external network.

3.1.8.3. Internet

A specific internet work, consisting of a worldwide interconnection of governmental, academic, public, and private networks based upon the Advanced Research Projects Agency Network (ARPANET) developed by ARPA of the U.S. Department of Defense – also home to the WWW and referred to as the 'Internet' with a capital 'I' to distinguish it from other generic internet works.

Participants on the Internet, or their service providers, use IP Addresses obtained from address registries that control assignments. Service providers and large enterprises also exchange information on the reachability of their address ranges through the BGP Border Gateway Protocol.

➢ Find the *synonyms* for the underlined words.

1. This gave rise to the cheap computers which have become ubiquitous in homes, schools and offices, and to the embedded computers which serve as controllers inside cameras, cars, washing machines and so on.
2. The computer revolution of the late 1990s, now continuing in the 21st century, involves computer networks, whose existence is enriching our society in countless different ways.
3. There are many types of servers, the most common being a file server. In a client/server network, the file server acts as a shared resource – a repository for files, such as documents, spreadsheets, databases, etc.
4. This helps ensure the long term integrity of the data. The use of dial-up services and the Internet has grown tremendously.
5. An inexpensive device called a router facilitates the sharing of your network's dedicated Internet connection, be it via dialup using a modem, ISDN, DSL, Cable Modem or T-1 line. In addition, networks can help to reduce other capital investment costs as well.
6. The prospect of moving information between computers probably doesn't sound very exciting at first, but when you remember what data means---movies, books, and music are all forms of data---then the usage of a network becomes more exciting.

7. Accounting documents, new orders for products and inventory reports can instantly be transferred from the employee in a warehouse to an executive in the main office. This drastically increases efficiency and makes work easier for everyone involved.
8. Computer networks are a relatively new technology, and they will likely change drastically as technology moves forward. Wireless networks, which have risen to popularity since the turn of the century, have broadened the range of networks substantially.
9. Internetworking can be extremely complex because it generally involves connecting networks that use different protocols. Internetworking is accomplished with routers, bridges, and gateways.
10. Participants in the Internet, or their service providers, use IP Addresses obtained from address registries that control assignments.

➢ Fill in the blank with the following words.

Fast, Advent, Basically, Widespread, Compel, Intensely, Specifically, Repetition

1. Within small organizations, the two most .... types of networks are "peer-to-peer" networks and "client/server" networks.
2. Instead of having multiple .... of documents and spreadsheets on disparate computers, files can be stored in a centralized location.
3. This growth has often .... the installation of a modem on each computer.
4. A more recently developed benefit of networks with the .... of the Internet is the remote access of email and files.
5. Distributed databases, e-mail, the World Wide Web and so on are examples of this. Here the sharing involves both LANs and wide area networks (WANs), ... the latter.
6. For businesses, networks allow the secure and .... transfer of vital information.
7. This .... increases efficiency and makes work easier for everyone involved.
8. Networks are a .... scalable concept.

> ➢ Write *antonyms* of following words.
> 1. Ubiquitous ....
> 2. Rise ....
> 3. Benefit ....
> 4. Disparate ....
> 5. Tremendously ....
> 6. Dedicated ....
> 7. Vital ....

3.1.9. Additional Information about Peer-to-Peer Network and Client/Server Network

Networks fall into two major types: peer-to-peer and client/server:

1. **Peer-to-Peer Networking:** This is a simple network configuration that requires some basic know-how to set up. Each of the interconnected machines share dual capability and responsibility on the network. That is to say, that each machine serves a dual purpose or role, i.e., they are both clients and servers to some extent. The server capability of the machines is very basic. The services provided by each, is no more than the ability to share resources like files, folders, disk drives and printers. They even have the ability to share Internet access.

   However, the server functionality of these machines stops there. They cannot grant any of the benefits mentioned previously, since these are functions provided only by a dedicated server operating system. Because all machines on the network have equal status, hence the term peers, there is no centralized control over shared resources. Sharing is endorsed or repealed by each machine's user. Passwords can be assigned to each individual shared resource whether it is a file, folder, drive or peripheral, again done by the user. Although this solution is workable on small networks, it introduces the possibility that users may have to know and remember the passwords assigned to every resource, and then re-learn them if the user of a particular machine decides to change them! Due to this flexibility and individual discretion, institutionalized chaos is the norm for peer-to-peer networks.

   Security can also be a major concern because users may give passwords to other unauthorized users, allowing them to access areas of the network that the company does not permit. Furthermore, due to lack of centralization, it is impossible for users to know and remember what data lives on what machine, and there are no restrictions to prevent them from over-writing the wrong files with older versions of the file. This of course cripples attempt to organize proper backups. It may appear that peer-to-peer networks are hardly worthwhile. However, they offer some powerful incentives, particularly for smaller organizations. Networks of this type are the cheapest and easiest to install, requiring only Windows 95, a network card for each machine and some cabling. Once connected, users can start to share information immediately and get access to devices.

As a result, networks of this type are not scalable and a limit of no more than 10 machines is the general rule.

Ø **Advantages:**

- Easy to install and configure.
- No dedicated server required.
- Users control their own resources.
- Inexpensive to purchase and operate.
- No specialist software required.
- No dedicated administrator to run the network required.

Ø **Disadvantages:**

- Difficult to employ security.
- Too many passwords for shared resources.
- Backups difficult to manage.
- No centralization.
- Limited users.

2. **Client/Server Networks:** Server based networks, or client/server networks as they are properly called, has a machine at the heart of its operations called the server. A server is a machine that provides services over a network by responding to client requests. Servers rarely have individuals operating it, and even then, it is usually to install, configure or manage its capabilities. The server's essential role on the network is to be continuously available to handle the many requests generated by its clients. Server-based networks provide centralized control of the entire network environment.

> The computer systems used for this role are generally more powerful than end-user machines, incorporating faster CPUs, more memory, larger disk drives and other drive types installed, like a tape drive for backup purposes. These are required because servers are dedicated to handling multiple simultaneous requests from their client communities.

Server based networks provide centralized verification of user accounts and passwords. Only valid account name and password combinations are allowed access to the network. Client/Server networks typically require a single login to the network itself, meaning that users need to remember long password lists to access various resources. Concentrations of resources on a single server, mean that they are easier to find, as opposed to the peer-to-peer model, where resources were distributed throughout the network since they were attached to multiple machines. The server being a central data repository, means that not only is data more accessible to users, but it also makes life much easier in terms of performing backups, since the data is in a location know to the administrator. Server-based networks are easier to scale. Peer-to-peer networks bog down seriously as they grow beyond 10 users, and serious slow up with 20 users. On the other hand, client/server networks can handle a few users, up to a 1,000 users as such networks grow to keep pace with an organization's growth and expansion.

Unlike peer-to-peer networks, client/server networks don't come cheap. The server machine itself may cost several thousands of pounds, along with the software to make it run; another 1,000 pounds. Because of the complex nature of this kind of networking environment, a dedicated administrator is required to be on site at all times to be involved in the day to day running of the network. Hiring an individual of this nature adds considerably to the cost of client/server networks.

Lastly, because the networks operability is so dependent upon the server, this introduces a single point of failure, if the server goes down the network goes down. There are measures available, that can legislate for such failures, however these techniques add even more cost to this solution.

Ø **Advantages:**

- Centralized user accounts, security, and access controls simplify network administration.
- More powerful equipment means more efficient access network resources.
- Single password login means access to all resources.

- Supports greater numbers of users, or networks where resources are heavily used.

Ø **Disadvantages:**

- More costly to install and maintain.
- Single point of failure, server goes down, the network goes down.
- Complex special-purpose software requires appointment of expert staff, increasing costs.
- Dedicated hardware and software increase costs.

3.2. COMMON TYPES OF COMPUTER NETWORKS

Computer network design can range from simple to very complex. Networking can be as simple as connecting two computers, or a computer and a printer, while more complex networks can involve the connection of millions of computers and devices. Below is a brief outline of different computer network types.

3.2.1. Personal Area Network (PAN)

A personal area network (PAN) is a computer network used for communication among computer devices close to one person. A PAN simply involves connecting one person's computer to a number of devices or peripherals. Usually, all devices, such as printers, PDAs, and telephones, are within a few feet of the computer. A PAN can also refer to a connection to the internet. Some examples of devices that may be used in a PAN are printers, fax machines, telephones, PDAs, or scanners. The reach of a PAN is typically within about 20–30 feet (approximately 4–6 Meters).

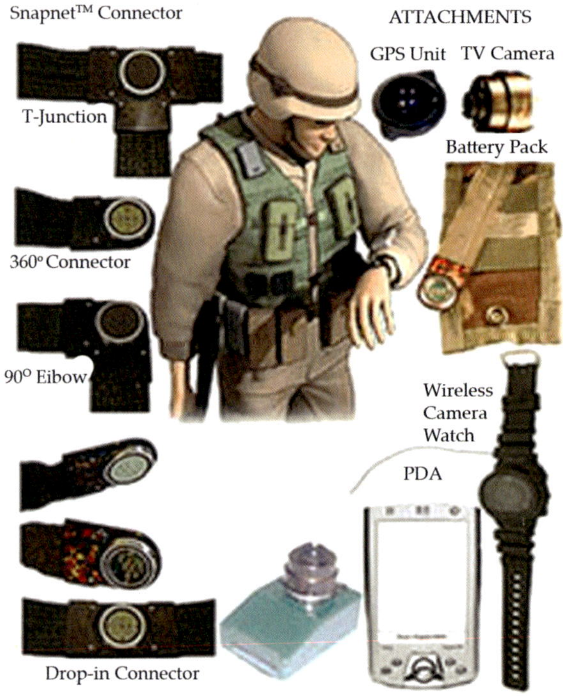

3.2.2. Local Area Network (LAN)

A network covering a small geographic area, like a home, office, or building. Current LANs are most likely to be based on Ethernet technology. For example, a library will have a wired or wireless LAN for users to interconnect local devices (e.g., printers and servers) connect to the internet. All of the PCs in the library are connected by category 5 (Cat5) cable, running the IEEE 802.3 protocol through a system of interconnection devices and eventually connect to the internet. The cables to the servers are on Cat 5e enhanced cable, which will support IEEE 802.3 at 1 Gbps.

The defining characteristics of LANs, in contrast to WANs, include their much higher data transfer rates, smaller geographic range, and lack of a need for leased telecommunication lines. Current Ethernet or other IEEE 802.3 LAN technologies operate at speeds up to 10 Gbit/s. This is the data transfer rate. IEEE has projects investigating the standardization of 100 Gbit/s, and possibly 40 Gbit/s. Inverse multiplexing is commonly used to build a faster aggregate from slower physical streams, such as bringing 4 Gbit/s aggregate stream into a computer or network element with four 1 Gbit/s interfaces.

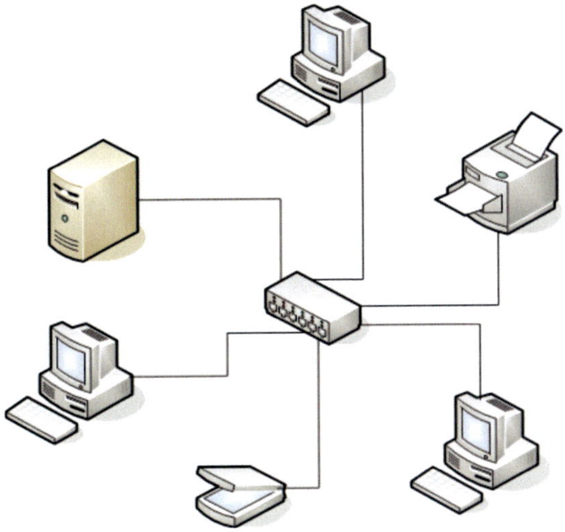

3.2.3. Campus Area Network (CAN)

A network that connects two or more LANs but that is limited to a specific and contiguous geographical area such as a college campus, industrial complex, or a military base. A CAN, may be considered a type of MAN (metropolitan area network), but is generally limited to an area that is smaller than a typical MAN.

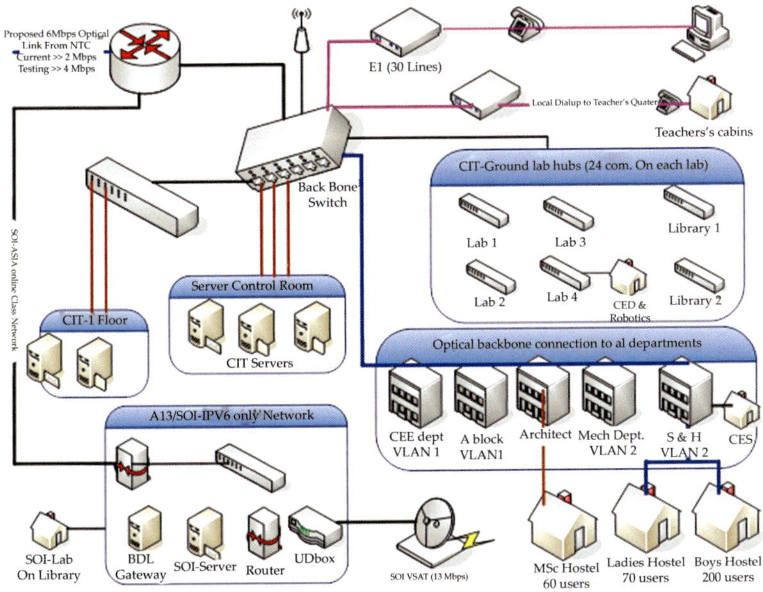

3.2.4. Campus Area Network (CAN)

CANs are so called because they are ideal for universities but are also found in industrial facilities where networks in a number of buildings need to be connected. This is usually accomplished through bridging and routing. Again, most CANs are based on Ethernet technology.

3.2.5. Metropolitan Area Network (MAN)

A MAN usually consists of a number of interconnected LANs and WANs but will not extend beyond the boundaries of a town, city, or metropolitan area. These are often operated at public utilities and are used by many businesses and individuals. MAN, technology has developed significantly in recent years with smaller networks within a MAN often interconnected wirelessly using radio, microwave, or infra-red laser links.

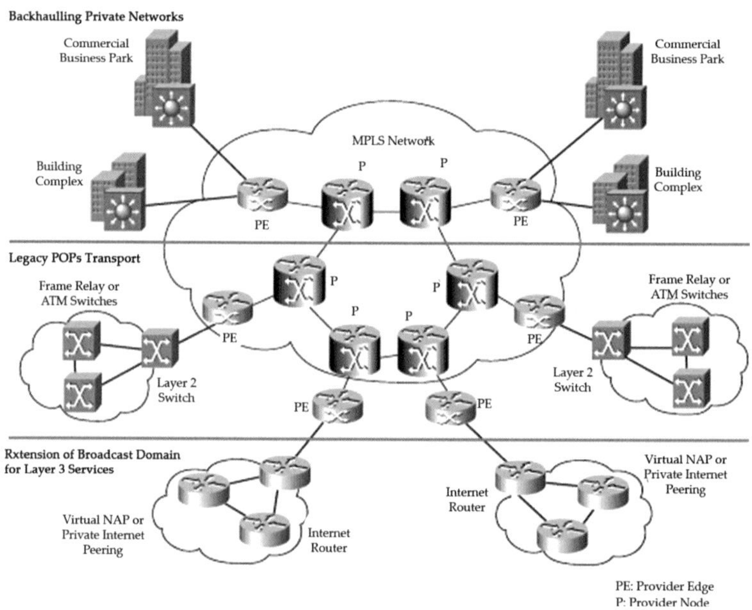

3.2.6. Wide Area Network (WAN)

The WAN is the next step up from the MAN because it can cross metropolitan or even national boundaries. The best-known WAN is the internet, and, like all WANs, it uses routers and public communication links to carry data. While the internet is open to all, many WANs are run by private companies and are restricted. A WAN is a data communications network that covers a relatively broad geographic area (i.e., one city to another and one country to another country) and that often uses transmission facilities provided by common carriers, such as telephone companies. WAN technologies generally function at the lower three layers of the OSI reference model: the physical layer, the data link layer, and the network Layer.

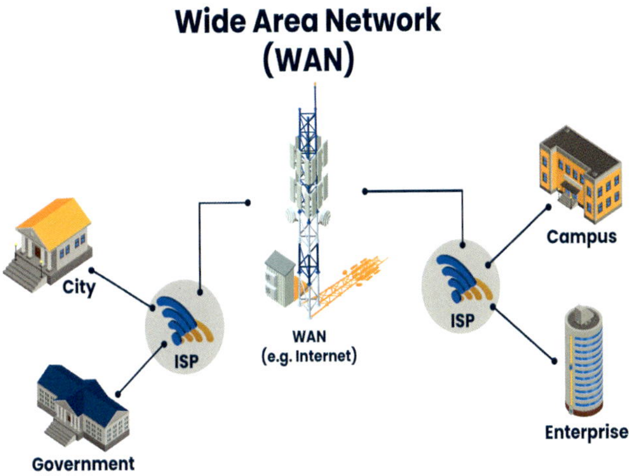

3.2.7. Global Area Networks (GAN)

Global area networks (GAN) specifications are in development by several groups, and there is no common definition. In general, however, a GAN is a model for supporting mobile communications across an arbitrary number of wireless LANs, satellite coverage areas, etc. The key challenge in mobile communications is "handing off" the user communications from one local coverage area to the next.

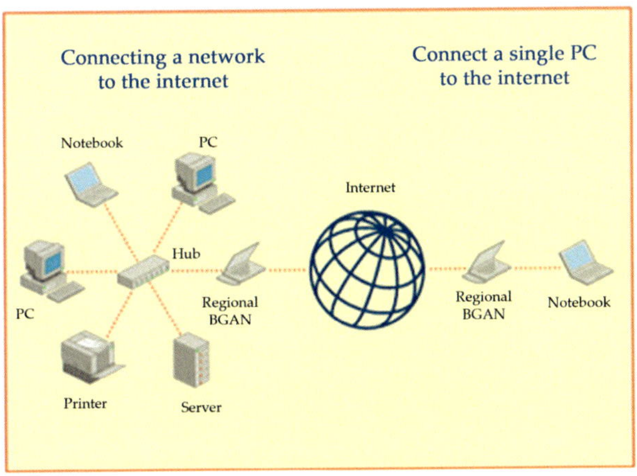

- Find the *synonyms* for the underlined words.

1. A network covering a small geographic area, like a home, office, or building. Current LANs are most likely to be based on Ethernet technology.
2. The defining characteristics of LANs, in contrast to WANs (wide area networks), include their much higher data transfer rates, smaller geographic range, and lack of a need for leased telecommunication lines.
3. Inverse multiplexing is commonly used to build a faster aggregate from slower physical streams.
4. A network that connects two or more LANs but that is limited to a specific and contiguous geographical area such as a college campus, industrial complex, or a military base.
5. CANs are so called because they are ideal for universities, but are also found in industrial facilities where networks in a number of buildings need to be connected.
6. MAN technology has developed significantly in recent years with smaller networks within a MAN often interconnected wirelessly using radio, microwave or infra-red laser links.
7. Global area networks (GAN) specifications are in development by several groups, and there is no common definition.
8. In general, however, a GAN is a model for supporting mobile communications across an arbitrary number of wireless LANs.
9. The key challenge in mobile communications is "handing off" the user communications from one local coverage area to the next.

- Fill in the blank with the following words.

Proportionately, Improve, Universal, Accomplished, Ordinarily, Be composed of, Inspecting

1. The cables to the servers are on Cat 5e enhanced cable, which will support IEEE 802.3 at 1 Gbps.
2. IEEE has projects .... the standardization of 100 Gbit/s, and possibly 40 Gbit/s.
3. A CAN, may be considered a type of MAN (metropolitan area network), but is .... limited to an area that is smaller than a typical MAN.
4. It uses routers and .... communication links to carry data.
5. A MAN usually .... a number of interconnected LANs and WANs.
6. A WAN is a data communications network that covers a .... broad geographic area.
7. This is usually .... through bridging and routing.

> ➢ Write *antonyms* of following words.
> 1. Complex ....
> 2. Brief ....
> 3. Inverse ....
> 4. Lack ....
> 5. Contiguous ....
> 6. Restricted ....
> 7. Lower ....

3.2.8. Additional Information about Simplex, Half-Duplex, and Full-Duplex Transmission

A data channel, over which a signal is sent, can operate in one of three ways: simplex, half-duplex, or full duplex. Full duplex is often just called duplex. The distinction is in the way that the signal can travel.

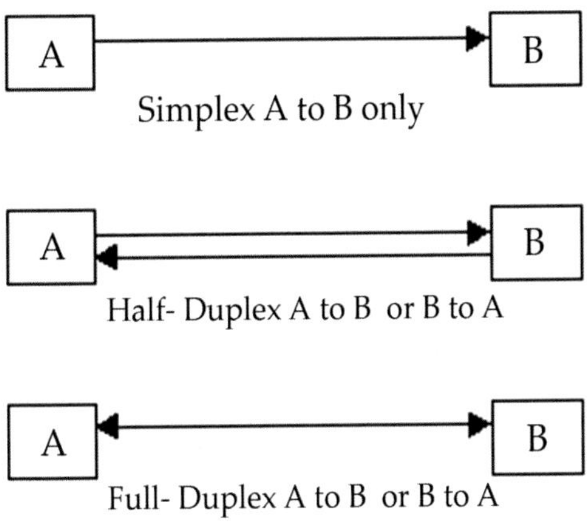

3.2.9. Simplex Transmission

Simplex transmission is a single one-way base band transmission. Simplex transmission, as the name implies, is simple. It is also called unidirectional because the signal travels in only one direction. An example of simplex transmission is the signal sent from the TV station to the home television.

3.2.10. Half-Duplex Transmission

Half-duplex transmission is an improvement over simplex because the traffic can travel in both directions. Unfortunately, the road is not wide enough to accommodate bidirectional signals simultaneously. This means that only one side can transmit at a time. Two-way radios, such as police or emergency communications mobile radios, work with half-duplex transmissions. When pressing the button on the microphone to transmit, nothing being said on the other end can be heard. If people at both ends try to talk at the same time, neither transmission gets through.

Ø *Note*: Modems are half-duplex devices. They can send and receive, but not at the same time. However, it is possible to create a full-duplex modem connection with two telephone lines and two modems.

3.2.11. Full-Duplex Transmission

Full-duplex transmission operates like a two-way, two-lane street. Traffic can travel in both directions at the same time. A land-based telephone conversation is an example of full-duplex communication. Both parties can talk at the same time, and the person talking on the other end can still be heard by the other party while they are talking. Although both parties talking at the same time might be difficult to understand what is being said.

Full-duplex networking technology increases performance because data can be sent and received at the same time. Digital subscriber line (DSL), two-way cable modem, and other broadband technologies operate in full-duplex mode. With DSL, for example, users can download data to their computer at the same time they are sending a voice message over the line.

3.3. NETWORK TOPOLOGY

Network topology is the study of the arrangement or mapping of the elements (links, nodes, etc.) of a network, especially the physical (real) and logical (virtual) interconnections between nodes.

There are two types of topologies: Physical and Logical. The physical topology of a network refers to the layout of cables, computers, and other peripherals. Try to imagine yourself in a room with a small network, you can see network cables coming out of every computer that is part of the network, then those cables plug into a hub or switch. What you're looking at is the physical topology of that network.

Logical topology is the method used to pass the information between the computers. In other words, looking at that same room, if you were to try to see how the network works with all the computers talking (think of the computers generating traffic and packets of data going everywhere on the network) you would be looking at the logical part of the network. The way the computers will be talking to each other, and the direction of the traffic is controlled by the various protocols (like Ethernet) or, if you like, rules.

Any particular network topology is determined only by the graphical mapping of the configuration of physical and/or logical connections between nodes – network topology is, therefore, technically a part of graph theory. Distances between nodes, physical interconnections, transmission rates, and/or signal types may differ in two networks and yet their topologies may be identical.

The physical arrangement of devices in networking is called Topology. In this the devices are connected by wire or without wire (wireless) to make a network so that the data may travel through each terminal with very least attenuation. The arrangement or mapping of the elements of a network gives rise to certain basic topologies which may then be combined to form more complex topologies (hybrid topologies).

The five different kinds of topologies are:

- Bus;
- Ring;
- Star;
- Tree; and
- Mesh.

3.3.1. Star Topology

Star Topology is the most common type of network topology that is used in homes and offices. In the Star Topology there is a central connection point called the hub which is a computer hub or sometimes just a switch. In a Star Network the best advantage is when there is a failure in cable then only one computer might get affected and not the entire network (Figure 3.1).

The star network topology typically needs more cable to be networked than the usual Bus topology. A common cable that is used in Star Network is the UTP or the unshielded twisted pair (UTP) cable. Another common cable that is used in star networks is the RJ45 or the Ethernet cables.

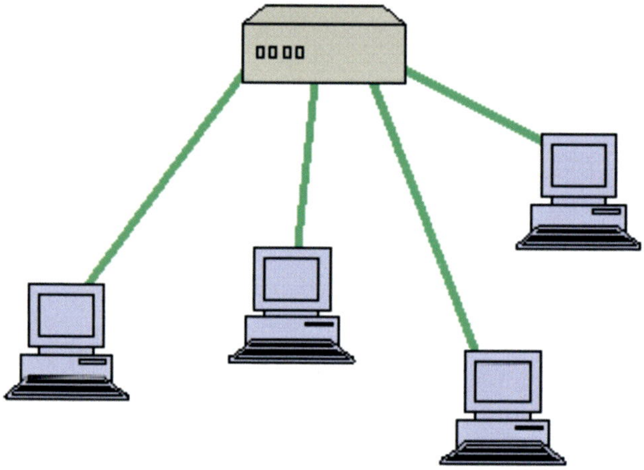

Figure 3.1. Star topology.

3.3.1.1. Extended Star

A type of network topology in which a network that is based upon the physical star topology has one or more repeaters between the central node (the 'hub' of the star) and the peripheral or 'spoke' nodes, the repeaters being used to extend the maximum transmission distance of the point-to-point links between the central node and the peripheral nodes beyond that which is supported by the transmitter power of the central node or beyond that which is supported by the standard upon which the physical layer of the physical star network is based (Figure 3.2).

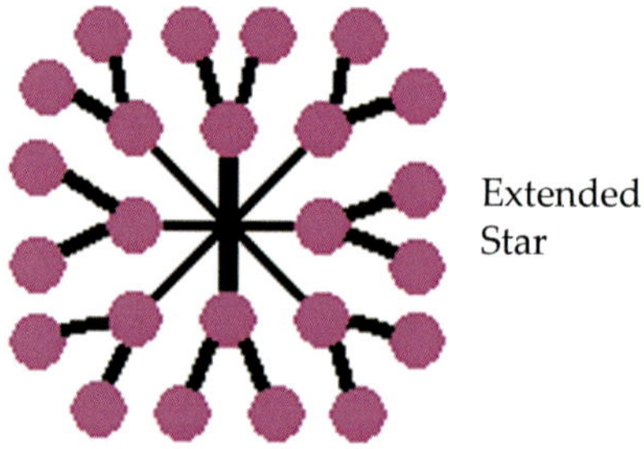

Figure 3.2. Extended star topology.

Ø *Note:* If the repeaters in a network that is based upon the physical extended star topology are replaced with hubs or switches, then a hybrid network topology is created that is referred to as a physical hierarchical star topology, although some texts make no distinction between the two topologies.

In a Star Network the entire network is dependent on the hub switch and is common in-home networks, so if the entire network is not working then there could be a problem with the hub. This feature makes it easy to troubleshoot by offering a single point for error connection ad at the same time the dependency is also very high on that single point. This diagram illustrates the star network topology. This diagram illustrates the star network topology. A star topology typically uses a network hub or switch and is common in-home networks.

3.3.1.2. Star Topology Advantages

1. **Performance:** Data packets do not travel through any unnecessary nodes. Communication between any two devices on the network involves at most three devices and two links. The isolation of traffic between nodes means that heavy utilization from one device is invisible to other devices on the network, provided that the central hub retains adequate capacity.
2. **Isolation:** Each device is isolated on its own link. This makes it easy to isolate individual devices from the network by disconnecting them from the hub. Any non-centralized failure will have very little effect on the network.
3. **Centralization:** The network can easily be scaled or expanded by adding to the capacity of the hub node, or by adding additional devices to the star. The fact that all traffic passes through the central hub means that the hub can easily be used to inspect or control traffic through the network.
4. **Simplicity:** The topology is easy to understand, establish, and navigate. Complex routing or message passing protocols is generally unnecessary. Individual nodes can easily be added or removed, and fault detection is simplified, as each link/device can be probed individually.

3.3.1.3. Star Topology Disadvantages

- The Star Topology is fully dependent on the hub and the entire working of the network depends on the hub or the switch.
- If there are many nodes and the cable is long then the network may slow down.

Since all the computers on the network have independent control of their networks and only dependent on the central hub computer, the failures in transmission and other possible problems in this area are less likely. Also, if the hub is safe then every computer in the network is safe. This type of network also offers more privacy than any other network.

All the computers in the network are communicating with one main centrally located computer and there is no peer-to-peer coordination. If the peer-to-peer coordination takes place it is routed through the central hub. This way the privacy of each and every computer on the network is maintained.

If one computer fails in the network, it does not affect any other computer in the network and the tasks of this computer can be easily switched very to the next computer easily using the hub controls. In a Star Network Topology, it is possible to have all the important data backups on the hub in a private folder and this way if the computer fails you can still use your data using the next computer in the network and accessing the backup files on the hub.

New devices or nodes can easily be added to the Star Network by just extending a cable from the hub. Since the hub controls everything the addition or removal of devices are done using g the hub. If the hub adds a device for example a printer or a fax machine, all the other computers on the network can access the new device by simply accessing the hub. The device need not be installed on all the computers in the network. The central function is cost effective and easier to maintain.

3.3.1.4. Star Topology Conclusion

A Star Network Topology is best suited for smaller networks and works efficiently when there is limited number of nodes. One has to ensure that the hub or the central node is always working, and extra security features should be added to the hub because it's the heart of the network.

3.3.2. Tree Topology

Among all the Network Topologies we can derive that the Tree Topology is a combination of the bus and the Star Topology. The tree like structure allows you to have many servers on the network and you can branch out the network in many ways. This is particularly helpful for colleges, universities, and schools so that each of the branches can identify the relevant systems in their own network and yet connect to the big network in some way.

A Tree Structure suits best when the network is widely spread and vastly divided into many branches. Like any other topologies, the Tree Topology has its advantages and disadvantages. A Tree Network may not suit small networks and it may be a waste of cable to use it for small networks. Tree Topology has some limitations, and the configuration should suit those limitations. This diagram illustrates the tree network topology. A tree topology integrates the star and bus topologies in a hybrid approach to improve network scalability (Figure 3.3).

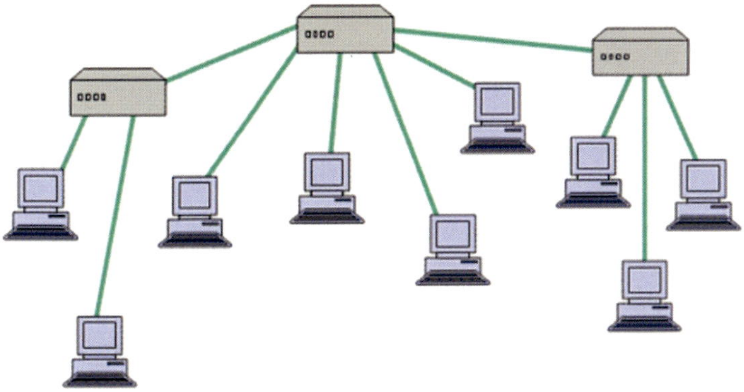

Figure 3.3. Tree topology.

3.3.2.1. Tree Network Topology Benefits

A Tree Topology is supported by many network vendors and even hardware vendors. A point-to-point connection is possible with Tree Networks. All the computers have access to the larger and their immediate networks. Best topology for branched out networks.

3.3.2.2. Tree Topology Limitations

In a Network Topology the length of the network depends on the type of cable that is being used. The Tree Topology network is entirely dependent on the trunk which is the main backbone of the network. If that has to fail, then the entire network would fail. Since the Tree Topology network is big it is difficult to configure and can get complicated after a certain point. The Tree Topology follows a hierarchical pattern where each level is connected to the next higher level in a symmetrical pattern. Each level in the hierarchy follows a certain pattern in connecting the nodes. Like the topmost level might have only one node or two nodes and the following level in the hierarchy might have few more nodes which work on the point-to-point connectivity and the third level also has asymmetrical node to node pattern and each of these levels are connected to the root level in the hierarchy. Think of a tree that branches out in various directions and all these branches need the roots and the tree trunk to survive. A Tree Structured network is very similar to this and that is why it is called the Tree Topology.

3.3.2.3. Tree Topology Features

There will be at least three levels of hierarchy in the Tree Network Topology and they all work based on the root node.

The Tree Topology has two kinds of topology integral in it, the star, and the linear way of connecting to nodes. The Tree Topology functions by taking into account the total number of nodes present in the network. It does not matter how many nodes are there on each level. Nodes can be added to any level of the hierarchy and there are no limitations a far as the total number of nodes do not exceed. The higher levels in the hierarchy are expected to perform more functions than the lower levels in the network.

3.3.2.4. Tree Topology Conclusion

The signals that are being transmitted by the root node are received by all the nodes at the same time. This increases the efficiency of the overall functioning of the network. The Tree Network topology can be extended easily to function and there are no limitations to how big it can be extended. Additional root nodes can be added, and they can be interconnected within one single network.

3.3.3. Mesh Topology

Mesh Network is a network where all the nodes are connected to each other and is a complete network. In a Mesh Network every node is connected to other nodes on the network through hops. Some are connected through single hops, and some may be connected with more than one hope.

3.3.3.1. Fully Connected Mesh

The type of network topology in which each of the nodes of the network is connected to each of the other nodes in the network with a point-to-point link – this makes it possible for data to be simultaneously transmitted from any single node to all of the other nodes.

3.3.3.2. Partially Connected Mesh

The type of network topology in which some of the nodes of the network are connected to more than one other node in the network with a point-to-point link – this makes it possible to take advantage of some of the redundancy that is provided by a physical fully connected mesh topology without the expense and complexity required for a connection between every node in the network.

While the data is traveling on the Mesh Network it is automatically configured to reach the destination by taking the shortest route which means the least number of hops. Data travels by hopping from one node to another and then reaches the destination node in a Mesh Topology Network. This diagram illustrates the mesh network topology. A mesh topology provides redundant communication paths between some or all devices (partial or full mesh) (Figure 3.4).

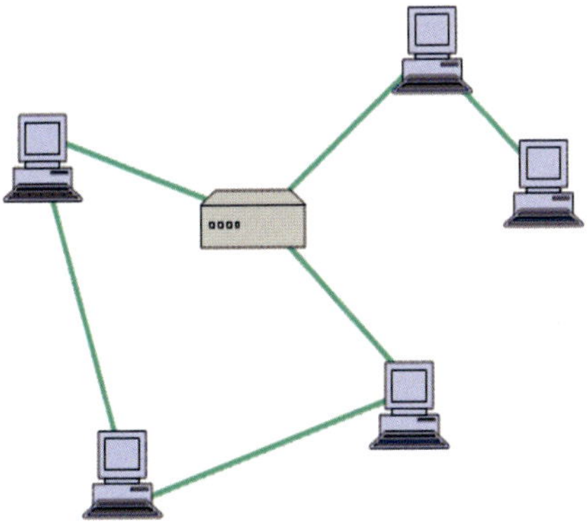

Figure 3.4. Mesh topology.

An example of a Mesh Network is the Mobile Ad hoc Network or MANet. The entire Mesh Network is continuously connected. Being completely connected does not mean that Mesh Network is dependent on each and every node of the network. Even if one node fails in the Mesh Network the network finds an alternate route to transfer the data. It is called the self-healing technology where it receives data one way or the other.

The Mesh Network is based on a very sensible concept and has lesser chances of a network breakdown. There are so many possible combinations of routes and hops a data transfer can take that it will reach the destination one way or the other. It is highly unlikely that all the nodes in a single Mesh Network will break down at any given point of time.

3.3.4. Hybrid Topology

With the hybrid topology, two or more topologies are combined to form a complete network. For example, a hybrid topology could be the combination of a star and bus topology. These are also the most common in use (Figure 3.5).

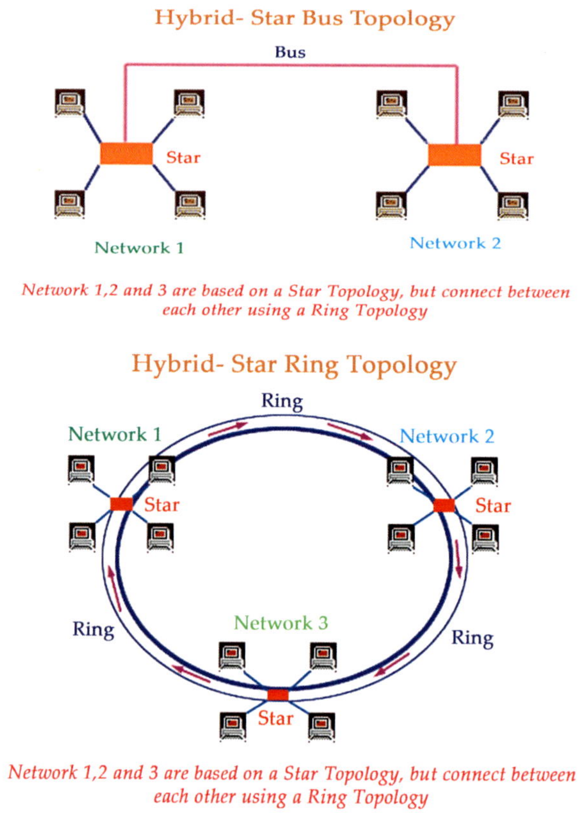

Figure 3.5. Hybrid topology.

3.3.4.1. Wireless Mesh Networks

Wireless mesh networks work based on the radio frequencies and was originally developed by the army to be able to communicate. The reliability factor is high in any kind of Mesh Network. There are three types of wireless mesh topologies:

- Fixed wireless connections;
- Peer to peer or ad hoc networks; and

- Node to node.

3.3.4.2. Fixed Mesh Networks

The fixed Mesh Networks will work only in the specified location, and they are not mobile networks. They are meant to be used in a limited surrounding with boundaries. The location of nodes in affixed Mesh Network is all predetermined and they are not interchangeable.

The fixed Mesh Network does not work online of sight like the other types of Mesh Networks. The total number of hops in a fixed Mesh Network is usually fixed and also short. There may not be many nodes as this kind of Mesh Networks exist within an office or building. More often than not the data travels ion a specific direction.

3.3.4.3. Peer to Peer Mobile Networks

In a peer-to-peer mobile network the individual devices connect to each other using the Mesh Network. The peer does not require connecting to the main node and they can still communicate from one device to another device by taking the shortest possible data transfer route. However, many experts believe that in the peer-to-peer Mesh Networks the problems with scalability in terms of time taken for data transfer is questionable. The device has to know to transmit the data in the most optimal path and the entire data transfer or depends on this single factor. If the device is incapable, then the whole purpose of using it in a peer-to-peer connection is lost.

3.3.5. Bus Topology

From the name of the network itself many inferences of the network can be derived. A bus topology in more technical terms means that it is a method of transmission on networks that uses a common vehicle for transmissions and thus it is categorized as shared communication. Imagine a bus picking up various people from one stop and dropping of people as it travels and then picking a few more. That is what happens in a bus network exactly.

However, in a Bus topology only one device is allowed to transmit at a given point of time. The DAP or the Distribute Access Protocol has the information about which station has to transmit the data. The data that is being transmitted have frames that will have the source name and the network address.

3.3.5.1. Bus Topology Functionality

The bus topology connects each computer on the network into something called the segment trunk. A bus is usually referred to a cable that connects end to end and this is used to transmit the signals from one end to the other end. At every end, a terminator is placed so that it understands in which direction the data is traveling and also the terminator is used to absorb the signals. If the terminator does not absorb the signal, then the same signal is reflected back to the bus confusing the whole data flow. The bus is considered to be a passive network because the computers are largely dependent on the signal that is being transmitted. This diagram illustrates the bus network topology. A bus topology such as 10Base-2 or 10Base-5 Ethernet uses a single communication backbone for all devices (Figure 3.6).

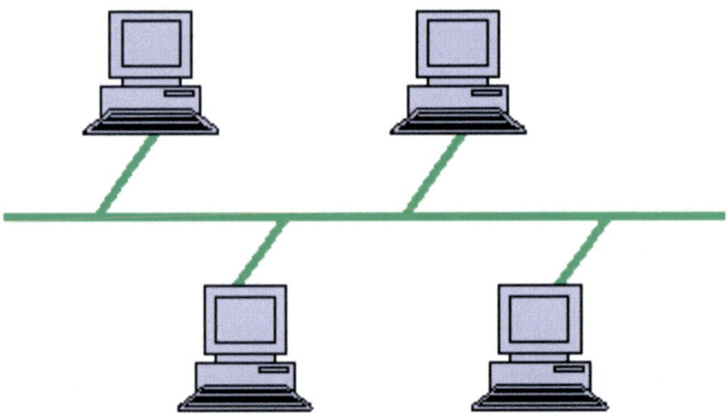

Figure 3.6. Bus topology.

3.3.5.2. Distributed Bus

The type of network topology in which all of the nodes of the network are connected to a common transmission medium which has more than two endpoints that are created by adding branches to the main section of the transmission medium – the physical distributed bus topology functions in exactly the same fashion as the physical linear bus topology (i.e., all nodes share a common transmission medium).

Ø ***Notes:***

1. All of the endpoints of the common transmission medium are normally terminated with a device called a 'terminator' (see the note under linear bus).

2. The physical linear bus topology is sometimes considered to be a special case of the physical distributed bus topology – i.e., a distributed bus with no branching segments.
3. The physical distributed bus topology is sometimes incorrectly referred to as a physical tree topology – however, although the physical distributed bus topology resembles the physical tree topology, it differs from the physical tree topology in that there is no central node to which any other nodes are connected, since this hierarchical functionality is replaced by the common bus (Figure 3.7).

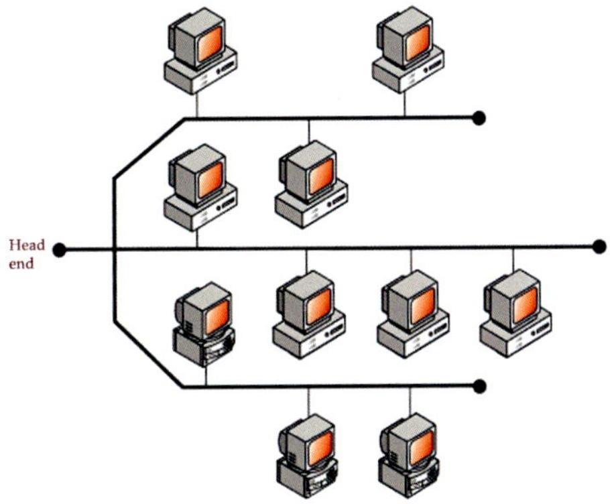

Figure 3.7. Distributed bus topology.

3.3.5.3. Bus Topology Advantages

The advantage of the Bus network is that if one computer fails in the network the others are still not affected and they continue to work. Bus network is very simple and easy to set up. If there is an urgent need to set up a network and perhaps be used on a short-term basis, then the Bus network is the best possibility. Bus networks use the least amount of cable to set up making it cost effective.

3.3.5.4. Bus Topology Limitations

In the bus network you will need a network connection in order to determine if the data is being transferred between two nodes. If the data transfer rate is high, then the Bus network does not perform very well because the data travels in a stream and cannot be overloaded. The bus network is a bit challenging when you have to troubleshoot the problems. Bus networks are not suitable as large networks as there are limitations to the number of nodes you can set up for one single cable. As the number of computers increase in the network the data transfer rate goes down accordingly and noticeably.

3.3.5.5. Bus Topology Conclusion

The bus networks in spite of its limitations are considered to be the easiest and the fastest network that can be set up compared to the other kinds of network. In bus networks there is a collision handling system which ensures that data travels without errors and data is delivered correctly.

3.3.6. Ring Topology

A ring topology is a network topology or circuit arrangement in which each network device is attached along the same signal path to two other devices, forming a path in the shape of a ring. Each device in the network that is also referred to as node handles every message that flows through the ring. Each node in the ring has a unique address. Since in a ring topology there is only one pathway between any two nodes, ring networks are generally disrupted by the failure of a single link. This diagram illustrates the ring network topology. A ring topology such as FDDI or SONET sends messages clockwise or counterclockwise through the shared link (Figure 3.8).

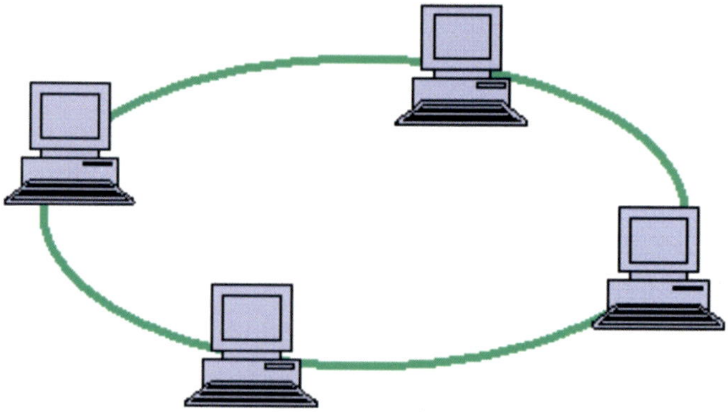

Figure 3.8. Ring topology.

The redundant topologies are used to eliminate network downtime caused by a single point of failure. All networks need redundancy for enhanced reliability. Network reliability is achieved through reliable equipment and network designs that are tolerant to failures and faults. The FDDI networks overcome the disruption in the network by sending data on a clockwise and a counterclockwise ring. In case there is a break in data flow, the data is wrapped back onto the complementary ring before it reaches the end of the cable thereby maintaining a path to every node within the complementary ring. The most well-known example of a ring topology is Token Ring.

3.3.6.1. Dual-Ring

The type of network topology in which each of the nodes of the network is connected to two other nodes in the network, with two connections to each of these nodes, and with the first and last nodes being connected to each other with two connections, forming a double ring – the data flows in opposite directions around the two rings, although, generally, only one of the rings carries data during normal operation, and the two rings are independent unless there is a failure or break in one of the rings, at which time the two rings are joined (by the stations on either side of the fault) to enable the flow of data to continue using a segment of the second ring to bypass the fault in the primary ring (Figure 3.9).

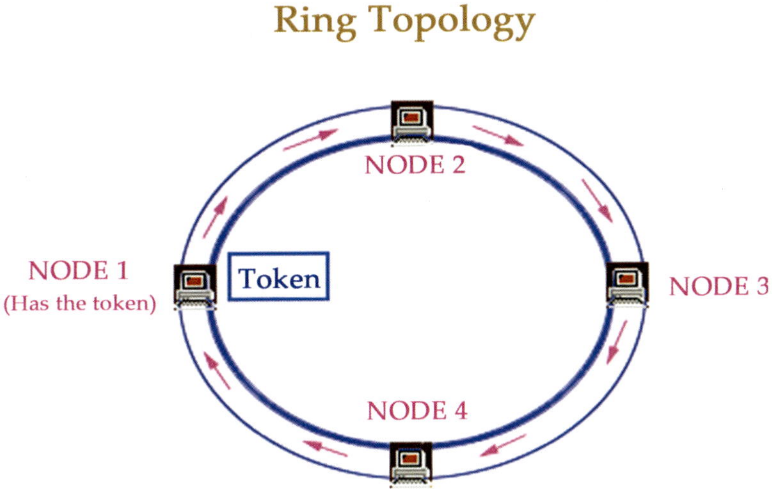

Figure 3.9. Dual-ring topology.

Ø **Advantages:**

- An orderly network where every device has access to the token and the opportunity to transmit.
- Under heavy network load performs better than a start topology.

- To manage the connectivity between the computers it does not need network server.

Ø **Disadvantages:**

- One malfunctioning workstation can throw away the entire network;
- Moves, adds, and changes of devices can affect the entire network;
- It is slower than an Ethernet network.

3.3.7. Cellular Topology

Wireless networks are commonly used in these days and there is no doubt that wireless communication will be the next generations' communication technology, 3G technologies can be given as an example to this. As in wired networks, wireless networks also have physical appearance. The physical topology in wireless networks is called cellular topology. In wireless networks access points are used instead of hubs and switches a sample access point. Access points are the connection points of wired and wireless networks, from this point of view access points also serve as a bridge and they enable such devices like a printer that doesn't have wireless property. In addition to this access points strengthens the incoming signals to transmit them further.

By using lots of access points, the length of the transfer distance of wireless network can be enhanced. Access points provides with a data transfer of 11 Mbps for up to 40 meters and 1 Mbps for up to 100 meters, with the help of more enhanced wireless bridges wireless networks can be provided for LAN type wired networks which has kilometers of distance in between and that may provide larger networks of MAN and WAN.

A cellular topology which composed from integration of access points. Every access point has a circular coverage area. In such a wireless network a computer that is in the coverage area of any access point can be connected wirelessly to the network as displayed in Figure 3.9 (mobile phone, palm, PDA, etc.).

Data transfer in wireless networks occurs within the scope of cellular topology mentioned above. Wireless network topologies don't have many alternatives like wired network topologies. In wireless networks star and mesh topologies are used that are mentioned in wired topologies (Figure 3.10).

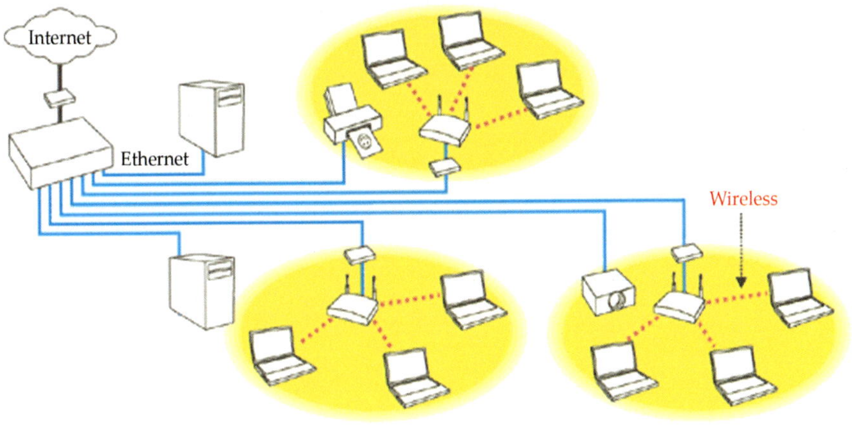

Figure 3.10. Wireless star topology.

3.3.8. Wireless Star Topology

In upon figure an example for wireless topology is shown. Mobile computers in a local network first of all connect to the wireless access point then to the switch and lastly connects to the internet by a router. In the upon figure mobile computers are connected to 3 access points are displayed. The red lines show that mobile computers in coverage area of an access point like physical star topology. Meanwhile, the access point which serves a bridge, makes the wireless and wired connections work in harmony.

3.3.9. Wireless Mesh Topology

At home and offices to make a wireless connection establishing a star topology connection will be sufficient. However, within the borders of country, when it is required to establish a wireless WAN (mobile phones) the question of what kind of topology is needed explains the reason for using mesh topology in wireless networks. In such a big area one access point won't be sufficient as a result of this more access points will be needed for establishing the connections. When it is required to enlarge the wireless network in the same form new access points are located as they can communicate with each other (Figure 3.11).

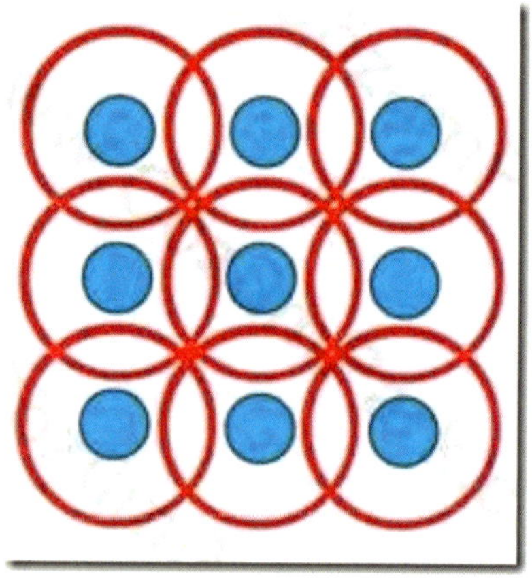

Figure 3.11. Wireless mesh topology.

The topology used for mobile phones are also cellular mesh topology. Base points might be regarded as access points. In wireless network environments like Bluetooth when the devices are in the coverage areas of other devices, they can transfer data from one point to other point without using any other hardware. In mobile phones this method is used for sharing files (Figure 3.12).

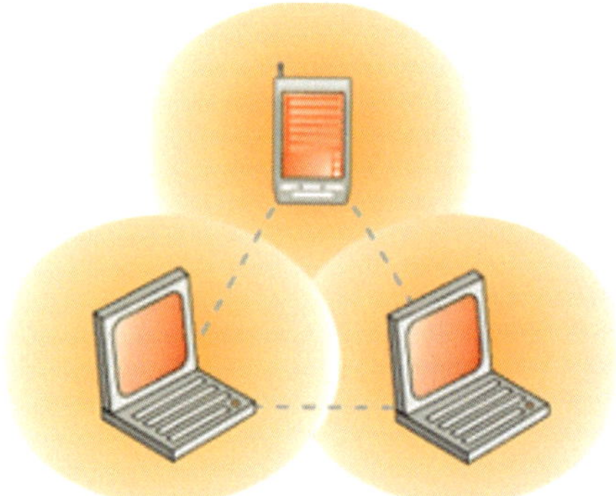

Figure 3.12. Ad hoc connection.

The systems that are not using access points can transfer data between each other with Ad Hoc method. These kinds of connections are used for sharing music and pictures.

3.3.10. Wireless Mesh Topologies

If we imagine wiring every single computer, wireless mesh topology provides great convenience to us. The greatest advantage of wireless mesh topology is it doesn't need any other carrier except atmosphere and space, the weakest part of it is the signal in the air can easily be listened and the security threads related to this.

> ➢ Find the *synonyms* for the underlined words.
>
> 1. The way the computers will be talking to each other and the direction of the traffic is controlled by the various protocols (like Ethernet) or, if you like, rules.
> 2. Memory plays a significant role in the following important aspects of your computer system.
> 3. In this the devices are connected by wire or without wire(wireless) to make a network so that the data may travel through each terminal with very least attenuation.
> 4. In a Star Network the best advantage is when there is a failure in cable then only one computer might get affected and not the entire network.
> 5. The isolation of traffic between nodes means that heavy utilization from one device is invisible to other devices on the network, provided that the central hub retains adequate capacity.
> 6. The topology is easy to understand, establish, and navigate.
> 7. Individual nodes can easily be added or removed, and fault detection is simplified, as each link/device can be probed individually.
> 8. A tree topology integrates the star and bus topologies in a hybrid approach to improve network scalability.
> 9. They are meant to be used in a limited surrounding with boundaries. The location of nodes in affixed Mesh Network is all pre determined and they are not interchangeable.
> 10. If the terminator does not absorb the signal then the same signal is reflected back to the bus confusing the whole data flow.

➢ Fill in the blank with the following words.

Order, Stretch, Guess, Scatter, Enlarged, Arrangement, Substitute for, Components

1. Network topology is the study of the .... or mapping of the elements.
2. Try to .... yourself in a room with a small network.
3. Any particular network topology is determined only by the graphical mapping of the .... of physical and/or logical connections between nodes.
4. The arrangement or mapping of the .... of a network gives rise to certain basic topologies which may then be combined to form more complex topologies
5. The repeaters being used to .... the maximum transmission distance of the point-to-point links between the central node and the peripheral nodes.
6. The repeaters in a network that is based upon the physical extended star topology are .... with hubs or switches.
7. The network can easily be scaled or .... by adding to the capacity of the hub node.
8. A Tree Structure suits best when the network is widely .... and vastly divided into many branches.

➢ Write *antonyms* of following words.

1. Invisible ....
2. Isolate ....
3. Entire ....
4. Privacy ....
5. Immediate ....
6. Asymmetrical ....
7. Boundaries ....

3.3.11. Additional Information about LAN Media-Access Methods

Media contention occurs when two or more network devices have data to send at the same time. Because multiple devices cannot talk on the network simultaneously, some type of method must be used to allow one device access to the network media at a time. This is done in two main ways: carrier sense multiple access collision detects (CSMA/CD) and token passing.

In networks using CSMA/CD technology such as Ethernet, network devices contend for the network media. When a device has data to send, it first listens to see if any other device is currently using the network. If not, it starts sending its data. After finishing its transmission, it listens again to see if a collision occurred. A collision occurs when two devices send data simultaneously. When a collision happens, each device waits a random length of time before resending its data. In most cases, a collision will not occur again between the two devices. Because of this type of network contention, the busier a network becomes, the more collisions occur. This is why performance of Ethernet degrades rapidly as the number of devices on a single network increase.

In token-passing networks such as Token Ring and FDDI, a special network packet called a token is passed around the network from device to device. When a device has data to send, it must wait until it has the token and then sends its data. When the data transmission is complete, the token is released so that other devices may use the network media. The main advantage of token-passing networks is that they are deterministic. In other words, it is easy to calculate the maximum time that will pass before a device has the opportunity to send data. This explains the popularity of token-passing networks in some real-time environments such as factories, where machinery must be capable of communicating at a determinable interval.

For CSMA/CD networks, switches segment the network into multiple collision domains. This reduces the number of devices per network segment that must contend for the media. By creating smaller collision domains, the performance of a network can be increased significantly without requiring addressing changes.

Normally CSMA/CD networks are half-duplex, meaning that while a device sends information, it cannot receive at the time. While that device is talking, it is incapable of also listening for other traffic. This is much like a walkie-talkie. When one person wants to talk, he presses the transmit button and begins speaking. While he is talking, no one else on the same frequency can talk. When the sending person is finished, he releases the transmit button and the frequency is available to others.

When switches are introduced, full-duplex operation is possible. Full-duplex works much like a telephone—you can listen as well as talk at the same time. When a network device is attached directly to the port of a network switch, the two devices may be capable of operating in full-duplex mode. In full-duplex mode, performance can be increased, but not quite as much as some like to claim. A 100-Mbps Ethernet segment is capable of transmitting 200 Mbps of data, but only 100 Mbps can travel in one direction at a time. Because most data connections are asymmetric (with more data traveling in one direction than the other), the gain is not as great as many claims. However, full-duplex operation does increase the throughput of most applications because the network media is no longer shared. Two devices on a full-duplex connection can send data as soon as it is ready.

Token-passing networks such as Token Ring can also benefit from network switches. In large networks, the delay between turns to transmit may be significant because the token is passed around the network.

3.3.12. LAN Transmission Methods

LAN data transmissions fall into three classifications: unicast, multicast, and broadcast. In each type of transmission, a single packet is sent to one or more nodes.

In a unicast transmission, a single packet is sent from the source to a destination on a network. First, the source node addresses the packet by using the address of the destination node. The package is then sent onto the network, and finally, the network passes the packet to its destination.

A multicast transmission consists of a single data packet that is copied and sent to a specific subset of nodes on the network. First, the source node addresses the packet by using a multicast address. The packet is then sent into the network, which makes copies of the packet and sends a copy to each node that is part of the multicast address.

A broadcast transmission consists of a single data packet that is copied and sent to all nodes on the network. In these types of transmissions, the source node addresses the packet by using the broadcast address. The packet is then sent on to the network, which makes copies of the packet and sends a copy to every node on the network.

3.4. OSI MODEL

The International Organization for Standardization (ISO) began developing the Open Systems Interconnection (OSI) reference model in 1977. It has since become the most widely accepted model for understanding network communication; once you understand how the OSI model works, you can use it to compare network implementations on different systems.

When you want to communicate with another person, you need to have two things in common: a communication language and a communication medium. Computer networks are no different; for communication to take place on a network composed of a variety of different network devices, both the language and medium must be clearly defined. The OSI model (and networking models developed by other organizations) attempts to define rules that cover both the generalities and specifics of networks:

- How network devices contact each other and, if they have different languages, how they communicate with each other.
- Methods by which a device on a network knows when to transmit data.
- Methods to ensure that network transmissions are received correctly and by the right recipient.
- How the physical transmission media is arranged and connected.
- How to ensure that network devices maintain a proper rate of data flow.
- How bits are represented on the network media.

The OSI model isn't a product. It's just a conceptual framework you can use to better understand the complex interactions taking place among the various devices on a network. It doesn't do anything in the communication process; appropriate software and hardware do the actual work. The OSI model simply defines which tasks need to be done and which protocols will handle those tasks at each of the seven layers of the model. The seven layers are as follows:

- Application (layer 7);
- Presentation (layer 6);
- Session (layer 5);
- Transport (layer 4);
- Network (layer 3);
- Datalink (layer 2);
- Physical (layer 1).

The main idea in OSI is that the process of communication between two end points in a telecommunication network can be divided into layers, with each layer adding its own set of special, related functions. Each communicating user or program is at a computer equipped with these seven layers of function. So, in a given message between users, there will be a flow of data through each layer at one end down through the layers in that computer and, at the other end, when the message arrives, another flow of data up through the layers in the receiving computer and ultimately to the end user or program. The actual programming and hardware that furnishes these seven layers of function is usually a combination of the computer operating system, applications (such as your Web browser), TCP/IP or alternative transport and network protocols, and the software and hardware that enable you to put a signal on one of the lines attached to your computer.

3.4.1. Basic Features of the OSI Model

The transmission of a message from one computer to another is a complex undertaking. The OSI model is designed to remove the complexity from the task. The specific object of the OSI model is to allow the timely and accurate transfer of the data across the communications network.

A message being transmitted on a communications network will pass through each of the seven layers at the transmitting and then the receiving end. Each layer of the OSI model has been given a specific role in ensuring the successful communication of messages.

The design of the OSI model is modular. This allows any level of the model to be modified as long as it follows the interfacing standards for the level above and below it. However, if a level is changed at one end of the communications network the connection will not work until the same level is modified at the other end. Each level of the OSI model has a one-to-one relationship with the same level at each end of the communications network.

The following are the broad guidelines for transmitting messages using the OSI model:

- All seven layers must be implemented in each end node on the communications network.
- Intermediate nodes do not require the seven layers to be implemented.
- When a layer is implemented on a node or intermediate node all layers below it must also be implemented.
- Each layer should be independent of the layers above and below it.
- The structure of the model must be modular to allow the replacement or modification of individual layers.
- If the two communicating nodes are incompatible at one of the

layers, an intermediate node is necessary to act as a protocol converter. The intermediate node must include all layers up to and including the incompatible node.

➢ Find the *synonyms* for the underlined words.

1. It has since become the most widely accepted model for understanding network communication.
2. Computer networks are no different; for communication to take place on a network composed of a variety of different network devices.
3. Methods to ensure that network transmissions are received correctly and by the right recipient.
4. How bits are represented on the network media.
5. You can use to better understand the complex interactions taking place among the various devices on a network.
6. Each communicating user or program is at a computer equipped with these seven layers of function.
7. The main idea in OSI is that the process of communication between two end points in a telecommunication network can be divided into layers
8. the software and hardware that enable you to put a signal on one of the lines attached to your computer.
9. This allows any level of the model to be modified as long as it follows the interfacing standards for the level above and below it.
10. If the two communicating nodes are incompatible at one of the layers, an intermediate node is necessary to act as a protocol converter.

➢ Fill in the blank with the following words.

Eventually, Goods, Obviously, Particular, Suitable, Mediator, Send, Executions

1. You can use it to compare network .... on different systems.
2. The language and medium must be .... defined.
3. Methods by which a device on a network knows when to .... data.
4. The OSI model isn't a .... It's just a conceptual framework.
5. It doesn't do anything in the communication process; .... software and hardware do the actual work.
6. When the message arrives, another flow of data up through the layers in the receiving computer and .... to the end user or program.
7. Each layer of the OSI model has been given a .... role in ensuring the successful communication of messages.

➢ Write *antonyms* of following words.

1. Incompatible ....
2. Above ....
3. Specific.........................
4. Successful ....
5. Accurate ....
6. Attached ....
7. Recipient ....

3.4.2. Additional Information about Networking Standards Organizations

Discuss the concept of standards. Explain that standards are vital for ensuring that products, processes, and services developed by different parties are able to work together. Mention that standards define a minimum set of specifications for acceptable performance.

3.4.3. ANSI

Explain that the American National Standards Institute (ANSI) is composed of many industry and governmental representatives and develops standards for a wide range of technical fields, including computers and networking.

If the classroom is equipped to do so, show the students ANSI's Web site to illustrate that standards documents can be obtained online.

3.4.4. EIA and TIA

Present a brief overview of the missions of the Electronic Industries Alliance (EIA) and the Telecommunications Industries Alliance (TIA). Mention the TIA/EIA 568-B Series of network cabling installation guidelines.

3.4.5. IEEE

Describe the overall goals and mission of the Institute of Electrical and Electronics Engineers (IEEE). Mention that IEEE technical publications are highly regarded and are used in the networking field. If the classroom is equipped to do so, show the students the IEEE Web site.

3.4.6. ISO

Discuss the mission of the ISO. Mention that this organization represents

146 countries and that the scope of its standards covers a wide range of industries and disciplines.

3.5. SEVEN LAYERS OF OSI MODEL

OSI divides telecommunication into seven layers. The layers are in two groups. The upper four layers are used whenever a message passes from or to a user. The lower three layers (up to the network layer) are used when any message passes through the host computer. Messages intended for this computer pass to the upper layers. Messages destined for some other hosts are not passed up to the upper layers but are forwarded to another host. The seven layers are discussed in subsections.

3.5.1. The Physical Layer

The Physical layer is responsible for sending bits from one computer to another. Physical layer components don't care what the bits mean; their job is to get the bits from point A to point B, using whatever kind of optical, electrical, or wireless connection that connects the points. This level defines physical and electrical details, such as what will represent a 1 or a 0, how many pins a network connector will have, how data will be synchronized, and when the network adapter may or may not transmit the data (Figure 3.13).

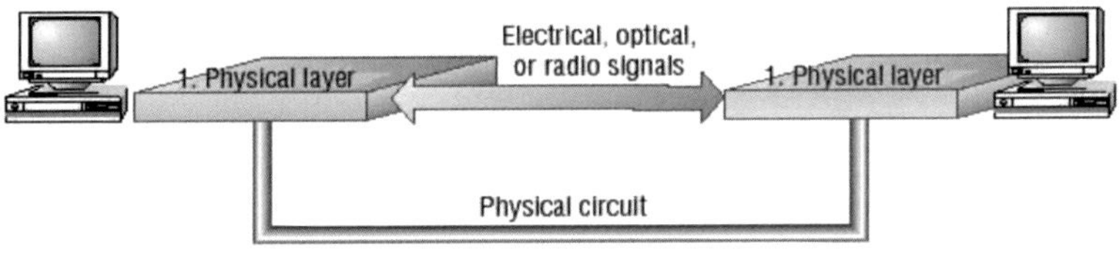

Figure 3.13. The physical layer makes a physical circuit with electrical, optical, or radio signals.

The Physical layer addresses all the minutiae of the actual physical connection between the computer and the network medium, including the following:

- Network connection types, including multipoint and point-to-point connections.
- Physical topologies, or how the network is physically laid out (e.g., bus, star, or ring topologies).

- Which analog and digital signaling methods are used to encode data in the analog and digital signals.
- Bit synchronization, which deals with keeping the sender and receiver in synch as they read and write data.
- Multiplexing, or the process of combining several data channels into one.
- Termination, which prevents signals from reflecting back through the cable and causing signal and packets errors. It also indicates the last node in a network segment.

3.5.2. The Data-Link Layer

The Data-Link layer provides for the flow of data over a single physical link from one device to another. It accepts packets from the Network layer and packages the information into data units called frames; these frames are presented to the Physical layer for transmission. The Data-Link layer adds control information, such as frame type, to the data being sent.

This layer also provides for the error-free transfer of frames from one computer to another. A cyclic redundancy check (CRC) added to the data frame can detect damaged frames, and the Data-Link layer in the receiving computer can request that the CRC information be present so that it can check incoming frames for errors. The Data-Link layer can also detect when frames are lost and request that those frames be sent again.

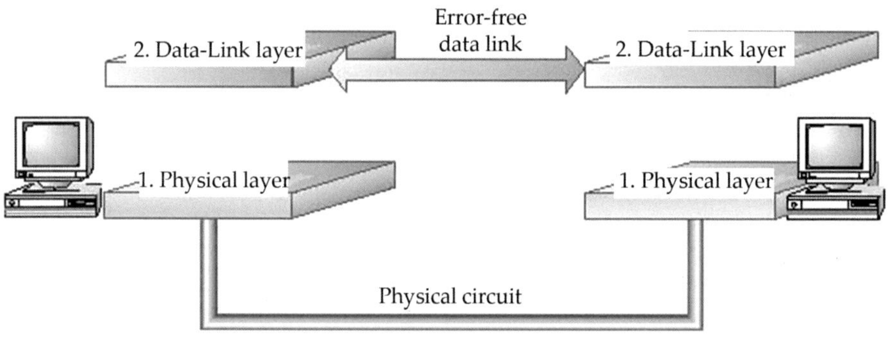

Figure 3.14. The data-link layer establishes an error-free link between two devices.

In broadcast networks such as Ethernet, all devices on the LAN receive the data that any device transmits. (Whether a network is broadcast, or point-to-point is determined by the network protocols used to transmit data over it.) The Data-Link layer on a particular device is responsible for recognizing frames addressed to that device and throwing the rest away, much as you might sort through your daily mail to separate good stuff from junk (Figure 3.14).

The IEEE developed a protocol specification known as IEEE 802.X. (802.2 is the standard that divides this layer into two sublayers. The MAC layer varies for different network types and is described further in standards 802.3 through 802.5.) As part of that specification (which today we know as Ethernet), the Data Link layer is split into two sublayers:

- The logical link control (LLC) layer establishes and maintains the logical communication links between the communicating devices.
- The media access control (MAC) layer acts like an airport control tower—it controls the way multiple devices share the same media channel in the same way that a control tower regulates the flow of air traffic into and out of an airport (Figure 3.15).

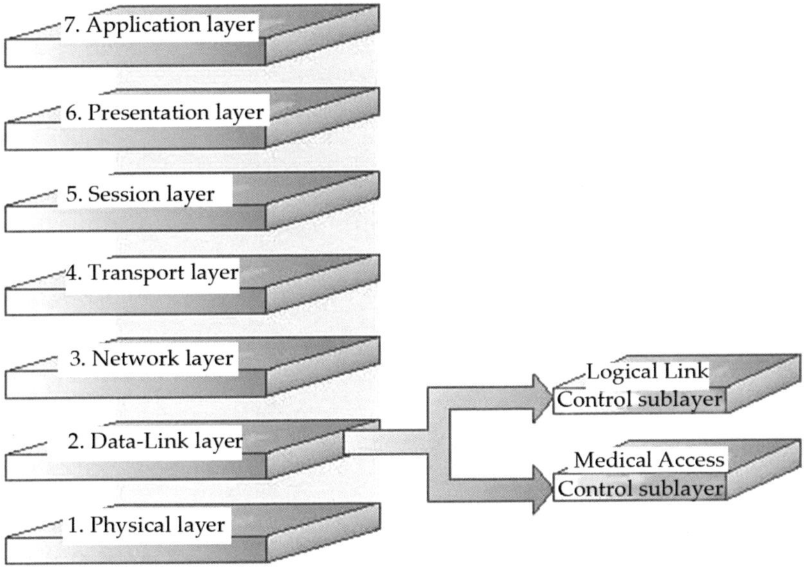

Figure 3.15. The IEEE split the ISO data-link layer into the LLC sublayer and the MAC sublayer.

The LLC sublayer provides service access points (SAPs) that other computers can refer to and use to transfer information from the LLC sublayer to the upper OSI layers. This is defined in the 802.2 standard. The MAC sublayer, the lower of the two sublayers, provides for shared access to the network adapter and communicates directly with network interface cards. Network interface cards have a unique 12-digit hexadecimal MAC address (frequently called the hardware Ethernet address) assigned before they leave the factory where they are made. The LLC sublayer uses MAC addresses to establish logical links between devices on the same LAN.

3.5.3. The Network Layer

The Network layer handles moving packets between devices that are more than one link away from each other. It makes routing decisions and forwards packets as necessary to help them travel to their intended destination. In larger networks, there may be intermediate devices and subnetworks between any two end systems. The network layer makes it possible for the Transport layer (and layers above it) to send packets without being concerned with whether the end system is on the same piece of network cable or on the other end of a large wide area network.

To do its job, the Network layer translates logical network addresses into physical machine addresses (MAC addresses, which operate at the Data-Link layer). The Network layer also determines the quality of service (QoS) (such as the priority of the message) and the route a message will take if there are several ways a message can get to its destination. The Network layer also may split large packets into smaller chunks if the packet is larger than the largest data frame the Data-Link layer will accept. The network reassembles the chunks into packets at the receiving end. Intermediate systems that perform only routing and relaying functions and do not provide an environment for executing user programs can implement just the first three OSI network layers (Figure 3.16).

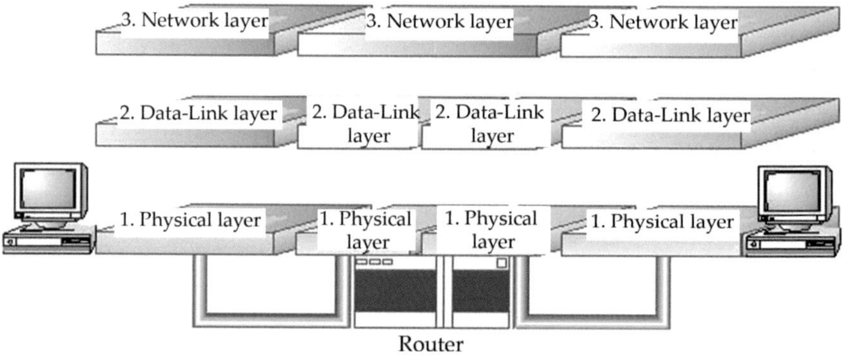

Figure 3.16. *The network layer moves packets across links to their destination.*

The Network layer performs several important functions that enable data to arrive at its destination. The protocols at this layer may choose a specific route through an internetwork to avoid the excess traffic caused by sending data over networks and segments that don't need access to it. The Network layer serves to support communications between logically separate networks. This layer is concerned with the following:

- Addressing, including logical network addresses and services addresses;
- Circuit, message, and packet switching;
- Route discovery and route selection;
- Connection services, including network layer flow control, Network layer error control, and packet sequence control.
- Gateway services.

In Windows Server 2000/2003, the various routing services for TCP/IP, AppleTalk, and internetwork packet exchange/sequenced packet exchange (IPX/SPX) perform Network layer services. In addition, the TCP/IP, AppleTalk, and IPX stacks provide routing capacity for those protocols.

3.5.4. The Transport Layer

The Transport layer ensures that data is delivered error free, in sequence, and with no losses or duplications. This layer also breaks large messages from the Session layer into smaller packets to be sent to the destination computer and reassembles packets into messages to be presented to the Network layer. The Transport layer typically sends an acknowledgment to the originator for messages received (Figure 3.17).

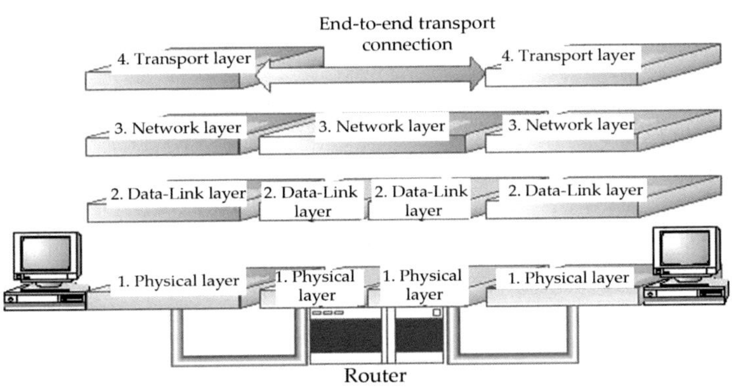

Figure 3.17. The transport layer provides end-to-end communication with integrity and performance guarantees.

3.5.5. The Session Layer

The Session layer allows applications on separate computers to share a connection called a session. This layer provides services, such as name lookup and security, which allow two programs to find each other and establish the communication link. The Session layer also provides for data synchronization and check pointing so that in the event of a network failure, only the data sent after the point of failure would need to be resent. This layer also controls the dialog between two processes and determines who can transmit and who can receive at what point during the communication (Figure 3.18).

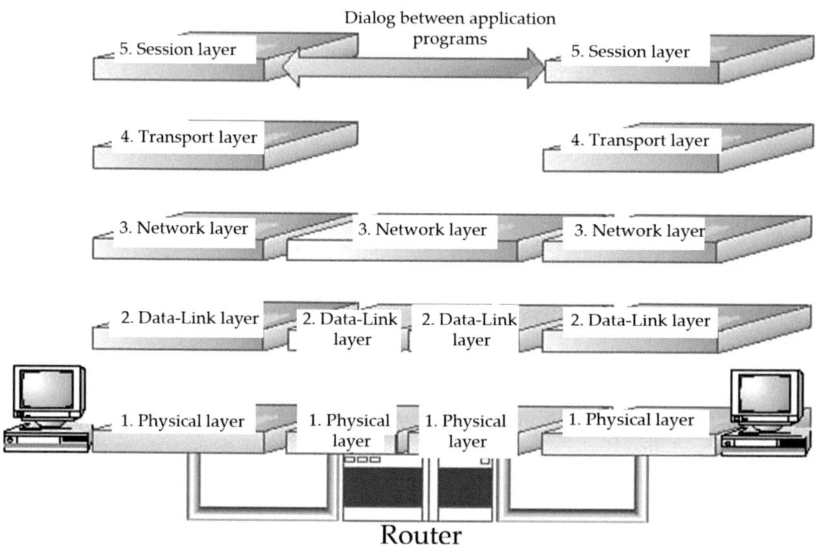

Figure 3.18. The session layer allows applications to establish communication sessions with each other.

3.5.6. The Presentation Layer

The Presentation layer translates data between the formats the network requires and the formats the computer expects. The Presentation layer performs protocol conversion; data translation, compression, and encryption; character set conversion; and the interpretation of graphics commands. The network redirector, long a part of Windows networking, operates at this level. The redirector is what makes the files on a file server visible to the client computer. The network redirector also makes remote printers act as though they are attached to the local computer (Figure 3.19).

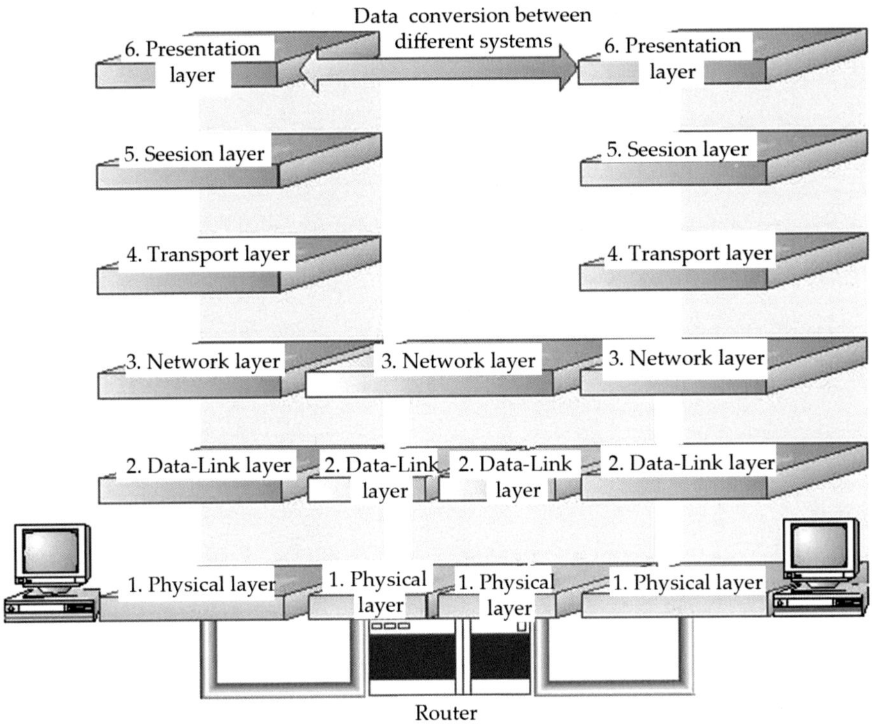

Figure 3.19. The presentation layer allows applications to establish communication sessions with each other.

3.5.7. The Application Layer

The Application layer is the topmost layer of the OSI model, and it provides services that directly support user applications, such as database access, e-mail, and file transfers. It also allows applications to communicate with applications on other computers as though they were on the same computer. When a programmer writes an application program that uses network services, this is the layer the application program will access. For example, Internet Explorer uses the Application layer to make its requests for files and web pages; the Application layer then passes those requests down the stack, with each succeeding layer doing its job (Figure 3.20).

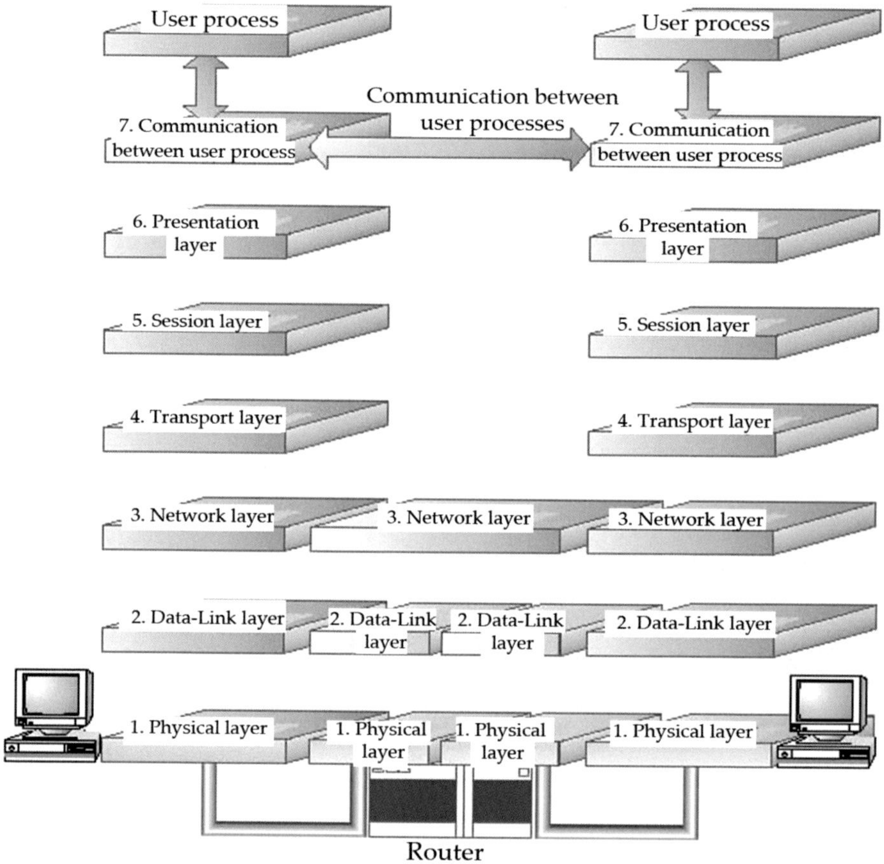

Figure 3.20. The application layer is where the applications function, using lower levels to get their work done.

➢ Find the *synonyms* for the underlined words.

1. This level defines physical and electrical details, such as what will represent a 1 or a 0, how many pins a network connector will have, how data will be synchronized, and when the network adapter may or may not transmit the data.
2. Physical topologies, or how the network is physically laid out.
3. Bit synchronization, which deals with keeping the sender and receiver in synch as they read and write data.
4. Termination, which prevents signals from reflecting back through the cable and causing signal and packets errors. It also indicates the last node in a network segment.
5. A cyclic redundancy check (CRC) added to the data frame can detect damaged frames, and the Data-Link layer in the receiving computer can request that the CRC information be present so that it can check incoming frames for errors.
6. The Data-Link layer on a particular device is responsible for recognizing frames addressed to that device and throwing the rest away, much as you might sort through your daily mail to separate good stuff from junk.
7. The *Logical Link Control (LLC)* layer establishes and maintains the logical communication links between the communicating devices.
8. This layer also breaks large messages from the Session layer into smaller packets to be sent to the destination computer and reassembles packets into messages to be presented to the Network layer. The Transport layer typically sends an acknowledgment to the originator for messages received.
9. The Presentation layer performs protocol conversion; data translation, compression, and encryption; character set conversion; and the interpretation of graphics commands.
10. The Application layer then passes those requests down the stack, with each succeeding layer doing its job.

➢ Fill in the blank with the following words.

Unite, Frame, Internetwork, Agree, Broadcast, More, Work, Petitions

1. Multiplexing, or the process of .... several data channels into one.
2. It .... packets from the Network layer and packages the information into data units called frames.
3. The Data-Link layer adds control information, such as .... type, to the data being sent.
4. In .... networks such as Ethernet, all devices on the LAN receive the data that any device transmits.
5. The MAC layer varies for different network types and is described .... in standards 802.3 through 802.5.
6. The Application layer to make its .... for files and web pages.
7. The network redirector also makes remote printers .... as though they are attached to the local computer.
8. The protocols at this layer may choose a specific route through an .... to avoid the excess traffic caused by sending data over networks and segments that don't need access to it.

➢ Write *antonyms* of following words.

1. Minutiae ....
2. Termination.........................
3. Present ....
4. Income ....
5. Separate ....
6. Regulate ....
7. Visible ....

3.5.8. Additional Information about the TCP/IP Model

Originally developed for the Unites States Department of Defense Advanced Research Project Agency, transmission control protocol/internet protocol (TCP/IP) is a stable, reliable, and efficient suite of protocols which is the basis for the internet and many intranets. The TCP/IP model contains five layers, the Physical layer, Data Link layer, Network layer, Transport layer, and Application layer.

During the early 1980s the Department of Defense developed TCP/IP to connect multiple networks (which were designed by different vendors) into one main network. Used to handle addressing on the ARPANet, TCP/IP was successful because it delivered basic services such as FTP, electronic mail, and remote logon. With the fear of a nuclear explosion, DOD used TCP/IP because it can automatically recover from and node or line failure. In 1982 the DOD decided to make TCP/IP the standard for their entire military network.

When comparing the TCP/IP model to the OSI model, you are able to see the importance of each component. The first notable difference is the number of layers each model contains. The TCP/IP model contains only five, while the OSI model contains seven. The OSI model has the same five as the TCP/IP model with the addition of the session and presentation layers. These layers were grouped with the application layer in the TCP/IP model because these layers do not exist as separate processes with standardized Application Programming Interfaces. The OSI model lacks several components towards the lower levels which support the workings of the IP suite.

Starting at the bottom, the Physical layer is what deals with hardware (wires, cables, satellite links, NICs, etc.). Utilizing the existing Physical layer, TCP/IP does not have to define its own, thus letting the layer be compatible with all network suites. This layer also encodes and transmits data over network communications media in the form of bits which are received by the Physical layer of the destination device. Often combined with this layer is the Data link layer which is responsible for moving packets from the network layer onto different hosts. Depending on the connection type, IP packets are transmitted using various methods. Dial-up modems transmit IP packets using PPP while broadband users transmit using PPoE. This layer is also where packets are intercepted to be sent over a virtual private network.

Traveling up the TCP/IP model the next layer is the Network layer. This layer routes and delivers data across similar networks or completely different networks. The Network layer is responsible for end-to-end packet delivery while maintaining routing, flow control, and error control functions. An example of this layer is the actual IP or the internet protocol security (IPSec).

Above the Network layer is the Transport layer. The Network layer can be thought of the actual vehicle which transports information. This layer categorizes end to end message transmissions or connecting applications as either TCP or user datagram protocol (UDP). TCP is a connection-oriented protocol which is considered to provide a reliable byte stream. Some characteristics of TCP are traffic congestion control, data arrives in order, data has minimal error, and duplicate data is discarded.

The top layer of the TCP/IP model is the Application layer which is used for network communication. Ports are used by programs to transfer data through this layer. For example, the File Transfer Protocol uses port 21 while the hypertext transfer protocol (HTTP) uses port 80.

TCP/IP has many benefits. TCP/IP enables cross-platform networking which is useful in this day-in-age. The ability for a Windows network to contain Windows, Mac, and UNIX workstations has boosted the popularity and functionality of TCP/IP. This suite also has superior failure recovery and the ability to add networks without interrupting existing services. The reliability of TCP/IP is also a huge benefit to using this protocol. The fact that if one part of the network goes down, other parts are still able to function is what has set TCP/IP above other networking protocols. TCP/IP is also easily expandable which allows for the unprecedented rate of growth which the Internet possesses.

Over the years, the TCP/IP model gained an extra layer. Originally, this model only consisted of four layers, but with the addition of the fifth (or more of a division of the physical and data layers) the model has evolved as technology has. Another adjustment made to TCP/IP was done by Van Jacobson, a networking expert. Jacobson discovered a way to compress TCP/IP headers from 40 bytes down to 4 bytes. He accomplished this by saving the state of TCP connections at both ends of the link and then only sent the differences in the header fields that changed. This data compression protocol is described in RFC 1144 and improved TCP/IP performance over slow connections.

The TCP/internet protocol is a beacon of ingenuity in the networking community and serves as the workings of the internet. Through proper research and development, this protocol suite was designed for reliability and expandability which is why it has not been replaced. This suite will continue to be protocols the world uses for many years to come.

3.6. PROTOCOL STACKS

The OSI model splits communication tasks into smaller pieces called subtasks. Protocol implementations are computer processes that handle these subtasks. Specific protocols fulfill subtasks at specific layers of the OSI model. When these protocols are grouped together to complete a whole task, the assemblage of code is called a *protocol stack*. The stack is just a group of protocols, arranged in layers, which implements an entire communication process. Each layer of the OSI model has a different protocol associated with it. When more than one protocol is needed to complete a communication process, the protocols are grouped together in a stack. An example of a protocol stack is TCP/IP, which is widely used by Unix and the Internet—the TCP and IP protocols are implemented at different OSI layers.

Each layer in the protocol stack receives services from the layer below it and provides services to the layer above it. It can be better explained like this: Layer N uses the services of the layer below it (layer N–1) and provides services to the layer above it (layer N+1).

For two computers to communicate, the same protocol stacks must be running on each computer. Each layer on both computers' stacks must use compatible protocols in order for the machines to communicate with each other. The computers can have different operating systems and still be able to communicate if they are running the same protocol stacks. For example, a DOS machine running TCP/IP can communicate with a Macintosh machine running TCP/IP (Figure 3.21).

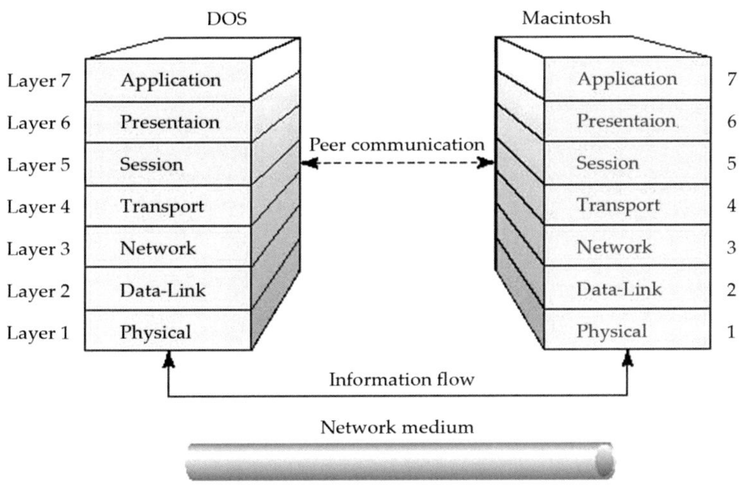

Figure 3.21. Each layer communicates with its counterparts on other network hosts.

3.6.1. Communication between Stacks

When a message is sent from one machine to another, it travels down the layers on one machine and then up the layers on the other machine (Figure 3.22).

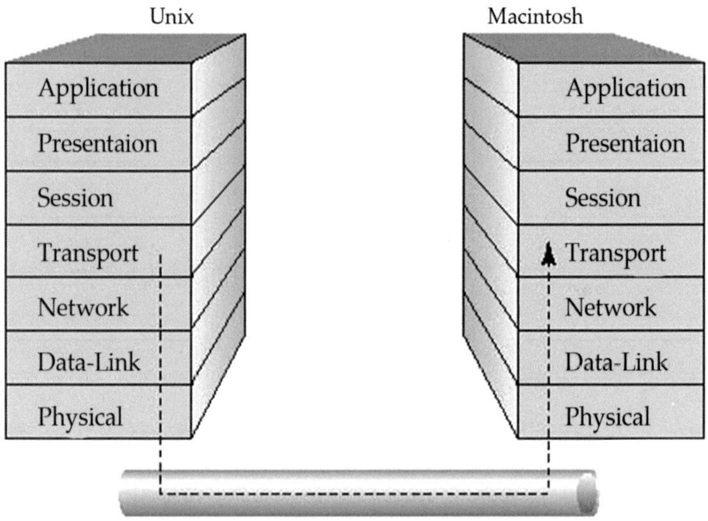

Figure 3.22. Traffic flows down through the stack on one computer and up the stack on the other.

As the message travels down the first stack, each layer it passes through (except the Physical layer) adds a header. These headers contain pieces of control information that are read and processed by the corresponding layer on the receiving stack. As the message travels up the stack of the other machine, each layer removes the header added by its peer layer and uses the information it finds to figure out what to do with the message contents (Figure 3.23).

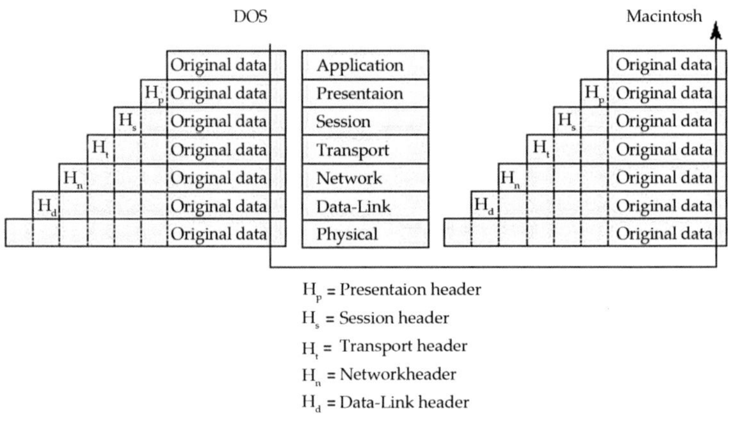

Figure 3.23. As packets flow up and down the stacks, each layer adds or removes necessary control information (data encapsulation).

As an example, consider the network we're using while writing this book. It's a TCP/IP network containing several Windows 2000, Windows Server 2003, Macintosh, and Windows NT machines, all connected using the TCP/IP protocol. When we mount a share from our Windows Server 2003 file server on the Mac desktop, at layer 7, the Mac Finder requests something from the Windows Server 2003. This request is sent to the Mac's layer 6, which receives the request as a data packet, adds its own header, and passes the packet down to layer 5. At layer 5, the process is repeated, and it continues until the packet makes it to the Physical layer.

The physical layer is responsible for actually moving the bits across the network wiring in the office, so it carries the request packet to a place where the Windows Server 2003 machine can "hear" it. At that point, the request packet begins its journey up the layers on the Windows Server 2003 file server. The header that was put on at the Data-Link layer of the Mac OS is stripped off at the Data-Link layer on the Windows Server 2003 machine. The Windows Data-Link layer driver performs the tasks requested in the header and passes the requests to the next, higher layer. This process is repeated until the Windows Server 2003 file server receives the packet and interprets the request. The Windows Server 2003 would then formulate an appropriate response and send it to the Mac.

3.6.2. The Basics of Network Protocols

Protocols are nothing more than an agreed-upon way in which two objects (people, computers, home appliances, etc.) can exchange information. There are protocols at various levels in the OSI model. In fact, it is the protocols at a particular level in the OSI model that provide that level's functionality. Protocols that work together to provide a layer or layers of the OSI model are known as a protocol stack or protocol suite. The following sections explain how network protocols move data between machines.

3.6.3. How Protocols Work?

A protocol is a set of basic steps that both computers must perform in the right order. For instance, for one computer to send a message to another computer, the first computer must perform the steps given in the following general example:

- Break the data into small sections called packets;
- Add addressing information to the packets, identifying the destination computer.

- Deliver the data to the network card for transmission over the network.

The receiving computer must perform these steps:

- Accept the data from the network adapter card;
- Remove the transmitting information that was added by the transmitting computer;
- Reassemble the packets of data into the original message.

Each computer needs to perform the same steps, in the same way and in the correct order, so that the data will arrive and be reassembled correctly. If one computer uses a protocol with different steps or even the same steps with different parameters (such as different sequencing, timing, or error correction), the two computers won't be able to communicate with each other.

3.6.4. Network Packets

Networks primarily send and receive small chunks of data called *packets*. Network protocols construct, modify, and disassemble packets as they move data down the sending stack, across the network, and back up the OSI stack of the receiving computer. Packets have the following components:

- A source address specifying the sending computer;
- A destination address specifying where the packet is being sent;
- Instructions that tell the computer how to pass the data along;
- Reassembly information (if the packet is part of a longer message);
- The data to be transmitted to the remote computer (often called the packet payload);
- Error-checking information to ensure that the data arrives intact.

These components are assembled into slightly larger chunks; each packet contains three distinct parts, and each part contains some of the components listed previously:

1. **Header:** A typical header includes an alert signal to indicate that the data is being transmitted, source, and destination addresses, and clock information to synchronize the transmission.
2. **Data:** This is the actual data being sent. It can vary (depending on the network type) from 48 bytes to 4 kilobytes.
3. **Trailer:** The contents of the trailer (or even the existence of a trailer) vary among network types, but it typically includes a

CRC. The CRC helps the network determine whether or not a packet has been damaged in transmission (Figure 3.24).

Figure 3.24. A packet consists of a header, the data, and a trailer.

- Find the *synonyms* for the underlined words.

1. Specific protocols fulfill subtasks at specific layers of the OSI model.
2. When these protocols are grouped together to complete a whole task, the assemblage of code is called a *protocol stack.*
3. Each layer on both computers' stacks must use compatible protocols in order for the machines to communicate with each other.
4. When a message is sent from one machine to another, it travels down the layers on one machine and then up the layers on the other machine.
5. As the message travels down the first stack, each layer it passes through (except the Physical layer) adds a header.
6. Each layer removes the header added by its peer layer and uses the information it finds to figure out what to do with the message contents.
7. We mount a share from our Windows Server 2003 file server on the Mac desktop.
8. This request is sent to the Mac's layer 6, which receives the request as a data packet, adds its own header, and passes the packet down to layer 5.
9. At that point, the request packet begins its journey up the layers on the Windows Server 2003 file server.
10. The header that was put on at the Data-Link layer of the Mac OS is stripped off at the Data-Link layer on the Windows Server 2003 machine.

➢ Fill in the blank with the following words.

Network, Divides, Arrange Similar, Associated, Various, Clarifies, Operating Systems

1. The OSI model .... communication tasks into smaller pieces called subtasks.
2. Each layer of the OSI model has a different protocol .... with it.
3. The computers can have different ....and still be able to communicate if they are running the same protocol stacks.
4. These headers contain pieces of control information that are read and processed by the .... layer on the receiving stack.
5. It's a TCP/IP network containing....... Windows 2000, Windows Server 2003, Macintosh
6. The physical layer is responsible for actually moving the bits across the .... wiring in the office.
7. This process is repeated until the Windows Server 2003 file server receives the packet and .... the request.
8. A protocol is a set of basic steps that both computers must perform in the right ....

➢ Write *antonyms* of following words.

1. Complete ....
2. Greatly ....
3. Share ....
4. Begin ....
5. Destination ....
6. Deliver ....
7. Right ....

3.6.5. Additional Information about Firewall

Firewall is a system designed to prevent unauthorized access to or from a private network. Firewalls can be implemented in both hardware and software, or a combination of both. They are frequently used to prevent unauthorized Internet users from accessing private networks connected to the Internet, especially intranets (a network belonging to an organization, usually a corporation, accessible only by the organization's members, employees, or others with authorization). All messages entering or leaving the intranet pass through the firewall, which examines each message and blocks those that do not meet the specified security criteria.

A firewall mostly enforces an access control policy between two networks. The actual means by which this is accomplished varies widely, but in principle, the firewall can be thought of as a pair of mechanisms: one which exists to block traffic, and the other which exists to permit traffic. Some firewalls place a greater emphasis on blocking traffic, while others emphasize permitting traffic. Probably the most important thing to recognize about a firewall is that it implements an access control policy.

There are several types of firewall techniques. One is a packet filter. This looks at each packet entering or leaving the network and accepts or rejects it based on user-defined rules. Packet filtering is fairly effective and transparent to users, but it is difficult to configure. In addition, it is susceptible to IP spoofing (a technique used to gain unauthorized access to computers, whereby the intruder sends messages to a computer with an IP address indicating that the message is coming from a trusted host).

The second type is application gateway. This applies security mechanisms to specific applications, such as FTP and Telnet servers. This is very effective but can impose performance degradation. The third type is circuit-level gateway. This applies security mechanisms when a TCP or UDP connection is established. Once the connection has been made, packets can flow between the hosts without further checking. The fourth type is proxy server. This technique intercepts all messages entering and leaving the network. The proxy server effectively hides the true network addresses. In practice, many firewalls use two or more of these techniques in concert.

3.6.6. Why Would I Want a Firewall?

Many traditional-style corporations and data centers have computing security policies and practices that must be adhered to. In a case where a company's policies dictate how data must be protected, a firewall is very important, since it is the embodiment of the corporate policy. Frequently, the hardest part of hooking to the Internet, if you're a large company, is not justifying the expense or effort, but convincing management that it's safe to do so. A firewall provides not only real security – it often plays an important role as a security blanket for management. Lastly, a firewall can act as your corporate "ambassador" to the Internet.

Many corporations use their firewall systems as a place to store public information about corporate products and services, files to download, bug-fixes, and so forth. Several of these systems have become important parts of the Internet service structure and have reflected well on their organizational sponsors.

3.6.7. What Can a Firewall Protect Against?

Some firewalls permit only email traffic through them, thereby protecting the network against any attacks other than attacks against the email service. Other firewalls provide less strict protections, and block services that are known to be problems.

Generally, firewalls are configured to protect against unauthenticated interactive logins from the "outside" world. This, more than anything, helps prevent vandals from logging into machines on your network. More elaborate firewalls block traffic from the outside to the inside but permit users on the inside to communicate freely with the outside. The firewall can protect you against any type of network-born attack if you unplug it.

Firewalls are also important since they can provide a single "choke point" where security and audit can be imposed. Unlike in a situation where a computer system is being attacked by someone dialing in with a modem, the firewall can act as an effective "phone tap" and tracing tool. Firewalls provide an important logging and auditing function; often, they provide summaries to the administrator about what kinds and amount of traffic passed through it, how many attempts there were to break into it, etc.

Providing this "choke point" can serve the same purpose on your network as a guarded gate can for your site's physical premises. That means anytime you have a change in "zones" or levels of sensitivity, such a checkpoint is appropriate. It is reasonable to expect layers of security on your network.

3.6.8. What Can't a Firewall Protect Against?

Firewalls can't protect against attacks that don't go through the firewall. Many corporations that connect to the Internet are very concerned about proprietary data leaking out of the company through that route. Unfortunately for those concerned, a magnetic tape can just as effectively be used to export data. Many organizations that are terrified (at a management level) of Internet connections have no coherent policy about how dial-in access via modems should be protected. There are a lot of organizations out there buying expensive firewalls and neglecting the numerous other backdoors into their network. For a firewall to work, it must be a part of a consistent overall organizational security architecture. Firewall policies must be realistic and reflect the level of security in the entire network. For example, a site with top secret or classified data doesn't need a firewall at all: they shouldn't be hooking up to the Internet in the first place, or the systems with the really secret data should be isolated from the rest of the corporate network.

Another thing a firewall can't really protect you against is traitors inside your network. While an industrial spy might export information through your firewall, he's just as likely to export it through a telephone, FAX machine, or floppy disk. Floppy disks are a far more likely means for information to leak from your organization than a firewall. Lastly, firewalls can't protect against tunneling over most application protocols. There are no magic bullets, and a firewall is not an excuse to not implement software controls on internal networks or ignore host security on servers. Tunneling "bad" things over HTTP, SMTP, and other protocols is quite simple and trivially demonstrated.

3.6.9. Can Firewalls Keep Out Viruses?

Firewalls can't protect very well against things like viruses. There are too many ways of encoding binary files for transfer over networks, and too many different architectures and viruses to try to search for them all. In other words, a firewall cannot replace security-consciousness on the part of your users. In general, a firewall cannot protect against a data-driven attack—attacks in which something is mailed or copied to an internal host where it is then executed. This form of attack has occurred in the past against various versions of send-mail, ghost-script, and scripting mail user agents like Outlook.

Organizations that are deeply concerned about viruses should implement organization-wide virus control measures. Rather than trying to screen viruses out at the firewall, make sure that every vulnerable desktop has virus scanning software that is run when the machine is rebooted. Blanketing your network with virus scanning software will protect against viruses that come in via floppy disks, modems, and Internet. Trying to block viruses at the firewall will only protect against viruses from the Internet – and the vast majority of viruses are caught via floppy disks.

Nevertheless, an increasing number of firewall vendors are offering "virus detecting" firewalls. They're probably only useful for naive users exchanging Windows-on-Intel executable programs and malicious-macro-capable application documents. There are many firewall-based approaches for dealing with problems like worms and Trojans and other attacks. Do not count on any protection from attackers with this feature. A strong firewall is never a substitute for sensible software that recognizes the nature of what it's handling—untrusted data from an unauthenticated party—and behaves appropriately.

If you don't have a good idea of what kind of access you want to allow or to deny, a firewall really won't help you. It's also important to recognize that the firewall's configuration because it is a mechanism for enforcing policy, imposes its policy on everything behind it. Administrators for firewalls managing the connectivity for a large number of hosts therefore have a heavy responsibility.

Firewalls are a very effective way to protect your system from many Internet security threats, and they're a critical component of today's computer network. A firewall is considered a first line of defense in protecting private information.

3.7. NETWORK DEVICES

3.7.1. Network Repeater

A repeater connects two segments of your network cable. It retimes and regenerates the signals to proper amplitudes and sends them to the other segments. When talking about, Ethernet topology, you are probably talking about using a hub as a repeater. Repeaters require a small amount of time to regenerate the signal. This can cause a propagation delay which can affect network communication when there are several repeaters in a row. Many network architectures limit the number of repeaters that can be used in a row. Repeaters work only at the physical layer of the OSI network model.

The LAN is a communications system that provides a connection among a number of independent computing stations within a small area, such as a single building or group of adjacent buildings. Ethernet is a local-area network (LAN) design which employs carrier sense multiple access with collision detection (CSMA/CD) as an access control method. A repeater transmits information by receiving the information on one cable segment and repeating the received information onto the other cable segment to which it is attached. The repeater may perform a variety of signal processing operations on the received data before it is repeated, such as signal amplification, signal retiming, preamble insertion, etc. Repeaters are widely used in the transmission of information throughout a system and are particularly useful in the transmission of information throughout a LAN. Repeaters in LANs are simple devices for broadcasting data packets originating at one port of the repeater to all other ports. Multiple end stations, i.e., data terminal equipment (DTEs), connect to repeaters via coaxial cables, or twisted-pair wiring, or optical fiber in the LAN. Repeaters are commonly used to increase the number of ports on a LAN. A typical repeater comprises a single integrated circuit (IC) chip. Because an IC chip has limited drive current, each chip has a limited number of ports. A network repeater typically has 4, 8, or 16 ports. Any transmission to any of the ports is repeated to all the other ports on the repeater. Thus, all the ports see transmissions from any of the repeater ports. In an Ethernet network, a typical Ethernet frame or packet includes a preamble, a header, data, and trailer components or sequences. When an Ethernet communication hub, such as an Ethernet repeater, receives a packet of data, a portion, if not the entire preamble sequence may be truncated. An Ethernet network repeater typically includes multiple transceivers for interfacing with other communication nodes through a transmission medium. The transceivers usually include circuitry for both the transmission and the reception of data packets. An Ethernet repeater typically includes core logic for coordinating the data traffic for the transceivers. The repeater performs signal amplitude and timing restoration on an incoming bit stream and repeats the bit stream to all of the ports connected to the repeater. By repeating data to all ports, the repeater acts as a logical coaxial cable so that any node connected to the network will see another node's transmission. A multi-port repeater is a device which performs signal conditioning on a received signal, wherein, the signal is amplified, and timing margins are restored. Multi-port repeaters, also referred to as hubs or wiring concentrators, allow interconnection of a number of network segments at the physical layer of the network protocol.

3.7.2. Hub

Network hubs are used to connect multiple workstations for routing through a single link to a server. In computer network systems, hubs, switches, repeaters, and routers are used when creating a network. Network switches are used to provide each network transmission with an independent path through the network free of collisions with other network transmissions. Network repeaters are used to extend the distance covered by the network, and routers are used to route communication signals through the network. As is well-known in LANs, computers may be connected to each other to enable them to communicate by way of a hub. Data signals sent from a transmitting component to a receiving component are transmitted to the hub and repeated at the hub for transmission to the receiving component. The network hub enables multiple computers, workstations, or file servers to share resources in a variety of applications. The simplest form of communications hub is what is known as a network repeater. Any communications sent by a computer would therefore be received by the repeater. The repeater simply retransmits any communication received on any port to all of the other ports, thereby enabling the communication to be received by all the other computers connected to the repeater. A typical network hub includes one or more devices for routing data transfers between a number of ports in a workgroup. Each port may be assigned to one or more individual users or one or more individual computers, workstations, or servers. Hubs typically have a limited number of input ports, so the number of workstations that can be connected is limited as well. To increase the number of ports available to a workgroup, multiple hubs may be connected. A network hub includes several attachment slots to hold line cards. Each line card contains one or more network devices attached to the hub. Internal data path resources within the hub are used to pass data between the multiple line cards. Hub connections are typically achieved by uplink cables, such as UTP cables, shielded twisted pair (STP) cables, or fiber optic cabling.

3.7.3. Bridge

A bridge reads the outermost section of data on the data packet, to tell where the message is going. It reduces the traffic on other network segments since it does not send all packets. Bridges can be programmed to reject packets from particular networks. Bridging occurs at the data link layer of the OSI model, which means the bridge cannot read IP addresses, but only the outermost hardware address of the packet. In our case the bridge can read the Ethernet data which gives the hardware address of the destination address, not the IP address. Bridges forward all broadcast messages. Only a special bridge called a translation bridge will allow two networks of different architectures to be connected. Bridges do not normally allow connection of networks with different architectures. The hardware address is also called the MAC address. To determine the network segment a MAC address belongs to, bridges use one of:

1. **Transparent Bridging:** They build a table of addresses (bridging table) as they receive packets. If the address is not in the bridging table, the packet is forwarded to all segments other than the one it came from. This type of bridge is used on Ethernet networks.
2. **Source Route Bridging:** The source computer provides path information inside the packet. This is used on Token Ring networks.

3.7.4. Router

A router is used to route data packets between two networks. It reads the information in each packet to tell where it is going. If it is destined for an immediate network, it has access to, it will strip the outer packet, readdress the packet to the proper Ethernet address, and transmit it on that network. If it is destined for another network and must be sent to another router, it will re-package the outer packet to be received by the next router and send it to the next router. Routing occurs at the network layer of the OSI model. They can connect networks with different architectures such as Token Ring and Ethernet. Although they can transform information at the data link level, routers cannot transform information from one data format such as TCP/IP to another such as IPX/SPX. Routers do not send broadcast packets or corrupted packets. If the routing table does not indicate the proper address of a packet, the packet is discarded.

3.7.5. Brouter

There is a device called a router which will function similar to a bridge for network transport protocols that are not routable and will function as a router for routable protocols. It functions at the network and data link layers of the OSI network model.

3.7.6. Gateway

A gateway can translate information between different network data formats or network architectures. It can translate TCP/IP to AppleTalk so computers supporting TCP/IP can communicate with Apple brand computers. Most gateways operate at the application layer but can operate at the network or session layer of the OSI model. Gateways will start at the lower level and strip information until it gets to the required level and repackage the information and work its way back toward the hardware layer of the OSI model. To confuse issues, when talking about a router that is used to interface to another network, the word gateway is often used. This does not mean the routing machine is a gateway as defined here, although it could be.

Gateways are the indispensable components in order to achieve communications between terminals connected to heterogeneous networks that use different protocols and have different network characteristics. Gateways are often used to enable users at remote locations to access different target systems (e.g., a computer system on a LAN). A network gateway provides the connectivity between remote systems (e.g., personal computers) at remote locations with the target systems of interest to enable different network applications. A gateway acts as the interface between proximity local area protocols and wide area protocols, such as TCP/IP on the Internet. A gateway also manages its client devices, aggregates their data, and performs other related tasks. The gateway provides mutual communication by performing communication protocol conversion between the public communication network and the private communication network. The gateway is also used in mutual protocol conversion between LANs that are constructed as private communication networks. The gateway routes user traffic to destinations in the local network or to an external network, such as the Internet. The gateway often functions as a service selection gateway (SSG) which allows users to connect to various subscribed, on-demand network services. A SSG facilitates a remote user to use various services provided using the Internetworking technologies.

3.7.7. Switch

A network switch is a device that provides a switching function in a data communications network. Data communication in a computer network involves the exchange of data between two or more entities interconnected by communication links and subnetworks. A network switch is an intermediate station which interconnects the communication links and sub networks to enable transmission of data between the end stations. Switching involves transferring information, such as digital data packets or frames, among entities of the network. A switch functions as an interchange and provides path switching for data being transported over a network. Typically, a switch supports one network protocol (e.g., Ethernet), meaning that the switch manages data in a particular format. Switched LANs use a network switch for supplying data frames between network stations or other network nodes (such as routers or gateways), where each network node is connected to the network switch by a media. A network switch for routing packets between network buses includes a set of input switch ports for receiving packets arriving on the network buses, a set of output switch ports for forwarding packets outward on the network buses, and a switch fabric for routing packets between the input and output switch ports. Each input switch port includes a memory for storing packets arriving on a network until the switch fabric can forward them to an output switch port. The input port may convert each packet arriving on a network bus to a sequence of cells of uniform size which can be efficiently stored in uniformly sized buffer memory storage locations until the input port can forward them in proper sequential order through the switch fabric to one of the switch's output ports. Each output switch port may also include a memory for storing packets it receives via the switch fabric until the port can forward them outward on a network bus. Each output switch port stores each cell sequence arriving from an input port in its own buffer memory. The output port later reassembles them into the packet from which they were derived, then forwards the packet outward on another network bus.

➢ Find the *synonyms* for the underlined words.

1. It retimes and regenerates the signals to proper amplitudes and sends them to the other segments.
2. A multi port repeater is a device which performs signal conditioning on a received signal, wherein, the signal is amplified and timing margins are restored.
3. Hub connections are typically achieved by uplink cables, such as unshielded twisted pair (UTP) cables, shielded twisted pair (STP) cables, or fiber optic cabling.
4. The section on routing explains the theory behind this and how routing tables are used to help determine packet destinations.
5. It can translate TCP/IP to AppleTalk so computers supporting TCP/IP can communicate with Apple brand computers.
6. To confuse issues, when talking about a router that is used to interface to another network, the word gateway is often used.
7. Gateways are the indispensable components in order to achieve communications between terminals connected to heterogeneous networks that use different protocols and have different network characteristics.
8. A gateway also manages its client devices, aggregates their data, and performs other related tasks.
9. The gateway is also used in mutual protocol conversion between LANs that are constructed as private communication networks.
10. The input port may convert each packet arriving on a network bus to a sequence of cells of uniform size which can be efficiently stored in uniformly-sized buffer memory storage locations until the input port can forward them in proper sequential order through the switch fabric to one of the switch's output ports.

➢ Fill in the blank with the following words.

Acceptance, Suitable, Inward, Make Capable, Between, Act, Like, Allocated

1. The transceivers usually include circuitry for both the transmission and the .... of data packets.
2. Each port may be .... to one or more individual users or one or more individual computers.
3. It will strip the outer packet, readdress the packet to the .... ethernet address.
4. There is a device called a router which will function .... a bridge for network transport protocols that are not routable.
5. Most gateways .... at the application layer, but can operate at the network or session layer of the OSI model.
6. A network gateway provides the connectivity between remote systems (e.g., personal computers) at remote locations with the target systems of interest to .... different network applications.
7. Switching involves transferring information, such as digital data packets or frames, ... entities of the network.
8. The source computer provides path information .... the packet.

➢ Write *antonyms* of following words.

1. Propagation.........................
2. Margin ....
3. Reject ....
4. Pair.........................
5. Confuse ....
6. Indispensable ....
7. Mutual ....

3.7.8. Additional Information About Network Cabling

Cable is the medium through which information usually moves from one network device to another. There are several types of cable which are commonly used with LANs. In some cases, a network will utilize only one type of cable, other networks will use a variety of cable types. The type of cable chosen for a network is related to the network's topology, protocol, and size. Understanding the characteristics of different types of cable and how they relate to other aspects of a network is necessary for the development of a successful network.

The types of cables used in networks:

- Unshielded twisted pair (UTP) cable;
- Shielded twisted pair (STP) cable;
- Coaxial cable;
- Fiber optic cable;
- Cable installation guides;
- Wireless LANs.

3.7.9. Unshielded Twisted Pair (UTP) Cable

Twisted pair cabling comes in two varieties: shielded and unshielded. UTP is the most popular and is generally the best option for school networks (Figure 3.25).

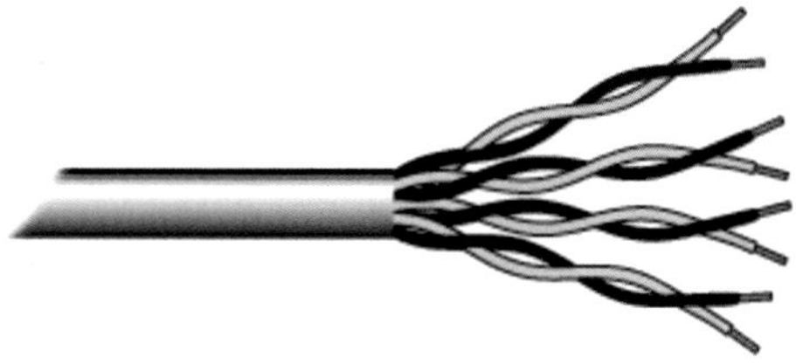

Figure 3.25. Unshielded twisted pair.

The quality of UTP may vary from telephone-grade wire to extremely high-speed cable. The cable has four pairs of wires inside the jacket. Each pair is twisted with a different number of twists per inch to help eliminate interference from adjacent pairs and other electrical devices. The tighter the twisting, the higher the supported transmission rate and the greater the cost per foot. The EIA/TIA (Electronic Industry Association/Telecommunication Industry Association) has established standards of UTP and rated six categories of wire (additional categories are emerging) (Table 3.1).

Table 3.1. Categories of Unshielded Twisted Pair

Category	Speed	Use
1	1 Mbps	Voice only (telephone wire)
2	4 Mbps	LocalTalk and telephone (rarely used)

3	16 Mbps	10BaseT ethernet
4	20 Mbps	Token ring (rarely used)
5	100 Mbps (2 pair) 1,000 Mbps (4 pair)	100BaseT Ethernet Gigabit Ethernet
5e	1,000 Mbps	Gigabit Ethernet
6	10,000 Mbps	Gigabit Ethernet

3.7.10. Unshielded Twisted Pair (UTP) Connector

The standard connector for UTP cabling is an RJ-45 connector. This is a plastic connector that looks like a large telephone-style connector. A slot allows the RJ-45 to be inserted only one way. RJ stands for Registered Jack, implying that the connector follows a standard borrowed from the telephone industry. This standard designates which wire goes with each pin inside the connector (Figure 3.26).

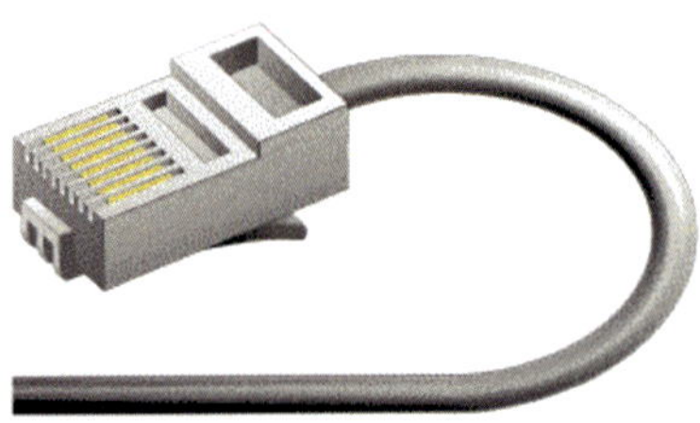

Figure 3.26. RJ-45 connector.

3.7.11. Shielded Twisted Pair (STP) Cable

Although UTP cable is the least expensive cable, it may be susceptible to radio and electrical frequency interference (it should not be too close to electric motors, fluorescent lights, etc.). If you must place cable in environments with lots of potential interference, or if you must place cable in extremely sensitive environments that may be susceptible to the electrical current in the UTP, STP may be the solution. Shielded cables can also help to extend the maximum distance of the cables.

STP cable is available in three different configurations:

- Each pair of wires is individually shielded with foil;

- There is a foil or braid shield inside the jacket covering all wires (as a group);
- There is a shield around each individual pair, as well as around the entire group of wires (referred to as double shield twisted pair).

3.7.12. Coaxial Cable

Coaxial cable is gradually becoming obsolete due to speed limitations of 10 megabits per second. However, it is still a reliable media for small 10 BASE T networks, in addition to having some unique characteristics that make it a good choice for a few special circumstances (Figure 3.27).

The most common type of coaxial data cable in use today is RG-58 Thin Net. It is used in a bus topology for 10 BASE T Ethernet networks. There can be a maximum of five segments, each segment can support up to 20 devices and cannot exceed 608 feet in length. In addition, only three of the segments can support devices. The other two segments must be linking segments, with repeaters used to boost the signal between segments. Due to the greater length possible with RG-58 segments, it is sometimes used in a star bus topology to link closets were trying to use twisted pair for a link would exceed the distance limitation of 328 feet. The braided shielding of RG-58 also makes it a decent choice where EMI/RFI is a problem. RG-58 can (and should) be grounded at one end, which makes it a somewhat better choice for linking buildings than twisted pair, although not nearly as good as fiber optic.

Ø **Advantages:**

- Low cost due to less total footage of cable, hubs not needed;
- Lower attenuation than twisted pair;
- Good immunity to EMI/RFI.

Ø **Disadvantages:**

- Limited in network speed;
- Limited in size of network;
- One bad connector can take down entire network.

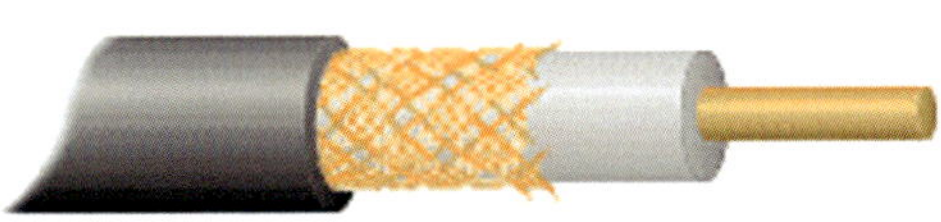

Figure 3.27. Coaxial cable.

3.7.13. Coaxial Cable Connectors

The most common type of connector used with coaxial cables is the Bayone-Neill-Concelman (BNC) connector (*see* Figure 3.28). Different types of adapters are available for BNC connectors, including a T-connector, barrel connector, and terminator. Connectors on the cable are the weakest points in any network.

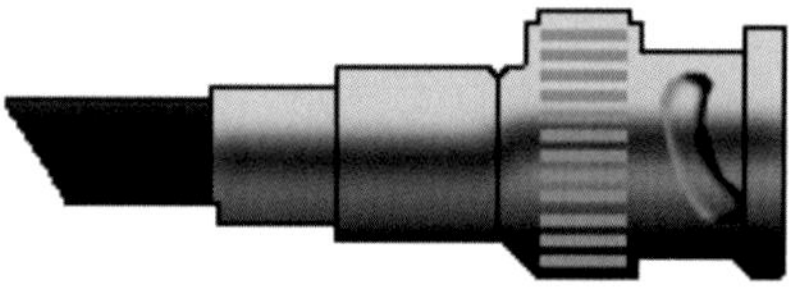

Figure 3.28. BNC connector.

3.7.14. Fiber Optic Cable

Data transmission over optical fiber has greatly increased over the last few years, although fiber to the desktop has not really caught on as expected. However, fiber optic plays an important role in many networks. In addition, it has some outstanding advantages over copper cabling for certain applications. There are a number of network topologies and standards based on fiber optic, such as 10 BASE FL and FDDI, which apply mainly to the backbone cabling of very large facilities and campus environments. The discussion will be limited here to the uses of fiber optic in star bus Ethernet network topologies.

When used as a link in a star bus topology, multi-mode fiber optic cable can transmit a maximum distance of 2,000 meters between all data closets, using a less expensive LED light source. While single mode fiber can transmit up to 3,000 meters, it requires a more expensive laser light source. By using fiber optic to link closets, it is possible to greatly extend the distance limitations in Ethernet networks using twisted pair only. Fiber optic is an outstanding choice for linking buildings together. In addition to the much greater distances possible, it is completely immune to over currents from lightning strikes and to ground potential problems. There is literally nothing metallic in a fiber optic cable to conduct current. It is an excellent choice for heavy manufacturing environments, such as a foundry, due to its immunity to EMI/RFI. Finally, it is the best choice where data of a highly sensitive nature is being transmitted. All copper cabling radiates a signal to a certain degree, making it at least possible for someone with sophisticated enough equipment to electronically eavesdrop. Fiber optic cable radiates no electrical signal at all, and the cable would be down for quite some time if someone tried to splice into it.

Ø **Advantages:**

- Very high speed;
- Very low attenuation;
- Completely immune to EMI/RFI, over current, lightning strike;
- Cannot electronically eavesdrop.

Ø **Disadvantages:**

- Most expensive type of cable;
- Most difficult type of cable to install;
- Network hardware more expensive.

Choosing the correct type of cabling depends on what type of network you have or intend to have, the number of network devices used, expected future growth, the speed requirements of your applications and the physical layout of your facility. Make this decision with the assistance of a professional, licensed, and insured network cabling company and a good information technology consultant (Figure 3.29).

Figure 3.29. Fiber optic cable.

3.7.15. Installing Cable – Some Guidelines

When running cable, it is best to follow a few simple rules:

- Always use more cable than you need. Leave plenty of slack;
- Test every part of a network as you install it. Even if it is brand new, it may have problems that will be difficult to isolate later;
- Stay at least 3 feet away from fluorescent light boxes and other sources of electrical interference;
- If it is necessary to run cable across the floor, cover the cable with cable protectors;
- Label both ends of each cable;

- Use cable ties (not tape) to keep cables in the same location together.

3.7.16. Wireless LANs

More and more networks are operating without cables, in the wireless mode. Wireless LANs use high frequency radio signals, infrared light beams, or lasers to communicate between the workstations and the file server or hubs. Each workstation and file server on a wireless network has some sort of transceiver/antenna to send and receive the data. Information is relayed between transceivers as if they were physically connected. For longer distance, wireless communications can also take place through cellular telephone technology, microwave transmission, or by satellite. Wireless networks are great for allowing laptop computers or remote computers to connect to the LAN. Wireless networks are also beneficial in older buildings where it may be difficult or impossible to install cables.

The two most common types of infrared communications used in schools are line-of-sight and scattered broadcast. Line-of-sight communication means that there must be an unblocked direct line between the workstation and the transceiver. If a person walks within the line-of-sight while there is a transmission, the information will need to be sent again. This kind of obstruction can slow down the wireless network. Scattered infrared communication is a broadcast of infrared transmissions sent out in multiple directions that bounces off walls and ceilings until it eventually hits the receiver. Networking communications with laser are virtually the same as line-of-sight infrared networks.

3.7.17. Wireless Standards and Speeds

The Wi-Fi Alliance is a global, non-profit organization that helps to ensure standards and interoperability for wireless networks, and wireless networks are often referred to as Wi-Fi (wireless fidelity). The original Wi-Fi standard (IEEE 802.11) was adopted in 1997. Since then, many variations have emerged (and will continue to emerge). Wi-Fi networks use the Ethernet protocol.

Standard	Max Speed	Typical Range
802.11a	54 Mbps	150 feet
802.11b	11 Mbps	300 feet
802.11g	54 Mbps	300 feet

Ø **Advantages of Wireless Networks:**

i. **Mobility:** With a laptop computer or mobile device, access can be available throughout a school, at the mall, on an airplane, etc. More and more businesses are also offering free Wi-Fi access.

ii. **Fast Setup:** If your computer has a wireless adapter, locating a wireless network can be as simple as clicking "Connect to a Network" – in some cases, you will connect automatically to networks within range.

iii. **Cost:** Setting up a wireless network can be much more cost effective than buying and installing cables.

iv. **Expandability:** Adding new computers to a wireless network is as easy as turning the computer on (as long as you do not exceed the maximum number of devices).

Ø **Disadvantages of Wireless Networks:**

i. **Security:** Wireless networks are much more susceptible to unauthorized use. If you set up a wireless network, be sure to include maximum security. You should always enable WEP (wired equivalent privacy) or WPA (Wi-Fi protected access), which will improve security and help to prevent virtual intruders and freeloaders.

ii. **Interference:** Because wireless networks use radio signals and similar techniques for transmission, they are susceptible to interference from lights and electronic devices.

iii. **Inconsistent Connections:** How many times have you hears "Wait a minute, I just lost my connection?" Because of the interference caused by electrical devices and/or items blocking the path of transmission, wireless connections are not nearly as stable as those through a dedicated cable.

iv. **Power Consumption:** The wireless transmitter in a laptop requires a significant amount of power; therefore, the battery life of laptops can be adversely impacted. If you are planning a laptop project in your classroom, be sure to have power plugs and/or additional batteries available.

v. **Speed:** The transmission speed of wireless networks is improving; however, faster options (such as gigabit Ethernet) are available via cables. In addition, if set up a wireless network at home, and you are connecting to the Internet via a DSL modem (at perhaps 3 Mbps), your wireless access to the Internet will have a maximum of 3 Mbps connection speed.

3.8. BASIC INTERNET CONCEPTS

The Internet is a worldwide system of interconnected computer networks. The computers and computer networks exchange information using TCP/IP to communicate with each other. The computers are connected via the telecommunications networks, and the Internet can be used for e-mailing, transferring files, and accessing information on the WWW. The Internet is easily accessible via modem and phone line, ISDN, direct cable/landline, or satellite. Regarding the delivery of information, the Internet is the most significant development since the printing press in the 15th-century.

Examples of information networks connected by the Internet include those of libraries, hospitals, research centers, government departments and universities. For example, the WHO Library is an international organization with an internet address http://www.who.int/library/.

3.8.1. What Is the Internet?

The Internet goes by many names: the Net, the Information Superhighway, Cyberspace. It is the largest computer system in the world, consisting of many thousands of connected networks. A network is a collection of computers linked together to share information. There is a lot of interesting information available on the Internet in many different languages. Most of it is free.

3.8.2. What Does the Internet Offer?

It connects you to the WWW. This is the place where you can access the following resources:

- Electronic mail (e-mail) is a fast, easy, inexpensive way to communicate with friends, family, colleagues, and people you meet on the Net with interests similar to yours.
- Information: You can look up information on any subject you can

imagine, learn how to do things (build a house, speak Rumanian!), read newspapers and magazines, enter libraries around the world, even listen to radio stations across the world.

- Computer programs, also known as software, can be downloaded (copied into) your own computer.
- Discussion groups (or mail servers lists) can send you information about topics that interest you. You can post messages to others in response.
- And… online shopping, entertainment, etc.

3.8.3. How Did the Internet Start?

In the 1960's, the U.S. Department of Defense created a network which connected military computers together. Around 20 years later, the National Science Foundation (NSF) used that same technology to allow universities and schools to be connected to each other. They improved the system, making it faster and allowing more information to transfer.

By the early 1990's, many companies began offering access to home users. This allowed anyone with a computer and a modem (a telephone connection to a computer) access to the Internet. The WWW was created by the European Laboratory for Particle Physics in order to allow researchers in different geographical areas to work together.

In 1993, the first web site accessible to the public was created. Now there are billions of sites! Internet Service Providers (known as ISP's), like the telephone companies, offer service for a fee. You can get better deals if you pay by the year. Many public libraries, museums, and schools offer computers with Internet connection where you can work for free. WWW is a part of the Internet and consists of billions of documents stored on computers around the world. The WWW is a system of internet servers that use HTTP to transfer documents formatted in HTML (Hypertext Mark-up Language). These are viewed by using software for web browsers such as Internet Explorer and Mozilla Firefox. Hypertext enables a document to be connected to other documents on the web through hyperlinks and makes it possible to move from one document to another via these links. In other words, the 'client' computer tells the remote 'server' (computer with the information) what information is wanted and the 'server' sends the material back to the 'client.' Regarding health information, the following types of information can be found on the WWW: electronic journals, online books, bibliographic databases, subject related gateways, reports, and gray literature (NGO and public sector publications), individual and organizations' websites, reference resources and news sources.

The URL (uniform resource locator) is the global address of documents and other resources on the web, e.g., http://www.who.int. The first part of the address indicates which protocol to use, e.g., http. The second part of the address identifies the domain name or the internet address where the information is located. The address bar is the toolbar displayed at the top of the screen when you open the internet browser (Figure 3.30).

Figure 3.30. Address bar.

Here's some vocabulary related to the web:

1. **Web Page:** A document on the Web which can include text, pictures, sound, and video.
2. **Web Site:** A collection of web pages maintained by a university, government agency, company or individual.
3. **Web Server:** A computer directly connected to the Internet that makes web pages available to the world.
4. **URL (Uniform Resource Locator):** The unique address of a web page.
5. **Hypertext:** Web pages are hypertext documents, that is, highlighted text connects you to other web pages. When you click on a word or phrase that is highlighted, another web page will open. You can easily navigate by jumping from one web page to another.
6. **Web Browser:** A software program that allows you to view and explore information on the Web. Two of the best known are Netscape and Internet Explorer.

3.8.4. How Do You Search the Internet?

Search tools are essential to help you find the information you want. Subject catalogs organize information by subjects or categories such as Arts, Business, Government, Health, and many more. Some examples are yahoo.com and infoseek.com.

Search engines ask you to state a topic and press a search button. The engine sends out automated systems called "spiders" that look for new pages that contain a reference to your specified topic. If you are not specific enough, you might wind up with a lot of unrelated references. Examples are google.com and infoseek.com.

3.8.5. Development

The Internet was initially developed to allow computers to share scientific and military information and was known as ARPANET in the late 1960s. Further development was funded by the NSF in the 1980s to develop internet communications to link several university computing departments. In 1989 Tim Berners-Lee and others working at CERN (Switzerland) proposed a new communications protocol for information transfer. This technology was based on a hypertext system and lead to the development of the WWW in the 1990s.

The Internet, often called "the Net," is a worldwide system of computer networks most commonly used for communication and information access. There are many Internet services and applications that allow for the exchange of information between individuals and organizations. These include E-mail, the WWW, Chat Rooms, Mailing Lists, Newsgroups, and others. Many people use the terms "internet" and "WWW" interchangeably, but the WWW is actually just one part of the Internet.

The Internet is useful to the telecenter manager for a number of reasons:

- It can increase access to information to improve telecenter management and increase the telecenter's success and ensure its long-term presence in the community.
- It can create more opportunities for cooperation and communication with colleagues and experts across greater distances.
- It can increase access to more information for the local community and improve the local standard of living. For example, one may be able to locate information quickly about ways to reduce mosquito-related diseases in the community by contacting experts across the world.
- It can increase efficiency, e.g., the Internet can increase the rate at which you or local officials can communicate with colleagues and gather information necessary for community projects. Work can therefore be completed more readily.

The Internet is often described as "electronic" or "digital." This refers to the fact that the Internet is set up on a numeric code that transforms these number codes into text, images, and sound.

- Find the *synonyms* for the underlined words.

1. The Internet is a worldwide system of interconnected computer networks
2. Regarding the delivery of information, the Internet is the most significant development since the printing press in the 15th century.
3. It is the largest computer system in the world, consisting of many thousands of connected networks.
4. Electronic mail (e-mail) is a fast, easy, inexpensive way to communicate with friends, family, colleagues and people you meet on the Net with interests similar to yours.
5. The World Wide Web was created by the European Laboratory for Particle Physics in order to allow researchers in different geographical areas to work together.
6. By the early 1990's, many companies began offering access to home users. This allowed anyone with a computer and a modem (a telephone connection to a computer) access to the Internet.
7. In other words, the 'client' computer tells the remote 'server' (computer with the information) what information is wanted and the 'server' sends the material back to the 'client'
8. The second part of the address identifies the domain name or the internet address where the information is located.
9. Search tools are essential to help you find the information you want.
10. It can increase access to information to improve telecenter management and increase the telecenter's success and ensure its long-term presence in the community.

➢ Fill in the blank with the following words.

Shows, Various, Themes, particular person, Approachable, Observed, Pass on, Joined

1. The Internet can be used for e-mailing, ………. files and accessing information on the World Wide Web
2. Examples of information networks ………. by the Internet include those of libraries, hospitals, research centers, government departments and universities
3. There is a lot of interesting information available on the Internet in many ………. languages.
4. Discussion groups (or mail servers lists) can send you information about ………. that interest you.
5. In 1993, the first web site ………. to the public was created. Now there are billions of sites! Internet Service Providers
6. These are ………. by using software for web browsers such as Internet Explorer and Mozilla Firefox.
7. The first part of the address ………. which protocol to use e.g. http.
8. Web Site – a collection of web pages maintained by a university, government agency, company or ……….

➢ Write *antonyms* of following words.

1. Increase ……………………
2. Reduce ……………………
3. Insure ……………………
4. Completed ……………………
5. Allowing ……………………
6. Downloaded ……………………
7. Significant ……………………

3.8.6. Additional Information about Wireless Application Protocol (WAP)

The wireless application protocol (WAP) is a hot topic that has been widely hyped in the mobile industry and outside of it. WAP is simply a protocol – a standardized way that a mobile phone talks to a server installed in the mobile phone network. The WAP is an important development in the wireless industry because of its attempt to develop an open standard for wireless protocols, independent of vendor and airlink. The WAP information is broken down under a number of headings as listed below. We hope that you find this information useful.

3.8.7. WAP Is Hot for Several Reasons

The WAP is a hot topic that has been widely hyped in the mobile industry and outside of it. WAP is simply a protocol – a standardized way that a mobile phone talks to a server installed in the mobile phone network. It is amazing how in just six months, it has become imperative for all information technology companies in Nordic countries and beyond to have a WAP division. Many advertising agencies and "dot.coms" have announced WAP services.

It provides a standardized way of linking the Internet to mobile phones, thereby linking two of the fastest growing industries anywhere Its founder members include the major wireless vendors of Nokia, Ericsson, and Motorola, plus a newcomer Phone.com The WAP Forum has over 120 member companies Mobile information services, a key application for WAP, have not been as successful as many network operators expected. WAP is seen as a way to rectify this situation. WAP also has its detractors and controversies. It is very difficult to configure WAP phones for new WAP services, with 20 or so different parameters needing to be entered to gain access to a WAP service. This is described in detail for the Nokia 7110 and Motorola L series in this new edition of "Data on WAP."

There are few mobile phones that support WAP and widespread WAP support in handsets is unlikely for a long time. Commercial quantities of WAP phones are not expected until towards the end of Quarter 1 2000.

WAP is a protocol that runs on top of an underlying bearer. None of the existing GSM bearers for WAP – the short message service (SMS), unstructured supplementary services data (USSD) and circuit switched data (CSD) are optimized for WAP.

The WAP standard is incomplete, with key elements such as Push (proactive sending of information to mobile devices) and wireless telephony (updating address reports and the like) not yet standardized (they will be standardized in WAP 1.2, due for standardization in late 1999 and first implementation in Spring, 2000).

There are many WAP Gateway vendors out there competing against each other with largely the same standardized product. This has led to consolidation such as the pending acquisition of APiON by Phone.com.

Other protocols such as SIM Application Toolkit and mobile station application execution environment (MexE) are respectively already widely supported or designed to supercede WAP.

WAP services are expected to be expensive to use since the tendency is to be on-line for a long CSD call as features such as interactivity and selection of more information are used by the end user. Without specific tariff initiatives, there are likely to be some surprised WAP users when they see their mobile phone bill for the first time after starting using WAP.

3.8.8. WAP Formation and Philosophy

3.8.8.1. Formation

Motorola, Nokia, Ericsson, and the US software company Phone.com (formerly Unwired Planet) were the initial partners that teamed up over two years ago in mid-1997 to develop and deploy the WAP. WAP is an attempt to define the standard for how content from the Internet is filtered for mobile communications. Content is now readily available on the Internet and WAP was designed as the (rather than one) way of making it easily available on mobile terminals.

The WAP Forum was formed after a US network operator Omnipoint issued a tender for the supply of mobile information services in early 1997. It received several responses from different suppliers using proprietary techniques for delivering the information such as Smart Messaging from Nokia and HDML from Phone.com (then called Unwired Planet). Omnipoint informed the tender responders that it would not accept a proprietary approach and recommended that various vendors get together to explore defining a common standard. After all, there was not a great deal of difference between the different approaches, which could be combined and extended to form a powerful standard. These events were the initial stimulus behind the development of the WAP, with Ericsson and Motorola joining Nokia and Unwired Planet as the founder members of the WAP Forum.

3.8.8.2. Philosophy

The WAP takes a client server approach. It incorporates a relatively simple micro browser into the mobile phone, requiring only limited resources on the mobile phone. This makes WAP suitable for thin clients and early smart phones. WAP puts the intelligence in the WAP Gateways whilst adding just a micro browser to the mobile phones themselves. Micro browser-based services and applications reside temporarily on servers, not permanently in phones. The WAP is aimed at turning a mass-market mobile phone into a "network-based smart phone." As a representative from Phone.com (formerly Unwired Planet) on the board of the WAP Forum commented "The philosophy behind WAP's approach is to utilize as few resources as possible on the handheld device and compensate for the constraints of the device by enriching the functionality of the network."

The WAP is envisaged as a comprehensive and scalable protocol designed for use with any mobile phone from those with a one line display to a smart phone, any existing or planned wireless service such as the SMS, CSD, USSD and general packet radio service (GPRS). Indeed, the importance of WAP can be found in the fact that it provides an evolutionary path for application developers and network operators to offer their services on different network types, bearers, and terminal capabilities. The design of the WAP standard separates the application elements from the bearer being used. This helps in the migration of some applications from SMS or CSD to GPRS for example, any mobile network standard such as code division multiple access (CDMA), global system for mobiles (GSM), or universal mobile telephone system (UMTS). WAP has been designed to work with all cellular standards and is supported by major worldwide wireless leaders such as AT&T wireless. Multiple input terminals such as keypads, keyboards, touchscreens, and styluses.

3.8.9. Technical Introduction

Please note that it is the purpose of this section to supplement the content of the WAP standards with context that allows readers to understand WAP's importance and related issues. As such, we will not be spending much time reproducing the published WAP standards that can be freely downloaded from the WAP Forum web site http://www.WAPforum.org/ by readers.

The WAP embraces and extends the previously conceived and developed wireless data protocols. Phone.com created a version of the standard HTML (hypertext markup language) IPs designed specifically for effective and cost-effective information transfer across mobile networks. Wireless terminals incorporated a HDML (handheld device markup language) micro browser, and Phone.com's handheld device transport protocol (HDTP) then linked the terminal to the UPLink Server Suite which connected to the Internet or intranet where the information being requested resides. The Internet site content was tagged with HDML.

This technology was incorporated into WAP – and renamed using some of the many WAP-related acronyms such as WMLS, WTP, and WSP. Someone with a WAP-compliant phone uses the in-built micro browser to Make a request in WML (wireless markup language), a language derived from HTML especially for wireless network characteristics.

This request is passed to a WAP Gateway that then retrieves the information from an Internet server either in standard HTML format or preferably directly prepared for wireless terminals using WML. If the content being retrieved is in HTML format, a filter in the WAP Gateway may try to translate it into WML. A WML scripting language is available to format data such as calendar entries and electronic business cards for direct incorporation into the client device.

The requested information is then sent from the WAP Gateway to the WAP client, using whatever mobile network bearer service is available and most appropriate.

3.8.10. WAP Protocol Stack

WAP has a layered architecture as shown in the diagram below:

- Wireless application environment (WAE);
- Wireless session protocol (WSP);
- Wireless transaction protocol (WTP);
- Wireless transport layer security (WTLS);
- Wireless datagram protocol (WDP);
- Bearers, e.g., data, SMS, USSD.

Let us take a look at each layer in the WAP protocol stack.

3.8.10.1. Wireless Application Environment

The WAE defines the user interface on the phone. The application development environment to facilitate the development of services that support multiple bearers. To achieve this, the WAE contains the WML, WMLScript – a scripting micro-language similar to JavaScript – and the wireless telephony application (WTA). These are the tools that allow WAP-based applications to be developed.

3.8.10.2. Wireless Session Protocol

A sandwich layer that links the WAE to two session services – one connection-oriented operating above the Wireless Transaction Protocol and a connectionless service operating above the wireless datagram protocol.

3.8.10.3. Wireless Transaction Protocol

Runs on top of a datagram service such as UDP; part of the standard suite of TCP/IP protocols, to provide a simplified protocol suitable for low bandwidth mobile stations. WTP offers three classes of transaction service, unreliable one-way request, reliable one-way request, and reliable two-way request respond. Interestingly, WTP supports Protocol Data Unit concatenation and delayed acknowledgement to help reduce the number of messages sent. This protocol therefore tries to optimize the user experience by providing the information that is needed when it is needed – it can be confusing to received confirmation of delivery messages when you are expecting the information itself. By stringing several messages together, the end user may well be able to get a better feel more quickly for what information is being communicated.

3.8.10.4. Wireless Transport Layer Security

WTLS incorporates security features that are based upon the established transport layer security (TLS) protocol standard. Includes data integrity checks, privacy on the WAP Gateway to client leg and authentication.

3.8.10.5. Wireless Datagram Protocol

Allows WAP to be bearer independent by adapting the transport layer of the underlying bearer. WDP presents a consistent data format to the higher layers of the WAP protocol stack thereby conferring the advantage of bearer independence to application developers.

3.8.11. Optimal WAP Bearer

3.8.11.1. Short Message Service (SMS)

See http://www.mobileSMS.com/ Given its limited length of 160 characters per short message, SMS may not be an adequate bearer for WAP because of the weight protocol of the protocol. The overhead of the WAP protocol that would be required to be transmitted in an SMS message would mean that even for the simplest of transactions several SMS messages may in fact have to be sent. This means that using SMS as a bearer can be a time consuming and expensive exercise. Only one network operator – SBC of the US – is known to be developing WAP services based on SMS.

3.8.11.2. Circuit Switched Data (CSD)

Most of the trial WAP based services use CSD as the underlying bearer. Since CSD has relatively few users currently, WAP could kick start usage of, and traffic generated by this bearer. However, CSD lacks immediacy – a dial up connection taking about 10 seconds is required to connect the WAP client to the WAP Gateway, and this is the best case scenario when there is an complete end to end digital call – in the case of the need for analog modem handshaking (because the WAP phone does not support V.110 the digital protocol, or the WAP Gateway does not have a digital direct connection such as ISDN into the mobile network), the connect time is increased to about 30 seconds.

3.8.12. Unstructured Supplementary Services Data (USSD)

See http://www.mobileUSSD.com/ unstructured supplementary services data (USSD) is a means of transmitting information or instructions over a GSM network. USSD has some similarities with SMS since both use the GSM network's signaling path. Unlike SMS, USSD is not a store and forward service and is session-oriented such that when a user accesses a USSD service, a session is established, and the radio connection stays open until the user, application, or time out releases it. This has more in common with CSD than SMS. USSD text messages can be up to 182 characters in length.

USSD has some advantages and disadvantages as a tool for deploying services on mobile networks Turnaround response times for interactive applications are shorter for USSD than SMS because of the session-based feature of USSD, and because it is NOT a store and forward service. According to Nokia, USSD can be up to seven times faster than SMS to carry out the same two-way transaction.

Users do not need to access any particular phone menu to access services with USSD – they can enter the USSD command direct from the initial mobile phone screen. Because USSD commands are routed back to the home mobile network's home location register (HLR), services based on USSD work just as well and in exactly the same way when users are roaming. USSD works on all existing GSM mobile phones. Both SIM Application Toolkit and the WAP support USSD.

USSD Stage 2 has been incorporated into the GSM standard. Whereas USSD was previously a one-way bearer useful for administrative purposes such as service access, Stage 2 is more advanced and interactive. By sending in a USSD2 command, the user can receive an information services menu. As such, USSD Stage 2 provides WAP-like features on EXISTING phones.

USSD strings are typically complicated for the user to remember, involving the use of the "*" and "#" characters to denote the start and finish of the USSD string. However, USSD) strings for regularly used services can be stored in the phonebook, reducing the need to remember and re-enter them. As such, USSD could be an ideal bearer for WAP on GSM networks.

3.8.13. General Packet Radio Service (GPRS)

See http://www.mobileGPRS.com/the general packet radio service (GPRS) is a new packet-based bearer that is being introduced on many GSM and TDMA mobile networks from the year 2000 onwards. It is an exciting new bearer because it is immediate (there is no dial up connection), relatively fast (up to 177.2 kbps in the very best theoretical extreme) and supports virtual connectivity, allowing relevant information to be sent from the network as and when it is generated.

At the time of writing in early August 1999, there has been no confirmation from any handset vendors that mobile terminated GPRS traffic (i.e., direct receipt of GPRS packets on the mobile phone) will be supported by the initial GPRS terminals. Availability or not of GPRS MT is a central question with critical impact on the GPRS business case such as application migration from other nonvoice bearers.

There are two efficient means of delivering proactively sending ("pushing") content to a mobile phone, by the SMS which is of course one of WAP bearers or by the user maintaining more or less a permanent GPRS (mobile originated) session with the content server. However, mobile terminated IP traffic might allow unsolicited information to reach the terminal. Internet sources originating such unsolicited content may not be chargeable. A possible worse case scenario would be that mobile users would have to pay for receiving unsolicited junk content. This is a potential reason for a mobile vendor NOT to support GPRS Mobile Terminate in their GPRS terminals. However, by originating the session themselves from their handset, users confirm their agreement to pay for the delivery of content from that service. Users could make their requests via a WAP session, which would not therefore need to be blocked. As such, a WAP session initiated from the WAP micro browser could well be the only way that GPRS users can receive information onto their mobile terminals.

Since all but the early WAP enabled phones will also support the GPRS, WAP, and GPRS could well be synergistic and be used widely together. For the kinds of interactive, menu-based information exchanges that WAP anticipates, CSD is not immediate enough because of the need to set up a call. Early prototypes of WAP services based on CSD were therefore close to unusable. SMS on the other hand is immediate but is ALWAYS store and forward, such that even when a subscriber has just requested information from their micro browser, the SMS Centre resources are used in the information transfer. As such, GPRS and WAP are ideal bearers for each other.

Additionally, WAP incorporates two different connection modes – WSP connection mode or WSP connectionless protocol. This is very similar to the two GPRS Point to Point services – connection oriented and connection less.

The predominant bearer for WAP-based services will depend on delays in availability of WAP handsets and delays in the availability of GPRS terminals. If WAP terminals are delayed until the year 2000, most WAP terminals will support GPRS as well. If the first WAP terminals support SMS and CSD, but not GPRS, then SMS could become the predominant initial WAP bearer.

WAP certainly will be important for the development of GPRS-based applications. Because the bearer level is separated from the application layer in the WAP protocol stack, WAP provides the ideal and defined and standardized means to port the same application to different bearers. As such, many application developers will use WAP to facilitate the migration of their applications across bearers once GPRS based WAP protocols are supported.

3.9. ROUTING

In internetworking, the process of moving a packet of data from source to destination. Routing is usually performed by a dedicated device called a router. Routing is a key feature of the Internet because it enables messages to pass from one computer to another and eventually reach the target machine. Each intermediary computer performs routing by passing along the message to the next computer. Part of this process involves analyzing a routing table to determine the best path.

Routing is often confused with bridging, which performs a similar function. The principal difference between the two is that bridging occurs at a lower level and is therefore more of a hardware function whereas routing occurs at a higher level where the software component is more important. And because routing occurs at a higher level, it can perform more complex analysis to determine the optimal path for the packet.

3.9.1. Routing Algorithm

So far, we have had a surface glance on two major reference models in network: OSI and TCP/IP. In this course we are mainly interested in one particular layer – the network layer, which is also divided into two approaches:

- Connectionless type; and
- Connection – oriented type.

The connection-oriented type refers to such protocols as ATM, telephony, and so on. This type of connection doesn't fit the hardware described below (CISCO Router 2600/11); thus, it will not be discussed here.

The independent packets of connectionless organization are called datagrams (in analogy with telegrams). In that kind of organization, the routing table telling which outgoing line to use for each possible destination router is built in every router. Each datagram must contain the full destination address. When the packet comes, the router looks up the outgoing line to use in the routing table and sends the packet on its way. Also, the establishment and release of network or transport layer connections do not require any special work on the part of the routers.

3.9.2. Routing Algorithms

The main function of the network layer is routing packets from source to destination. The algorithms that choose the routes and the data structures that they use area major area of network layer design.

The routing algorithm is that part of the network layer software responsible for deciding which output line an incoming packet should be transmitted on. If the subnet uses datagrams internally, this decision must be made anew for every arriving data packet since the best route may have changed since last time. In the subnet using virtual circuits such decision is made ones per session. Routing algorithms can be grouped into two major classes: nonadaptive and adaptive.

1. **Nonadaptive Algorithms:** These do not base their routing decisions on measurements or estimates of the current traffic and topology. Instead, the choice of the route to use to get from I to J is computed in advance, of-line, and downloaded to the routers when the network is booted. This procedure is sometimes called static routing.
2. **Adaptive Algorithms:** In contrast, change their routing decisions to reflect changes in the topology, and usually the traffic as well. Adaptive algorithms differ in where the get their information, when they change the routes, and what metric is used for optimization. They are also called dynamic.

3.9.3. The Optimality Principle

To start with algorithm's overview, we should see some helpful theoretical explanations. The optimality principle states that if router J is on the optimal path from router I to router K, then the optimal path from J to K also falls along the same route. As a consequence of that principle, we can see that the set of optimal routes from all sources to a given destination form a tree rooted at the destination. Such tree is called a sink tree. In the next three sections, we will look at three static routing algorithms, subsequently we will move to dynamic ones.

3.9.4. Shortest Path Routing

The following technique is widely used in many forms because it is simple and easy to understand. The idea is to build a graph of the subnet, with each node of the graph representing a router and each arc representing a communication line (link). To choose a rout between a given pair of routers, the algorithm just finds the shortest path between them on the graph. The shortest path concept includes definition of the way of measuring path length. Deferent metrics like number of hops, geographical distance, the mean queuing, and transmission delay of router can be used. In the most general case, the labels on the arcs could be computed as a function of the distance, bandwidth, average traffic, communication cost, mean queue length, measured delay, and other factors.

There are several algorithms for computing shortest path between two nodes of a graph. One of them due to Dijkstra.

3.9.5. Flooding

That is another static algorithm, in which every incoming packet is sent out on every outgoing line except the one it arrived on. Flooding generates infinite number of duplicate packets unless some measures are taken to damp the process.

One such measure is to have a hop counter in the header of each packet, which is decremented at each hop, with the packet being discarded when the counter reaches zero. Ideally, the hop counter is initialized to the length of the path from source to destination. If the sender does not know the path length, it can initialize the counter to the worst case, the full diameter of the subnet.

An alternative technique is to keep track of which packets have been flooded, to avoid sending then out a second time. To achieve this goal the source router put a sequence number in each packet it receives from its hosts. Then each router needs a list per source router telling which sequence numbers originating at that source have already been seen. Any incoming packet that is on the list is not flooded. To prevent list form growing, each list should be augmented by a counter, k, meaning that all sequence numbers through k have been seen.

A variation of flooding named selective flooding is slightly more practical. In this algorithm the routers do not send every incoming packet out on every line, but only on those going approximately in the right direction. (There is usually little point in sending a westbound packet on an eastbound line unless the topology is extremely peculiar). Flooding algorithms are rarely used, mostly with distributed systems or systems with tremendous robustness requirements at any instance.

3.9.6. Flow-Based Routing

The algorithms seen above took only topology into account and did not consider the load. The following algorithm considers both and is called flow-based routing. In some networks, the mean data flow between each pair of nodes is relatively stable and predictable. Under conditions in which the average traffic from i to j is known in advance and to a reasonable approximation, constant in time, it is possible to analyze the flows mathematically to optimize the routing.

The idea behind the analysis is that for a given line, if the capacity and average flow are known, it is possible to compute the mean packet delay on that line from queuing theory. From the mean delays on all the lines, it is straightforward to calculate a flow-weighted average to get the mean packet delay for the whole subnet. The routing problem then reduces to finding the routing algorithm that produces the minimum average delay for the subnet.

This technology demands certain information in advance. First the subnet topology, second the traffic matrix, third the capacity matrix and finally a routing algorithm (further explanation look at the same reference as above).

3.9.7. Distance Vector Routing

Modern computer networks generally use dynamic routing algorithms rather than static ones described above. Two dynamic algorithms in particular, distance vector and link state routing are the most popular. In this section we will look at the former algorithm. In the following one we will study the later one.

Distance vector routing algorithms operate by having each router maintain a table giving he best known distance to each destination and which line to use to get there. These table are updated by exchanging information with the neighbors.

The distance vector routing algorithm is sometimes called by other names including Bellman-Ford or Ford-Fulkerson. It was the original ARPANET routing algorithm and was also used on the Internet under the name RIP and in early versions of DECnet and Novell's IPX. AppleTalk and CISCO routers use improved distance vector protocols.

In that algorithm each router maintains a routing table indexed by and containing one entry for each router in the subnet. This entry contains two parts: the preferred outgoing line to use for that destination and an estimate of the time or distance to that destination. The metric used might be number of hops, time delay in milliseconds, total number of packets queued along the path or something similar.

The router is assumed to know the "distance" to each of its neighbors. In the hops metric the distance is one hop, for queue length metrics the router examines each queue, for the delay metric the route can measure it directly with special ECHO packets that the receiver just timestamps and sends back as fast as it can.

Distance vector routing works in theory but has a serious drawback in practice: although it converges to the correct answer, it may be done slowly.

Good news propagates at linear time through the subnet, while bad ones have the count-to-infinity problem: no router ever has a value more than one higher than the minimum of all its neighbors. Gradually, all the routers work their way up to infinity, but the number of exchanges required depends on the numerical value used for infinity. One of the solutions to this problem is split horizon algorithm that defines the distance to the X router is reported as infinity on the line that packets for X are sent on. Under that behavior bad news propagate also at linear speed through the subnet.

3.9.8. Link State Routing

The idea behind link state routing is simple and can be stated as five parts. Each router must:

- Discover its neighbors and learn their network addresses;
- Measure the delay or cost to each of its neighbors;
- Construct a packet telling all it has just learned;
- Send the packet to all other routers;
- Compute the shortest path to every other router.

In effect, the complete topology, and all delays re experimentally measured and distributed to every router. Then Dijkstra's algorithm can be used to find the shortest path to every other router.

3.9.9. Hierarchical Routing

As the network grows larger the amount of resources necessary to take care or routing table becomes enormous and makes routing impossible. Here appears the idea of hierarchical routing that suggests that routers should be divided into regions, with each router knowing all the details about how to route packets within its own region, but knowing nothing about the internal structure of other regions.

Unfortunately, the gains in routing table size and CPU time are not free, the penalty of increasing path length has to be paid.

It has been discovered that the optimal number of nested levels for an N router subnet is ln N, requiring a total of eln N entries per router.

3.9.10. Routing for Mobile Hosts

Through the last years more and more people purchase portable computer under natural assumption that they can be used all over the world. These mobile hosts introduce new complication: to route a packet to a mobile host the network first has to find it. Generally, that requirement is implemented through creation of two new issues in LAN foreign agent and home agent.

Each time any mobile host connects to the network it collects a foreign agent packet or generates a request for foreign agent, as a result they establish connection between them, and the mobile host supplies the foreign agent with its home and some security information.

After that the foreign agent contacts the mobile host's home agent and delivers the information about the mobile host.

Subsequently the home agent examines the received information and if it authorizes the security information of mobile host it allows the foreign agent to proceed. As the result the foreign agent enters the mobile host into its routing table.

When the packet for the mobile host arrives its home agent it encapsulates it and redirects to the foreign agent where the mobile host is hosting. Then it returns encapsulation data to the router that sent the packet so that all next packets would be directly sent to correspondent router (foreign agent).

3.9.11. Broadcast Routing

For some applications, hosts need to send messages to many or all other hosts. Broadcast routing is used for that purpose. Some deferent methods were proposed for doing that.

- The source should send the packet to all the necessary destinations. One of the problems of this method is that the source has to have the complete list of destinations.
- Flooding routing. As it was discussed before the problem of that method is generating duplicate packets.
- Multi destination routing. In that method each packet includes list or a bitmap indicating desired destinations. When a packet arrives router checks all the destinations to determine the set of output lines that will be needed, generates a new copy of the packet for each output line to be used and includes in each packet only those destinations that are to use the line. In effect, the destination set is partitioned between the lines. After a sufficient number of hops, each packet will carry only one destination and can be treated as a normal packet.
- This routing method makes use of spanning tree of the subnet. If

each router knows which of its lines belong to the panning tree, it can copy an incoming broadcast packet onto all the spanning tree lines except the one it arrived on. Problem: each router has to know the spanning tree.

- Reverse path-forwarding algorithm at the arrival of the packet checks if the line that packet arrived on is the same one through which the packets are send to the source, if yes it sends it through all other lines, otherwise discards it.

3.9.12. Multicast Routing

Sending messages to well-defined groups that are numerically large in size, but small compared to the network as a whole is called multicasting. To do multicasting, group management is required, but that is not concern of routers. What is of concern is that when a process joins a group, it informs its host of this fact. It is important that routers know which of their hosts belong to which group. Either hosts must inform their routers about changes in group membership, or routers must query their hosts periodically.

To do multicast routing, each router computes a spanning tree covering all other routers in the subnet. When a process sends a multicast packet to a group, the first router examines its spanning tree ad prunes it, removing all lines that do not lead to hosts that are members of the group.

The simplest way of pruning the panning tree is under Link State routing when each router is aware of the complete subnet topology, including which hosts belong to which groups. Then the spanning tree can be pruned by staring at the end to each path and working toward the root, removing all routers that do not belong the group in question.

A different pruning strategy is followed with distance vector routing, reverse path forwarding algorithm. Whenever a router with no hosts interested in a particular group and no connections to other routers receives a multicast message for that group, it responds with a PRUNE message, telling the sender not to send it any more multicasts for that group. When a router with no group members among its own hosts has received such messages on all its lines, it, too, can respond with a PRUINE message. In this way, the subnet is recursively pruned. One potential disadvantage of this algorithm is that it scales poorly to large networks. An alternative design uses core-base trees. Here a single spanning tree per group is computed, with the root (the core) near the middle of the group. To send a multicast message, a host sends it to the core, which then does the multicast along the spanning tree. Although this tree will not be optimal for all sources, the reduction in storage costs from *m* trees to one tree per group is a major saving.

> ➢ Find the *synonyms* for the underlined words.
>
> 1. More of a hardware function whereas routing occurs at a higher level where the software component is more important.
> 2. So far we have had a surface glance on two major reference models in network: OSI and TCP/IP.
> 3. The independent packets of connectionless organization are called datagrams.
> 4. As a consequence of that principle, we can see that the set of optimal routes from all sources to a given destination form a tree rooted at the destination.
> 5. In the most general case, the labels on the arcs could be computed as a function of the distance, bandwidth, average traffic, communication cost, mean queue length, measured delay, and other factors.
> 6. Flooding generates infinite number of duplicate packets unless some measures are taken to damp the process.
> 7. It is straightforward to calculate a flow-weighted average to get the mean packet delay for the whole subnet.
> 8. In that algorithm each router maintains a routing table indexed by and containing one entry for each router in the subnet.
> 9. Good news propagates at linear time through the subnet.
> 10. One of the solutions to this problem is split horizon algorithm that defines the distance to the X router is reported as infinity on the line that packets for X are sent on.

> ➢ Fill in the blank with the following words.
> Occasionally, Best, Punishment, Supposed, Exclude, Discarded, Diameter, Appraise
>
> 1. It can perform more complex analysis to determine the .... path for the packet.
> 2. Nonadaptive algorithms do not base their routing decisions on measurements or .... of the current traffic and topology.
> 3. That is another static algorithm, in witch every incoming packet is sent out on every outgoing line .... the one it arrived on.
> 4. In the header of each packet, which is decremented at each hop, with the packet being .... when the counter reaches zero.
> 5. If the sender does not no the path length, it can initialize the counter to the worst case, the full .... of the subnet.
> 6. The distance vector routing algorithm is .... called by other names including Bellman-Ford or Ford-Fulkerson.
> 7. The router is .... to know the "distance" to each of its neighbors.
> 8. Unfortunately the gains in routing table size and CPU time are not free, the .... of increasing path length has to be paid.

> ➢ Write *antonyms* of following words.
>
> 1. Principal ....
> 2. Confuse ....
> 3. Release ....
> 4. Decrement ....
> 5. 5. Infinite ....
> 6. 6. Augmented ....
> 7. 7. Entry ....

3.9.13. Additional Information About Quality of Service (QoS)

With the increased use of the IP based networks, including the Internet, there has been a large focus on providing necessary network resources to certain applications.

That is, it has become better understood that some applications are more "important" than others, thereby demanding preferential treatment throughout an internetwork. Additionally, applications have different demands, such as real-time requirements of low latency and high bandwidth. This chapter discusses the topic of traffic prioritization, or QoS. It explains why QoS can be desirable in an intranet, as well as on the Internet, and presents the two main approaches to implementing QoS in TCP/IP networks:

- Integrated services; and
- Differentiated services (DS).

3.9.14. Why QoS?

On the Internet and intranets of today, bandwidth is an important subject. More and more people are using the Internet for private and business purposes. The amount of data that is being transmitted through the Internet is increasing exponentially. Multimedia applications, such as IP telephony and videoconferencing systems, need a lot more bandwidth than the applications that were used in the early years of the Internet. While traditional Internet applications, such as WWW, FTP, or Telnet, cannot tolerate packet loss but are less sensitive to variable delays, most real-time applications show just the opposite behavior, meaning they can compensate for a reasonable amount of packet loss but are usually very critical toward high variable delays.

This means that without any bandwidth control, the quality of these real time streams depends on the bandwidth that is currently available. Low or unstable bandwidth causes bad quality in real-time transmissions by leading to, for example, dropouts, and hangs. Even the quality of a transmission using the real-time protocol (RTP) depends on the utilization of the underlying IP delivery service.

Therefore, certain concepts are necessary to guarantee a specific QoS for real-time applications on the Internet. A QoS can be described as a set of parameters that describe the quality (for example, bandwidth, buffer usage, priority, and CPU usage) of a specific stream of data. The basic IP protocol stack provides only one QoS, which is called best-effort. Packets are transmitted from point to point without any guarantee for a special bandwidth or minimum time delay.

With the best-effort traffic model, Internet requests are handled with the first come, first serve strategy. This means that all requests have the same priority and are handled one after the other. There is no possibility to make bandwidth reservations for specific connections or to raise the priority for special requests. Therefore, new strategies were developed to provide predictable services for the Internet. Today, there are two main rudiments to bring QoS to the Internet and IP based internetworks: integrated services and DS.

3.9.15. Integrated Services

Integrated services bring enhancements to the IP network model to support real-time transmissions and guaranteed bandwidth for specific flows. In this case, we define a flow as a distinguishable stream of related datagrams from a unique sender to a unique receiver that results from a single user activity and requires the same QoS. For example, a flow might consist of one video stream between a given host pair. To establish the video connection in both directions, two flows are necessary. Each application that initiates data flows can specify which QoSs are required for this flow. If the videoconferencing tool needs a minimum bandwidth of 128 kbps and a minimum packet delay of 100 ms to assure a continuous video display, such a QoS can be reserved for this connection.

To support the Integrated Services model, an Internet router must be able to provide an appropriate QoS for each flow, in accordance with the service model. The router function that provides different qualities of service is called traffic control. It consists of the following components:

1. **Packet Scheduler:** It manages the forwarding of different packet streams in hosts and routers, based on their service class, using queue management and various scheduling algorithms. The packet scheduler must ensure that the packet delivery corresponds to the QoS parameter for each flow. A scheduler can also police or shape the traffic to conform to a certain level of service. The packet scheduler must be implemented at the point where packets are queued. This is typically the output driver level of an operating system and corresponds to the link layer protocol.
2. **Packet Classifier:** It identifies packets of an IP flow in hosts and routers that will receive a certain level of service. To realize effective traffic control, each incoming packet is mapped by the classifier into a specific class. All packets that are classified in the same class get the same treatment from the packet scheduler. The choice of a class is based on the source and destination IP address and port number in the existing packet header or an additional classification number, which must be added to each packet. A class can correspond to a broad category of flows. For example, all video flows from a video conference with several participants can belong to one service class. But it is also possible that only one flow belongs to a specific service class.
3. **Admission Control:** It contains the decision algorithm that a

router uses to determine if there are enough routing resources to accept the requested QoS for a new flow. If there are not enough free routing resources, accepting a new flow would impact earlier guarantees and the new flow must be rejected. If the new flow is accepted, the reservation instance in the router assigns the packet classifier and the packet scheduler to reserve the requested QoS for this flow. Admission control is invoked at each router along a reservation path to make a local accept/reject decision at the time a host requests a real-time service. The admission control algorithm must be consistent with the service model. Admission control is sometimes confused with policy control, which is a packet-by-packet function, processed by the packet scheduler. It ensures that a host does not violate its promised traffic characteristics. Nevertheless, to ensure that QoS guarantees are honored, the admission control will be concerned with enforcing administrative policies on resource reservations. Some policies will be used to check the user authentication for a requested reservation. Unauthorized reservation requests can be rejected. As a result, admission control can play an important role in accounting costs for Internet resources in the future.

3.9.16. Differentiated Services (DS)

DS mechanisms do not use per-flow signaling, and as a result, do not consume per-flow state within the routing infrastructure. Different service levels can be allocated to different groups of users, which means that all traffic is distributed into groups or classes with different QoS parameters. This reduces the amount of maintenance required in comparison to Integrated Services. The DS concept is currently under development at the IETF DS working group. The DS specifications are defined in some IETF Internet drafts. There is no RFC available yet.

The goal of DS development is to provide differentiated classes of service for Internet traffic to support various types of applications and meet specific business requirements. DS offers predictable performance (delay, throughput, packet loss, and so on) for a given load at a given time. The difference between integrated services, and DS provides scalable service discrimination on the Internet without the need for per-flow state and signaling at every hop. It is not necessary to perform a unique QoS reservation for each flow. With DS, the Internet traffic is split into different classes with different QoS requirements.

A central component of DS is the service level agreement (SLA). An SLA is a service contract between a client and a service provider that specifies the details of the traffic classifying and the corresponding forwarding service a client should receive. A client can be a user organization or another DS domain. The service provider must assure that the traffic of a client, with whom it has an SLA, gets the contracted QoS. Therefore, the service provider's network administration must set up the appropriate service policies and measure the network performance to guarantee the agreed traffic performance. To distinguish the data packets from different clients in DS-capable network devices, the IP packets are modified in a specific field. A small bit-pattern, called the *DS field*, in each IP packet is used to mark the packets that receive a particular forwarding treatment at each network node. The DS field uses the space of the former TOS octet in the IPv4 IP header and the traffic class octet in the IPv6 header. All network traffic inside of a domain receives a service that depends on the traffic class that is specified in the DS field. To provide SLA conform services, the following mechanisms must be combined in a network:

- Setting bits in the DS field (TOS octet) at network edges and administrative boundaries.
- Using those bits to determine how packets are treated by the routers inside the network.
- Conditioning the marked packets at network boundaries in accordance with the QoS requirements of each service.

3.10. INTRODUCTION TO NEURAL NETWORKS

3.10.1. What Is a Neural Network?

An artificial neural network (ANN) is an information processing paradigm that is inspired by the way biological nervous systems, such as the brain, process information. The key element of this paradigm is the novel structure of the information processing system. It is composed of a large number of highly interconnected processing elements (neurons) working in unison to solve specific problems. ANNs, like people, learn by example. An ANN is configured for a specific application, such as pattern recognition or data classification, through a learning process. Learning in biological systems involves adjustments to the synaptic connections that exist between the neurons. This is true of ANNs as well.

3.10.2. Historical Background

Neural network simulations appear to be a recent development. However, this field was established before the advent of computers, and has survived at least one major setback and several eras.

Many important advances have been boosted by the use of inexpensive computer emulations. Following an initial period of enthusiasm, the field survived a period of frustration and disrepute. During this period when funding and professional support was minimal, important advances were made by relatively few researchers. These pioneers were able to develop convincing technology which surpassed the limitations identified by Minsky and Papert. They published a book (in 1969) in which they summed up a general feeling of frustration (against neural networks) among researchers, and was thus accepted by most without further analysis. Currently, the neural network field enjoys a resurgence of interest and a corresponding increase in funding.

The first artificial neuron was produced in 1943 by the neurophysiologist Warren McCulloch and the logician Walter Pits. But the technology available at that time did not allow them to do too much.

3.10.3. Why Use Neural Networks?

Neural networks, with their remarkable ability to derive meaning from complicated or imprecise data, can be used to extract patterns and detect trends that are too complex to be noticed by either humans or other computer techniques. A trained neural network can be thought of as an "expert" in the category of information it has been given to analyze. This expert can then be used to provide projections given new situations of interest and answer "what if" questions. Other advantages include:

1. **Adaptive Learning:** An ability to learn how to do tasks based on the data given for training or initial experience.
2. **Self-Organization:** An ANN can create its own organization or representation of the information it receives during learning time.
3. **Real Time Operation:** ANN computations may be carried out in parallel, and special hardware devices are being designed and manufactured which take advantage of this capability.
4. **Fault Tolerance via Redundant Information Coding:** Partial destruction of a network leads to the corresponding degradation

of performance. However, some network capabilities may be retained even with major network damage.

3.10.4. Neural Networks versus Conventional Computers

Neural networks take a different approach to problem solving than that of conventional computers. Conventional computers use an algorithmic approach, i.e., the computer follows a set of instructions in order to solve a problem. Unless the specific steps that the computer needs to follow are known the computer cannot solve the problem. That restricts the problem-solving capability of conventional computers to problems that we already understand and know how to solve. But computers would be so much more useful if they could do things that we don't exactly know how to do.

Neural networks process information in a similar way the human brain does. The network is composed of a large number of highly interconnected processing elements (neurons) working in parallel to solve a specific problem. Neural networks learn by example. They cannot be programmed to perform a specific task. The examples must be selected carefully otherwise useful time is wasted or even worse the network might be functioning incorrectly. The disadvantage is that because the network finds out how to solve the problem by itself, its operation can be unpredictable.

On the other hand, conventional computers use a cognitive approach to problem solving; the way the problem is too solved must be known and stated in small unambiguous instructions. These instructions are then converted to a high-level language program and then into machine code that the computer can understand. These machines are totally predictable; if anything goes wrong is due to a software or hardware fault.

Neural networks and conventional algorithmic computers are not in competition but complement each other. There are tasks are more suited to an algorithmic approach like arithmetic operations and tasks that are more suited to neural networks. Even more, a large number of tasks, require systems that use a combination of the two approaches (normally a conventional computer is used to supervise the neural network) in order to perform at maximum efficiency.

3.10.5. Human and Artificial Neurons – Investigating the Similarities

3.10.5.1. How the Human Brain Learns?

Much is still unknown about how the brain trains itself to process information, so theories abound. In the human brain, a typical neuron collects signals from others through a host of fine structures called dendrites. The neuron sends out spikes of electrical activity through a long, thin stand known as an *axon*, which splits into thousands of branches. At the end of each branch, a structure called a *synapse* converts the activity from the axon into electrical effects that inhibit or excite activity from the axon into electrical effects that inhibit or excite activity in the connected neurons. When a neuron receives excitatory input that is sufficiently large compared with its inhibitory input, it sends a spike of electrical activity down its axon. Learning occurs by changing the effectiveness of the synapses so that the influence of one neuron on another changes (Figures 3.31 and 3.32).

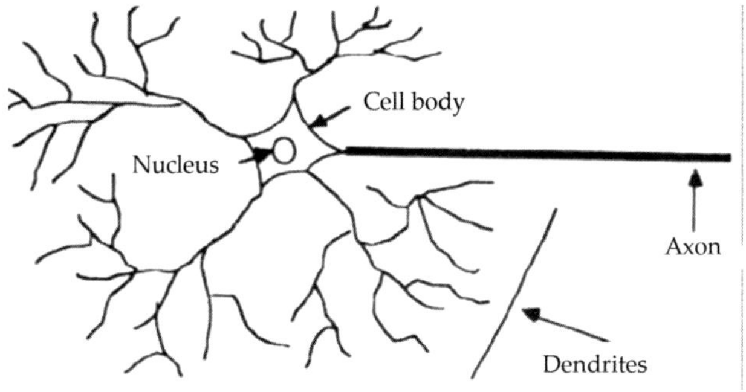

Figure 3.31. *Components of a neuron.*

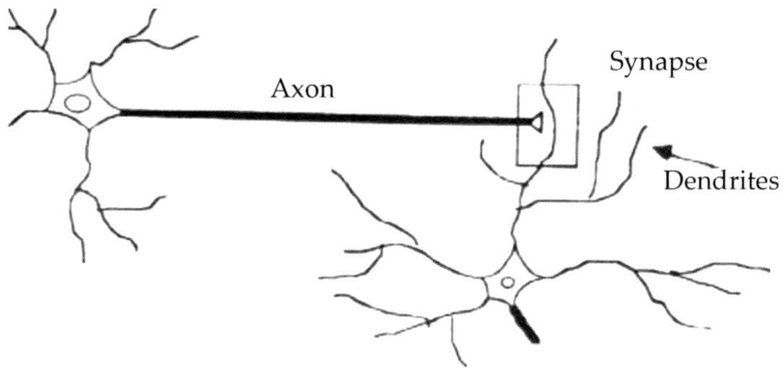

Figure 3.32. The synapse.

3.10.5.2. From Human Neurons to Artificial Neurons

We conduct these neural networks by first trying to deduce the essential features of neurons and their interconnections. We then typically program a computer to simulate these features. However, because our knowledge of neurons is incomplete and our computing power is limited, our models are necessarily gross idealizations of real networks of neurons (Figure 3.33).

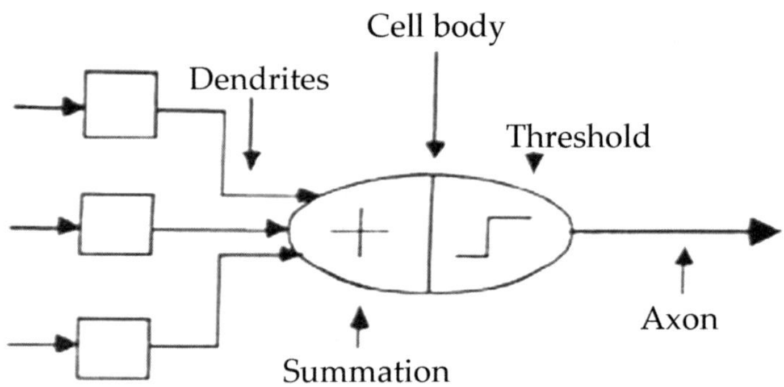

Figure 3.33. The neuron models.

3.10.6. An Engineering Approach

3.10.6.1. A Simple Neuron

An artificial neuron is a device with many inputs and one output. The neuron has two modes of operation; the training mode and the using mode. In the training mode, the neuron can be trained to fire (or not), for particular input patterns. In the using mode, when a taught input pattern is detected at the input, its associated output becomes the current output. If the input pattern does not belong in the taught list of input patterns, the firing rule is used to determine whether to fire or not (Figure 3.34).

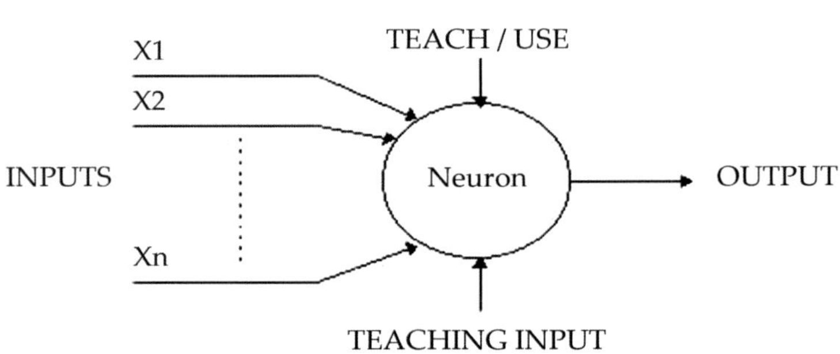

Figure 3.34. A simple neuron.

3.10.6.2. Firing Rules

The firing rule is an important concept in neural networks and accounts for their high flexibility. A firing rule determines how one calculates whether a neuron should fire for any input pattern. It relates to all the input patterns, not only the ones on which the node was trained.

A simple firing rule can be implemented by using Hamming distance technique. The rule goes as follows.

Take a collection of training patterns for a node, some of which cause it to fire (the 1-taught set of patterns) and others which prevent it from doing so (the 0-taught set). Then the patterns not in the collection cause the node to fire if, on comparison, they have more input elements in common with the 'nearest' pattern in the 1-taught set than with the 'nearest' pattern in the 0-taught set. If there is a tie, then the pattern remains in the undefined state.

For example, a 3-input neuron is taught to output 1 when the input (X1, X2, and X3) is 111 or 101 and to output 0 when the input is 000 or 001. Then, before applying the firing rule, the truth table is:

X1:	0	0	0	0	1	1	1	1
X2:	0	0	1	1	0	0	1	1
X3:	0	1	0	1	0	1	0	1
OUT:	0	0	0/1	0/1	0/1	1	0/1	1

As an example of the way the firing rule is applied, take the pattern 010. It differs from 000 in 1 element, from 001 in 2 elements, from 101 in 3 elements and from 111 in 2 elements. Therefore, the 'nearest' pattern is 000 which belongs in the 0-taught set. Thus the firing rule requires that the neuron should not fire when the input is 001. On the other hand, 011 is equally distant from two taught patterns that have different outputs and thus the output stays undefined (0/1).

By applying the firing in every column the following truth table is obtained:

X1:	0	0	0	0	1	1	1	1
X2:	0	0	1	1	0	0	1	1
X3:	0	1	0	1	0	1	0	1
OUT:	0	0	0	0/1	0/1	1	1	1

The difference between the two truth tables is called the *generalization of the neuron*. Therefore, the firing rule gives the neuron a sense of similarity and enables it to respond 'sensibly' to patterns not seen during training.

3.10.7. Pattern Recognition – An Example

An important application of neural networks is pattern recognition. Pattern recognition can be implemented by using a feed-forward (Figure 3.35) neural network that has been trained accordingly. During training, the network is trained to associate outputs with input patterns. When the network is used, it identifies the input pattern and tries to output the associated output pattern. The power of neural networks comes to life when a pattern that has no output associated with it, is given as an input. In this case, the network gives the output that corresponds to a taught input pattern that is least different from the given pattern.

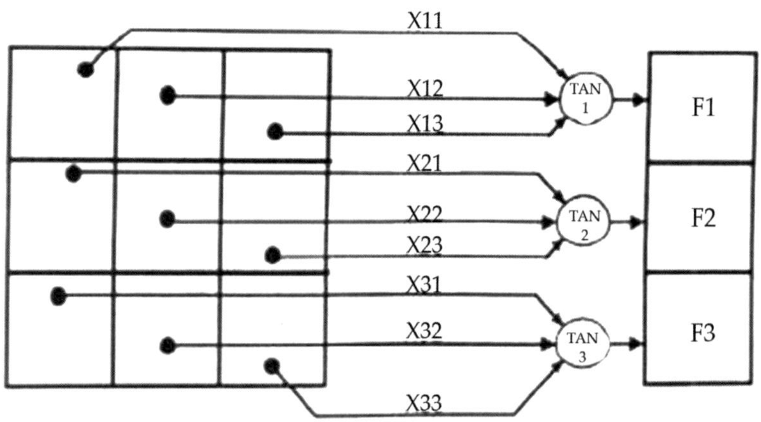

Figure 3.35. An illustration of pattern recognition

- Ø **For example:** The network of Figure 3.35 is trained to recognize the patterns T and H. The associated patterns are all black and all white respectively as shown below.

If we represent black squares with 0 and white squares with 1 then the truth tables for the 3 neurons after generalization are:

X11:	0	0	0	0	1	1	1	1
X12:	0	0	1	1	0	0	1	1
X13:	0	1	0	1	0	1	0	1
OUT:	0	0	1	1	0	0	1	1

Ø **Top Neuron:**

X21:	0	0	0	0	1	1	1	1
X22:	0	0	1	1	0	0	1	1
X23:	0	1	0	1	0	1	0	1
OUT:	1	0/1	1	0/1	0/1	0	0/1	0

Ø **Middle Neuron:**

X21:	0	0	0	0	1	1	1	1
X22:	0	0	1	1	0	0	1	1
X23:	0	1	0	1	0	1	0	1
OUT:	1	0	1	1	0	0	1	0

Ø **Bottom Neuron:** From the tables it can be seen the following associations can be extracted:

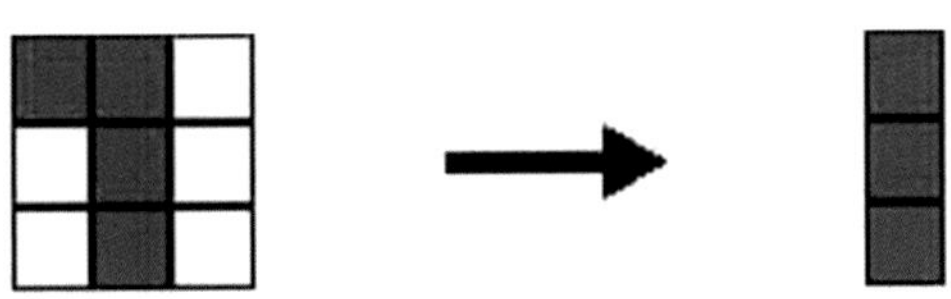

INPUT OUTPUT

In this case, it is obvious that the output should be all blacks since the input pattern is almost the same as the 'T' pattern.

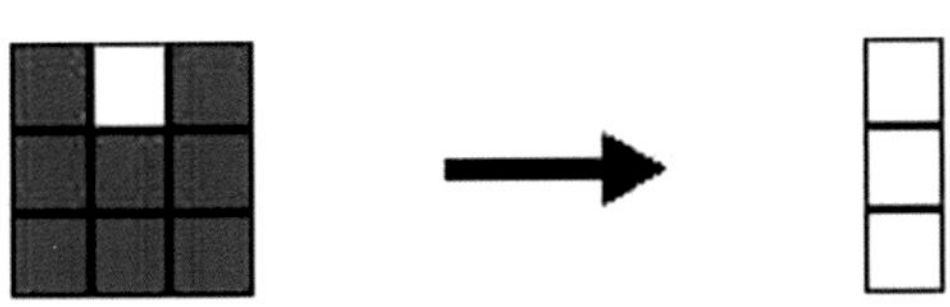

INPUT OUTPUT

Here also, it is obvious that the output should be all whites since the input pattern is almost the same as the 'H' pattern.

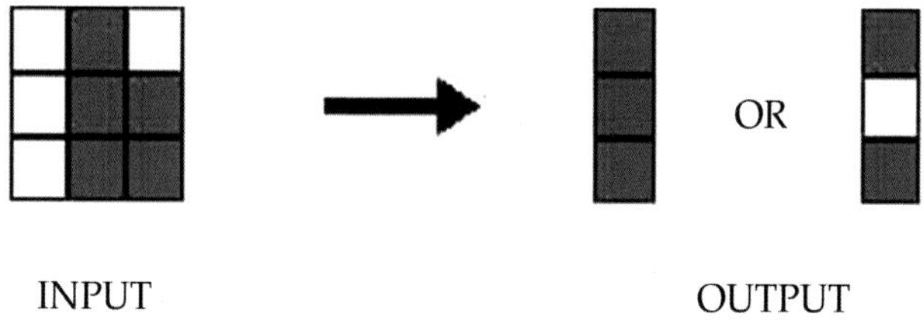

Here, the top row is 2 errors away from a T and 3 from an H. So, the top output is black. The middle row is 1 error away from both T and H, so the output is random. The bottom row is 1 error away from T and 2 away from H. Therefore, the output is black. The total output of the network is still in favor of the T shape.

3.10.8. A More Complicated Neuron

The previous neuron doesn't do anything that conventional computers don't do already. A more sophisticated neuron (Figure 3.36) is the McCulloch and Pitts (MCP) model (MCP). The difference from the previous model is that the inputs are 'weighted,' the effect that each input has at decision making is dependent on the weight of the particular input. The weight of an input is a number which when multiplied with the input gives the weighted input. These weighted inputs are then added together and if they exceed a pre-set threshold value, the neuron fires. In any other case the neuron does not fire.

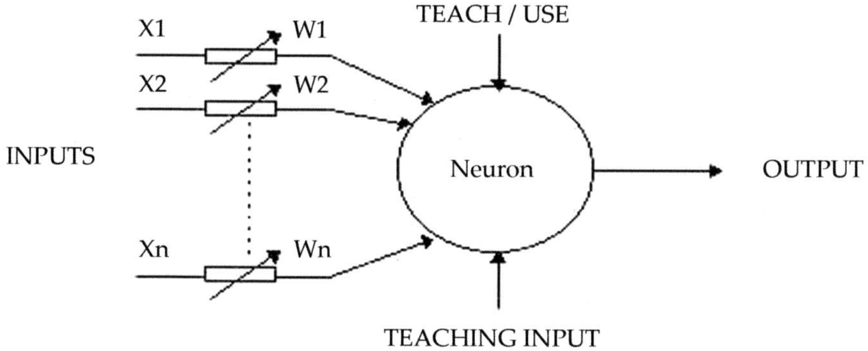

Figure 3.36. An MCP neuron.

In mathematical terms, the neuron fires if and only if:

$$X1W1 + X2W2 + X3W3 + \ldots > T$$

The addition of input weights and of the threshold makes this neuron a very flexible and powerful one. The MCP neuron has the ability to adapt to a particular situation by changing its weights and/or threshold. Various algorithms exist that cause the neuron to 'adapt;' the most used ones are the Delta rule and the back error propagation. The former is used in feed-forward networks and the latter in feedback networks.

3.10.9. Architecture of Neural Networks

3.10.9.1. Feed-Forward Networks

Feed-forward ANNs (Figure 3.37) allow signals to travel one way only; from input to output. There is no feedback (loops), i.e., the output of any layer does not affect that same layer. Feed-forward ANNs tend to be straight forward networks that associate inputs with outputs. They are extensively used in pattern recognition. This type of organization is also referred to as bottom-up or top-down.

3.10.9.2. Feedback Networks

Feedback networks (Figure 3.37) can have signals traveling in both directions by introducing loops in the network. Feedback networks are very powerful and can get extremely complicated. Feedback networks are dynamic; their 'state' is changing continuously until they reach an equilibrium point. They remain at the equilibrium point until the input changes and a new equilibrium needs to be found. Feedback architectures are also referred to as interactive or recurrent, although the latter term is often used to denote feedback connections in single-layer organizations (Figures 3.37 and 3.38).

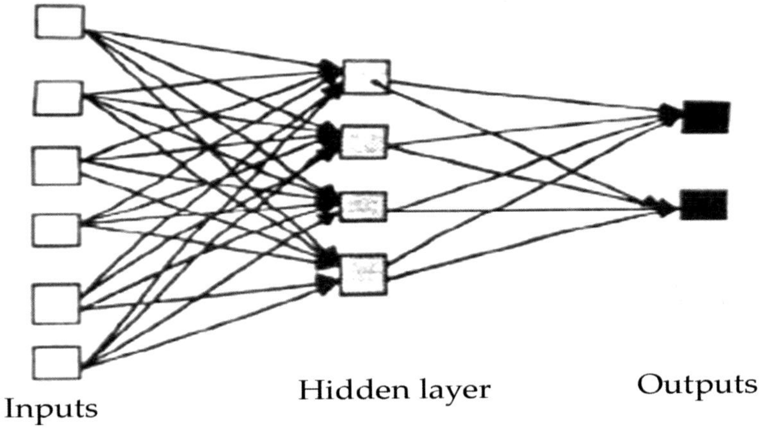

Figure 3.37. An example of a simple feed forward network.

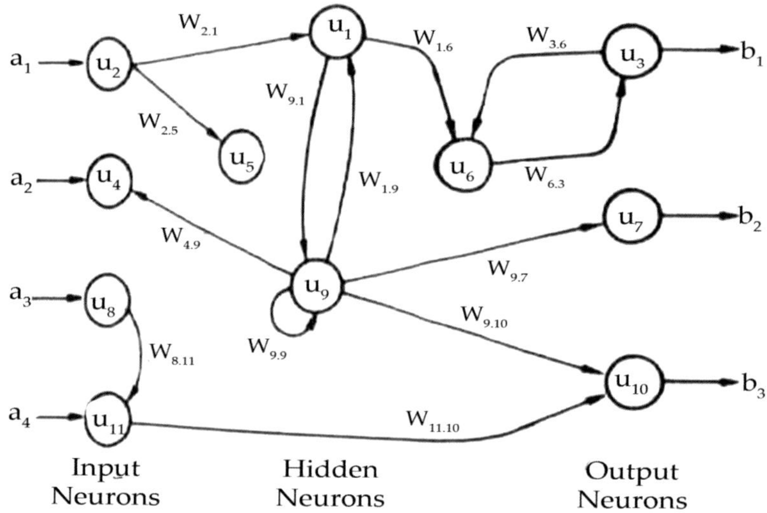

Figure 3.38. An example of a complicated network.

3.10.10. Network Layers

The commonest type of ANN consists of three groups, or layers, of units: a layer of "input" units is connected to a layer of "hidden" units, which is connected to a layer of "output" units (*see* Figure 3.1):

- The activity of the input units represents the raw information that is fed into the network.
- The activity of each hidden unit is determined by the activities of the input units and the weights on the connections between the input and the hidden units.
- The behavior of the output units depends on the activity of the hidden units and the weights between the hidden and output units.

This simple type of network is interesting because the hidden units are free to construct their own representations of the input. The weights between the input and hidden units determine when each hidden unit is active, and so by modifying these weights, a hidden unit can choose what it represents.

We also distinguish single-layer and multi-layer architectures. The single-layer organization, in which all units are connected to one another, constitutes the most general case and is of more potential computational power than hierarchically structured multi-layer organizations. In multi-layer networks, units are often numbered by layer, instead of following a global numbering.

3.10.11. Perceptrons

The most influential work on neural nets in the 60's went under the heading of 'perceptrons' a term coined by Frank Rosenblatt. The perceptron (Figure 3.39) turns out to be an MCP model (neuron with weighted inputs) with some additional, fixed, pre-processing. Units labeled A_1, A_2, A_j, Ap are called association units and their task is to extract specific, localized featured from the input images. Perceptrons mimic the basic idea behind the mammalian visual system. They were mainly used in pattern recognition even though their capabilities extended a lot more.

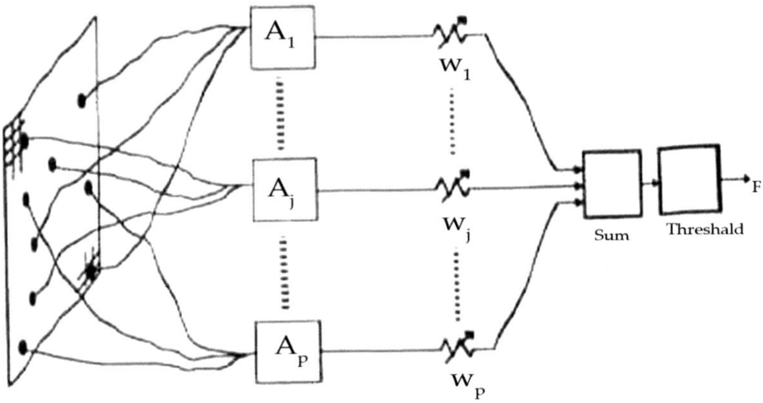

Figure 3.39. An example of Perceptrons.

In 1969 Minsky and Papert wrote a book in which they described the limitations of single layer Perceptrons. The impact that the book had was tremendous and caused a lot of neural network researchers to lose their interest. The book was very well written and showed mathematically that *single layer* perceptrons could not do some basic pattern recognition operations like determining the parity of a shape or determining whether a shape is connected or not. What they did not realized, until the 80's, is that given the appropriate training, multilevel perceptrons can do these operations.

3.10.12. The Learning Process

The memorization of patterns and the subsequent response of the network can be categorized into two general paradigms:

1. **Associative Mapping:** in which the network learns to produce

a particular pattern on the set of input units whenever another particular pattern is applied on the set of input units. The associative mapping can generally be broken down into two mechanisms:

i. **Auto-Association:** An input pattern is associated with itself, and the states of input and output units coincide. This is used to provide pattern competition, i.e., to produce a pattern whenever a portion of it or a distorted pattern is presented. In the second case, the network actually stores pairs of patterns building an association between two sets of patterns.

ii. **Hetero-Association:** is related to two recall mechanisms:

a. **Nearest-Neighbor Recall:** Where the output pattern produced corresponds to the input pattern stored, which is closest to the pattern presented.

b. **interpolative Recall:** Where the output pattern is a similarity dependent interpolation of the patterns stored corresponding to the pattern presented. Yet another paradigm, which is a variant associative mapping is classification, i.e., when there is a fixed set of categories into which the input patterns are to be classified.

2. **Regularity Detection:** in which units learn to respond to particular properties of the input patterns. Whereas in associative mapping the network stores the relationships among patterns, in regularity detection the response of each unit has a particular 'meaning.' This type of learning mechanism is essential for feature discovery and knowledge representation.

Every neural network possesses knowledge which is contained in the values of the connections weights. Modifying the knowledge stored in the network as a function of experience implies a learning rule for changing the values of the weights.

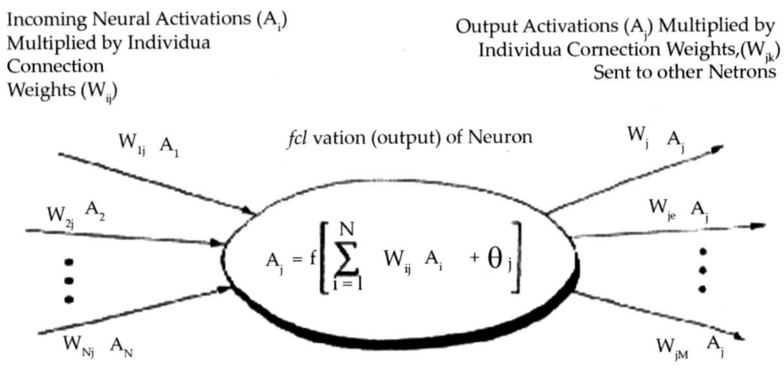

Information is stored in the weight matrix W of a neural network. Learning is the determination of the weights. Following the way learning is performed, we can distinguish two major categories of neural networks:

1. **Fixed Networks:** In which the weights cannot be changed, i.e., dW/dt=0. In such networks, the weights are fixed a priori according to the problem to solve.
2. **Adaptive Networks:** In which are able to change their weights, i.e., dW/dt not= 0.

All learning methods used for adaptive neural networks can be classified into two major categories:

i. **Supervised Learning:** In which incorporates an external teacher, so that each output unit is told what its desired response to input signals ought to be. During the learning process global information may be required. Paradigms of supervised learning include error-correction learning, reinforcement learning and stochastic learning. An important issue concerning supervised learning is the problem of error convergence, i.e., the minimization of error between the desired and computed unit values. The aim is to determine a set of weights which minimizes the error. One well-known method, which is common to many learning paradigms is the least mean square (LMS) convergence.

ii. **Transfer Function:** The behavior of an ANN depends on both the weights and the input-output function (transfer function) that is specified for the units. This function typically falls into one of three categories:

a. Linear (or ramp);

b. Threshold; and

c. Sigmoid.

For linear units, the output activity is proportional to the total weighted output. For threshold units, the output is set at one of two levels, depending on whether the total input is greater than or less than some threshold value. For sigmoid units, the output varies continuously but not linearly as the input changes. Sigmoid units bear a greater resemblance to real neurons than do linear or threshold units, but all three must be considered rough approximations. To make a neural network that performs some specific tasks, we must choose how the units are connected to one another (*see* Figure 4.1), and we must set the weights on the connections appropriately. The connections determine whether it is possible for one unit to influence another. The weights specify the strength of the influence.

We can teach a three-layer network to perform a particular task by using the following procedure:

- We present the network with training examples, which consist of a pattern of activities for the input units together with the desired pattern of activities for the output units.
- We determine how closely the actual output of the network matches the desired output.
- We change the weight of each connection so that the network produces a better approximation of the desired output.

3.10.13. An Example to Illustrate the Above Teaching Procedure

Assume that we want a network to recognize hand-written digits. We might use an array of, say, 256 sensors, each recording the presence or absence of ink in a small area of a single digit. The network would therefore need 256 input units (one for each sensor), 10 output units (one for each kind of digit) and a number of hidden units.

For each kind of digit recorded by the sensors, the network should produce high activity in the appropriate output unit and low activity in the other output units.

To train the network, we present an image of a digit and compare the actual activity of the 10 output units with the desired activity. We then calculate the error, which is defined as the square of the difference between the actual and the desired activities. Next, we change the weight of each connection so as to reduce the error. We repeat this training process for many different images of each different images of each kind of digit until the network classifies every image correctly.

To implement this procedure, we need to calculate the error derivative for the weight (EW) in order to change the weight by an amount that is proportional to the rate at which the error changes as the weight is changed. One way to calculate the EW is to perturb a weight slightly and observe how the error changes. But that method is inefficient because it requires a separate perturbation for each of the many weights.

Another way to calculate the EW is to use the Back-propagation algorithm which is described below and has become nowadays one of the most important tools for training neural networks. It was developed independently by two teams, one (Fogelman-Soulie, Gallinari, and Le Cun) in France, the other (Rumelhart, Hinton, and Williams) in U.S.

3.10.14. The Back-Propagation Algorithm

In order to train a neural network to perform some tasks, we must adjust the weights of each unit in such a way that the error between the desired output and the actual output is reduced. This process requires that the neural network compute the error derivative of the weights (EW). In other words, it must calculate how the error changes as each weight is increased or decreased slightly. The back propagation algorithm is the most widely used method for determining the EW.

The back-propagation algorithm is easiest to understand if all the units in the network are linear. The algorithm computes each EW by first computing the EA, the rate at which the error changes as the activity level of a unit is changed. For output units, the EA is simply the difference between the actual and the desired output. To compute the EA for a hidden unit in the layer just before the output layer, we first identify all the weights between that hidden unit and the output units to which it is connected. We then multiply those weights by the EAs of those output units and add the products. This sum equals the EA for the chosen hidden unit. After calculating all the EAs in the hidden layer just before the output layer, we can compute in like fashion the EAs for other layers, moving from layer to layer in a direction opposite to the way activities propagate through the network. This is what gives back propagation its name. Once the EA has been computed for a unit, it is straight forward to compute the EW for each incoming connection of the unit. The EW is the product of the EA and the activity through the incoming connection. Note that for non-linear units, (*see* Appendix C) the back-propagation algorithm includes an extra step. Before back-propagating, the EA must be converted into the EI, the rate at which the error changes as the total input received by a unit are changed.

3.10.15. Applications of Neural Networks

3.10.15.1. Neural Networks in Practice

Given this description of neural networks and how they work, what real world applications are they suited for? Neural networks have broad applicability to real world business problems. In fact, they have already been successfully applied in many industries.

Since neural networks are best at identifying patterns or trends in data, they are well suited for prediction or forecasting needs including:

- Sales forecasting;
- Industrial process control;
- Customer research;
- Data validation;
- Risk management;
- Target marketing.

But to give you some more specific examples; ANN are also used in the following specific paradigms: recognition of speakers in communications; diagnosis of hepatitis; recovery of telecommunications from faulty software; interpretation of multi meaning Chinese words; undersea mine detection; texture analysis; three-dimensional object recognition; hand-written word recognition; and facial recognition.

3.10.15.2. Neural Networks in Medicine

ANNs are currently a 'hot' research area in medicine, and it is believed that they will receive extensive application to biomedical systems in the next few years. At the moment, the research is mostly on modeling parts of the human body and recognizing diseases from various scans (e.g., cardiograms, CAT scans, ultrasonic scans, etc.).

Neural networks are ideal in recognizing diseases using scans since there is no need to provide a specific algorithm on how to identify the disease. Neural networks learn by example so the details of how to recognize the disease are not needed. What is needed is a set of examples that are representative of all the variations of the disease. The quantity of examples is not as important as the 'quantity.' The examples need to be selected very carefully if the system is to perform reliably and efficiently.

3.10.16. Modeling and Diagnosing the Cardiovascular System

Neural Networks are used experimentally to model the human cardiovascular system. Diagnosis can be achieved by building a model of the cardiovascular system of an individual and comparing it with the real time physiological measurements taken from the patient. If this routine is carried out regularly, potential harmful medical conditions can be detected at an early stage and thus make the process of combating the disease much easier.

A model of an individual's cardiovascular system must mimic the relationship among physiological variables (i.e., heart rate, systolic and diastolic blood pressures, and breathing rate) at different physical activity levels. If a model is adapted to an individual, then it becomes a model of the physical condition of that individual. The simulator will have to be able to adapt to the features of any individual without the supervision of an expert. This calls for a neural network.

Another reason that justifies the use of ANN technology, is the ability of ANNs to provide sensor fusion which is the combining of values from several different sensors. Sensor fusion enables the ANNs to learn complex relationships among the individual sensor values, which would otherwise be lost if the values were individually analyzed. In medical modeling and diagnosis, this implies that even though each sensor in a set may be sensitive only to a specific physiological variable, ANNs are capable of detecting complex medical conditions by fusing the data from the individual biomedical sensors.

3.10.17. Electronic Noses

ANNs are used experimentally to implement electronic noses. Electronic noses have several potential applications in telemedicine. Telemedicine is the practice of medicine over long distances via a communication link. The electronic nose would identify odors in the remote surgical environment. These identified odors would then be electronically transmitted to another site where a door generation system would recreate them. Because the sense of smell can be an important sense to the surgeon, telesmell would enhance telepresent surgery.

3.10.18. Instant Physician

An application developed in the mid-1980s called the "instant physician" trained an auto associative memory neural network to store a large number of medical records, each of which includes information on symptoms, diagnosis, and treatment for a particular case. After training, the net can be presented with input consisting of a set of symptoms; it will then find the full stored pattern that represents the "best" diagnosis and treatment.

3.10.19. Neural Networks in Business

Business is a diverted field with several general areas of specialization such as accounting or financial analysis. Almost any neural network application would fit into one business area or financial analysis. There is some potential for using neural networks for business purposes, including resource allocation and scheduling. There is also a strong potential for using neural networks for database mining, that is, searching for patterns implicit within the explicitly stored information in databases. Most of the funded work in this area is classified as proprietary. Thus, it is not possible to report on the full extent of the work going on. Most work is applying neural networks, such as the Hopfield-Tank network for optimization and scheduling.

3.10.20. Marketing

There is a marketing application which has been integrated with a neural network system. The Airline Marketing Tactician (a trademark abbreviated as AMT) is a computer system made of various intelligent technologies including expert systems. A feed forward neural network is integrated with the AMT and was trained using back propagation to assist the marketing control of airline seat allocations. The adaptive neural approach was amenable to rule expression. Additionally, the application's environment changed rapidly and constantly, which required a continuously adaptive solution. The system is used to monitor and recommend booking advice for each departure. Such information has a direct impact on the profitability of an airline and can provide a technological advantage for users of the system (Hutchison & Stephens, 1987).

While it is significant that neural networks have been applied to this problem, it is also important to see that this intelligent technology can be integrated with expert systems and other approaches to make a functional system. Neural networks were used to discover the influence of undefined interactions by the various variables. While these interactions were not defined, they were used by the neural system to develop useful conclusions. It is also noteworthy to see that neural networks can influence the bottom line.

3.10.21. Credit Evaluation

The HNC company, founded by Robert Hecht-Nielsen, has developed several neural network applications. One of them is the Credit Scoring system which increase the profitability of the existing model up to 27%. The HNC neural systems were also applied to mortgage screening. A neural network automated mortgage insurance under writing system was developed by the Nestor Company. This system was trained with 5048 applications of which 2597 were certified. The data related to property and borrower qualifications. In a conservative mode the system agreed on the under writers on 97% of the cases. In the liberal model the system agreed 84% of the cases. This is system run on an Apollo DN3000 and used 250 K memory while processing a case file in approximately 1 sec.

> ➢ Find the *synonyms* for the underlined words.
>
> 1. An Artificial Neural Network (ANN) is an information processing paradigm that is inspired by the way biological nervous systems, such as the brain, process information
> 2. An ANN is configured for a specific application, such as pattern recognition or data classification, through a learning process.
> 3. Neural network simulations appear to be a recent development. However, this field was established before the advent of computers, and has survived at least one major setback and several eras.
> 4. These pioneers were able to develop convincing technology which surpassed the limitations identified by Minsky and Papert. Minsky and Papert, published a book in which they summed up a general feeling of frustration among researchers.
> 5. Partial destruction of a network leads to the corresponding degradation of performance.
> 6. When a neuron receives excitatory input that is sufficiently large compared with its inhibitory input, it sends a spike of electrical activity down its axon.
> 7. Feed-forward ANNs tend to be straight forward networks that associate inputs with outputs.

8. Feedback architectures are also referred to as interactive or recurrent, although the latter term is often used to denote feedback connections in single-layer organizations.
9. The single-layer organization, in which all units are connected to one another, constitutes the most general case and is of more potential computational power than hierarchically structured multi-layer organizations.
10. An important issue concerning supervised learning is the problem of error convergence, ie the minimization of error between the desired and computed unit values.

➢ Fill in the blank with the following words.

Neurons, Synaptic, Mapping, Axon, Odors Weights, Machine code, Hidden

1. Learning in biological systems involves adjustments to the .... connections that exist between the neurons.
2. These instructions are then converted to a high level language program and then into .... that the computer can understand.
3. The neuron sends out spikes of electrical activity through a long, thin stand known as an ...., which splits into thousands of branches.
4. We conduct these neural networks by first trying to deduce the essential features of .... and their interconnections.
5. The MCP neuron has the ability to adapt to a particular situation by changing its .... and/or threshold.
6. The behavior of the output units depends on the activity of the .... units and the weights between the hidden and output units.
7. associative .... in which the network learns to produce a particular pattern on the set of input units.
8. These identified .... would then be electronically transmitted to another site where an door generation system would recreate them.

> ➢ Write *antonyms* of following words.
>
> 1. Highly ....
> 2. Boosted ....
> 3. Resurgence ....
> 4. Deduce ....
> 5. Novel ....
> 6. Equilibrium.........................
> 7. Influential ....

3.10.22. Additional Information about Neural Networks

The history of neural networks can be divided into several periods:

1. **First Attempts:** There were some initial simulations using formal logic. MCP (1943) developed models of neural networks based on their understanding of neurology. These models made several assumptions about how neurons worked. Their networks were based on simple neurons which were considered to be binary devices with fixed thresholds. The results of their model were simple logic functions such as "a or b" and "a and b." Another attempt was by using computer simulations. Two groups (Farley & Clark, 1954; Rochester, Holland, Haibit, & Duda, 1956). The first group (IBM researchers) maintained closed contact with neuroscientists at McGill University. So, whenever their models did not work, they consulted the neuroscientists. This interaction established a multi-disciplinary trend which continues to the present day.
2. **Promising and Emerging Technology:** Not only was neuroscience influential in the development of neural networks, but psychologists and engineers also contributed to the progress of neural network simulations. Rosenblatt (1958) stirred considerable interest and activity in the field when he designed and developed the Perceptron. The Perceptron had three layers with the middle layer known as the association layer. This system could learn to connect or associate a given input to a random output unit. Another system was the ADALINE (adaptive linear element) which was developed in 1960 by Widrow and Hoff (of Stanford University). The ADALINE was an analog electronic device made from simple components. The method used for learning was different to that of the Perceptron, it employed the Least-Mean-Squares (LMS) learning rule.

3. **Period of Frustration and Disrepute:** In 1969 Minsky and Papert wrote a book in which they generalized the limitations of single layer Perceptrons to multilayered systems. In the book they said: "...our intuitive judgment that the extension (to multilayer systems) is sterile." The significant result of their book was to eliminate funding for research with neural network simulations. The conclusions supported the disenchantment of researchers in the field. As a result, considerable prejudice against this field was activated.

4. **Innovation:** Although public interest and available funding were minimal, several researchers continued working to develop neuromorphically based computational methods for problems such as pattern recognition.

   During this period, several paradigms were generated which modern work continues to enhance. Grossberg's (Steve Grossberg and Gail Carpenter in 1988) influence founded a school of thought which explores resonating algorithms. They developed the ART (adaptive resonance theory) networks based on biologically plausible models. Anderson and Kohonen developed associative techniques independent of each other. Klopf (A. Henry Klopf) in 1972, developed a basis for learning in artificial neurons based on a biological principle for neuronal learning called heterostasis. Werbos (Paul Werbos, 1974) developed and used the back-propagation learning method, however several years passed before this approach was popularized. Back-propagation nets are probably the most well-known and widely applied of the neural networks today. In essence, the back-propagation net is a Perceptron with multiple layers, a different threshold function in the artificial neuron, and a more robust and capable learning rule. Amari (Shun-Ichi, 1967) was involved with theoretical developments: he published a paper which established a mathematical theory for a learning basis (error-correction method) dealing with adaptive pattern classification. While Fukushima (F. Kunihiko) developed a step wise trained multilayered neural network for interpretation of handwritten characters. The original network was published in 1975 and was called the Cognitron.

5. **Re-Emergence:** Progress during the late 1970s and early 1980s was important to the re-emergence on interest in the neural network field. Several factors influenced this movement. For

example, comprehensive books and conferences provided a forum for people in diverse fields with specialized technical languages, and the response to conferences and publications was quite positive. The news media picked up on the increased activity and tutorials helped disseminate the technology. Academic programs appeared and courses were introduced at most major Universities (in US and Europe). Attention is now focused on funding levels throughout Europe, Japan, and the US and as this funding becomes available, several new commercial with applications in industry and financial institutions are emerging.

6. **Today:** Significant progress has been made in the field of neural networks-enough to attract a great deal of attention and fund further research. Advancement beyond current commercial applications appears to be possible, and research is advancing the field on many fronts. Neutrally based chips are emerging and applications to complex problems developing. Clearly, today is a period of transition for neural network technology.

References

1. David Clark (1997). Interoperation, Open Interfaces, and Protocol Architecture. The Unpredictable Certainty: White Papers. National Research Council. ISBN 9780309060363
2. Patterson, D. A., and Hennessy, J.L., "Computer Organization and Design:The Hardware/Software Interface", 3rd Edition, Elsevier, 2005.
3. William Stallings, "Computer Organization and Architecture – Designing for Performance", 6th Edition, Pearson Education, 2003.
4. Hayes, J.P., "Computer Architecture and Organization", 3rd Edition, Tata Mc-Graw Hill, 1998.
5. Bliss, T., and Lømo, T. (1973). Long-lasting potentiation of synaptic transmission in the dentate area of the anaesthetized rabbit following stimulation of the perforant path. J. Physiol. 232, 331–356. doi: 10.1113/jphysiol.1973.sp010273
6. Briglia, J., Servajean, P., Michalland, A. H., Brunel, L., and Brouillet, D. (2018). Modeling an enactivist multiple-trace memory. ATHENA: a fractal model of human memory. J. Math. Psychol. 82, 97–110. doi: 10.1016/j.jmp.2017.12.002
7. Atkinson, R.C. & Shiffrin, R.M. (1968). Human memory: A proposed system and its control processes. In The psychology of learning and motivation: II Oxford, England: Academic Press.
8. LeDoux J.E. (2007) Consolidation: Challenging the traditional view. In: Roediger, H.L., Dudai, Y. and Fitzpatrick S.M., eds. Science of Memory: Concepts. New York: Oxford University Press, pp. 171–175.

9. Hassani, M. M., & Berangi, R. (2019). Impact of secondary user block on the TCP throughput in cognitive Radio sensor networks. Wireless Personal Communication, 109(4), 2221–2238.

10. David Clark (1997). Interoperation, Open Interfaces, and Protocol Architecture. The Unpredictable Certainty: White Papers. National Research Council. ISBN 9780309060363

11. Sadrozinski, Hartmut F.-W.; Wu, Jinyuan (2010). Applications of Field-Programmable Gate Arrays in Scientific Research. Taylor & Francis. ISBN 978-1-4398-4133-4.

12. Mitra, Jubin (2018). "An FPGA-Based Phase Measurement System". IEEE Transactions on Very Large Scale Integration (VLSI) Systems. IEEE. **26**: 133–142. doi:10.1109/TVLSI.2017.2758807. S2CID 4920719.

13. Groth, David; Toby Skandier (2005). Network+ Study Guide, Fourth Edition. Sybex, Inc. ISBN 0-7821-4406-3

INDEX

C

D

E

J

K

L

M

N

S

T